'Cinderella', I wish!

Dominiquè DeVeraux

Matador
9 Priory Business Park,
Wistow Road, Kibworth Beauchamp,
Leicestershire. LE8 0RX
Tel: 0116 279 2299
Email: books@troubador.co.uk
Web: www.troubador.co.uk/matador
Twitter: @matadorbooks

ISBN 978 1789018 059

British Library Cataloguing in Publication Data.
A catalogue record for this book is available from the British Library.

Printed and bound in Great Britain by 4edge Limited
Typeset in 12pt Adobe Caslon Pro by Troubador Publishing Ltd, Leicester, UK

Matador is an imprint of Troubador Publishing Ltd

This book is dedicated to those who truly loved me.
And those who empowered me to aim high.
To people who misunderstood me.

I dedicate this book to me,
for pushing through the pain and struggle,
to claim a new beginning.

Foreword

Dominiquè's life is a prime example that your childhood does not determine your life. Even if you have a bad start you can turn it around with determination and drive.

Remember, nothing lasts forever.
Find your inner happiness
Push forward and be who you want to be.

Written by Ernesta Moore

DISCLAIMER

I have written my story to inspire and empower those in need of a hope. Whilst the events are accurate from my experience and perspective, I have changed names and places to protect the identity of those who wish to remain anonymous.

1

FULL CIRCLE

Music has played such a vital role in my life, listen to my playlist, as you journey through my life. Pages 352–368. Or go to YouTube: 'Cinderella', I Wish! Memoir Vol 1, 2, 3, 4.

∽

I'm uncertain about where to start, but one thing is a guarantee; all roads lead to me asking why me? As I sit here at the age of fifty, I'm still puzzled by my life. One thing is charmingly clear; love: three, heartbreak: a trillion!

But as I finally listen to my spirit, I must admit this ending had been written earlier, but the idiosyncrasies of my mind refused to face the truth, choosing instead to cling to hope.

Unfortunately, my cycle grew from a childhood and matured in tandem with my so-called mother's viciousness. The power of this negativity fuelled my determination to be successfully loved but despite the dedication of an Olympian, I have failed in spectacular style.

While I recount, my purpose is not to pick my belly fluff or play sad violins, but to string together all my pearls which I wear as wisdom wings as I conquer this familiar terrain for the last time, fingers crossed, I will rise above and soar.

∽

I had better explain. My starting point is at the age of about two. I remember looking out of the car window and seeing the street lights flashing by and I said to myself, "Oh no, not here again!"

My 'old soul' awareness frightened me for a split second and then I just carried on living, I guess. My memories of life with Nanny and Granddad, my white foster parents, are wonderful.

Nanny and Granddad were old; Nanny was fifty-six and Granddad was fifty-eight. They had been together since they were teenagers. They had a daughter called Pam. Pam was grown up, married with two boys, Gary and Richard, who were older than me; probably about six and eight.

Pam lived around the corner from us, and we saw them often. Nanny and Granddad also fostered an older girl; I think her name was Audrey. Audrey was rarely at home, hence I'm not 100% sure what her name was.

So really it was just me with Nanny and Granddad. They spoiled me rotten. I had all the toys in the world, and I had a playroom under the stairs, where I had many tea parties with friends, with real tea and cakes. In keeping with child rearing in the 70s Nanny and Grandad allowed me to roam free; I played out in our close or in the park.

One of my fondest memories is doing the milk round with the milkman on a Saturday morning. I would sit on the back of the milk van and at every stop I would jump off and run and put the milk on a doorstep, and then I would run back and sit on the back of the milk van.

I loved the buzz of my first job. I felt all important, and all my neighbours knew me; they'd wave and smile at me. Every day with Nanny and Granddad was fun, but Fridays stood out; we'd always have treats on Friday evening.

We usually toasted bread in front of the fire and Granddad let me hold the long toasting fork while I sat on his lap. Once slightly toasted we'd apply lashings of butter on the toast and eat it while it was hot. It was wonderful.

Growing up I didn't realise I was different from Nanny and Granddad, but Nanny would always say to me that I was special and kiss me. I never really knew what she meant until sometime later when I was living in hell.

However, until then, I grew up in a loving family. Being special meant every Sunday I had to go to our neighbour's, Mrs Green's, house. Mrs Green came from Jamaica; she had a house full of children.

Her house always smelt of cooked food and ripe coconuts. Every Sunday Mrs Green plaited my hair and creamed my skin with coconut oil and Vaseline. I enjoyed visiting Mrs Green; she was warm and caring.

Nevertheless, I loved to go home. Life at Nanny and Granddad's was perfect except for the occasional visit from my so-called mother. She'd turn up out of the blue and stay for but a minute. Even so, the whole time I would sit on Nanny's lap.

Nanny encouraged me to go to my so-called mother, but I wouldn't go near her. For years, I thought my so-called mother was in the singing group The Three Degrees; I'm not sure why, probably because she resembled them. Occasionally my so-called mother wouldn't turn up for the visit but then The Three Degrees would come on *The Larry Grayson Show*, and it didn't seem to matter.

One day, my so-called mother brought a man with her; I must have been about three or four. The man looked so stern as he sat in silence. For some strange reason, I don't know why, as he was leaving, I whispered, "Bye Daddy."

His head spun round so his eyes could show me his disdain.

"I'm not your daddy!"

And that was the last time he came for a visit. It didn't matter; I loved being with Nanny and Granddad, they were always warm and loving.

My home life was perfect until Nanny got sick; she was taken to a hospital. I remember going to the hospital. I hated the smell;

everyone was lying in beds with crisp white sheets. Walking through the corridors I had this sickly feeling, and this sense of impending doom.

As Granddad and I approached Nanny's bed this woman got out of bed; I don't know where she was going, but she started walking and then she fell to the floor.

Terrified, I watched as nurses came and picked her up and put her back into bed. This incident compounded my feelings. I hated being around sick people, and, to make it worse, every now and then an ambulance would arrive with the siren ringing out.

My heart pounded like I was going to have a heart attack. I remember feeling so scared. I kept peering at Nanny; she looked fine to me, she still had her lovely warm smile, and she gave me a nice hug. Nanny told me she felt much better and would be coming home soon.

Thankfully, Nanny came home. I don't know how long she was in hospital; I was just so happy I didn't have to go to the hospital to visit her. However, things were not quite back to normal; Nanny stayed in bed every day.

I'd go in to see her; I remember thinking how pale she looked, and she didn't say much. I'd sit next to her bed, but I was scared to touch her.

I remember smelling a sickly odour in her room. Nanny kept coughing, and spitting something in her handkerchief, and in between coughing she'd eat something like a sweet but she said they were for the catarrh. Granddad wasn't his usual chirpy self, but he kept telling me Nanny would be fine.

One sunny spring day, I was about seven, I was in class sitting on the mat in the book corner, listening to a story, when, after receiving a note my teacher told me to go to the headmistress's office.

I wondered why. I was really curious about going to see the headmistress. I had never been sent to the headmistress's office before, so it was all quite fascinating to me.

I pondered it over in my mind on the short walk to her office. I knocked at the door and poked my head around the door. The headmistress looked at me sweetly and beckoned me in. I sat down in front of her desk, and she looked at me intensely as she spoke.

"Nanny has died!"

Everything in me stopped. She was speaking, but I couldn't hear what she was saying. Everything looked like it was happening in film, and I was in a fish bowl. I couldn't feel anything. I couldn't hear anything. The headmistress led me out of her office. In a blink, I was at home. I don't know how I got there.

Granddad looked ashen grey and there were people at the house whom I didn't recognise, or did I? I'm not sure; everything happened with a swish and a whoosh. People spoke to me, but I don't know what they said. Nothing felt right.

At night I slept in fear. Nanny was gone, and death took her. I felt so frightened. I didn't want to see a ghost. I feared the night, but daytime wasn't any better.

I woke to swishing and whooshing. Nothing was the same. Nanny was gone. I couldn't understand what was going on. I overheard conversations about the funeral, but I was not allowed to go. I don't know why, there was some discussion about the pros and cons of a small child attending a funeral, and I guess the cons won.

I found out the outcome by chance. I remember playing hopscotch in the school playground at break time. I don't know what pulled my attention towards the road, but I looked up to see a purple coffin in a hearse, with funeral cars following behind full of faces which seemed familiar.

I remember I felt a pang of fear from my head, which fell deep into my stomach. For many years, well into my adulthood, I struggled against the fear of death and, in particular, funerals. I felt that funerals must be bad or worse if I wasn't allowed to go to Nanny's funeral, so I avoided death and funerals with a passion.

Sometime after the funeral my so-called mother arrived to take me away. I don't know how long after the funeral because I remained in the fish bowl; things moved in a swish and a whoosh, everything just happened without explanation or meaning.

As the realisation of what was happening hit me, I cried my heart out while clinging to Granddad, but my so-called mother, emotionless, unpeeled my arms and legs, which were wrapped around Granddad.

He didn't speak but a single tear trickled slowly down his cheek as he stood at the front door. I was bundled into a car, sobbing. As the car moved, I looked back at the house; the house, which had always shone so brightly and oozed happiness, looked so dim and so sad the further away it got from my eyes.

2

'Cinderella', I Wish!

I bawled, sobbed and cried nonstop until I had no more tears left and only the sound of pain was left. My so-called mother drove without a word or an offer of compassion. I don't know how long the journey had taken but suddenly the car stopped in front of a tall grey building; we went down the stairs to a basement flat. It was dark and dingy-looking.

My so-called mother rang the doorbell. The door was opened by a fat, red-skinned old woman who had a sweet sickly smile with a gold tooth. This is your Auntie Viola, I was told. The red-skinned woman led my so-called mother and me into a tiny cramped flat. As she opened another door, little dogs bounded towards us. Auntie Viola shouted at the dogs, in a thick accent. Nevertheless, they just kept coming; they licked me up and down.

"Don't let them lick your face," Auntie Viola snapped.

However, she didn't tell me how to stop them.

"Sit down!" she barked.

I followed the command and so did the dogs, all three of them; they sat on me! The room was like nothing I had seen before. It was small and full of ornaments of every description, little and big, dogs and cats, elephants. The walls were covered with pictures of dogs and cats, sheep, 'Jesus and the Last Supper', flowers, the room was full of stuff. There were crocheted things on every chair; every inch of the place was occupied with something!

But what struck me most of all was this unbelievable smell. The air was thick with it. The smell was repugnant; urine, shit, disinfectant and dust, I think. I was so overwhelmed with it all I sat staring.

"She can't speak?" asked Auntie Viola.

My so-called mother let out a fake laugh as she answered, "Yes, she can," while poking me.

I still didn't speak.

"You want a drink?"

Auntie Viola seemed determined to hear my voice.

My so-called mother shot me a look, and I knew I had better speak. I could only manage a whisper.

"Yes please."

She came from the kitchen with a little bottle, which she thrust at me. I took a sip of the drink, it was nice except for the hair, dog hair, I think.

I wiped the hair away and drank quickly. The taste was lovely. I think it was the first time I had ever had Cresta cream soda. I loved the cute little bottle with a picture of a polar bear on it.

I was so into my cream soda that I hadn't noticed my so-called mother had got up from her seat. She was now at the door, which led to the front door. I got up and walked towards her. I wanted to go with her.

"Bye."

And with that, my so-called mother was gone. We couldn't have been there more than an hour. Auntie Viola told me to put my things in my room. She led me through a dark corridor into a small dingy room which smelled of damp mixed with the other smells of the place, piss, shit, disinfectant and dust.

I surveyed the room, which was crowded with dark wood furniture, a wardrobe, chest of drawers and a cabinet with lots of china in it. I put my bags on the floor. Suddenly, Auntie Viola started shouting in her thick accent.

"You ain't got no slaves around here. They may have thought you were special, but you are just a little black bitch that nobody wants. So, you better be of some use! Get them good clothes off and put on your house clothes."

I just sat there trying to make sense of what she was saying and what was going on. This just made matters worse.

Boof, she punched me in the face. Suddenly, the fish bowl was broken, and I could feel nothing but pain, from my face to my feet; everything hurt.

"Move. You don't hear me talking to you? You is an idiot or what?"

I jumped up, hot tears streaming down my face.

"Wait you crying, you must really want me to give you something to cry for."

She towered over me with her fist clenched. Just then I heard a voice.

"Viola, don't hit the child."

Auntie Viola spun around towards the voice and they began arguing aggressively. I was frightened, I thought they were going to fight.

"Toni, don't come in here telling me what to do, mind your own business."

Auntie Viola walked off into the other room, where the voice had come from.

This reprieve gave me a minute to try to do what she had asked; the only problem was that I didn't know what she was talking about. So I decided to just change my clothes and hope for the best. This seemed to work as she didn't return to the bedroom.

I was summoned into the dining/front room, where I was introduced to Auntie Toni. The introduction confused me because Auntie Toni was a white woman, with a short skinny frame, except she looked like an old man. She was wearing a man's oversized shirt, with the sleeves rolled up to the elbows, and trousers, which also looked like menswear. So she couldn't be my auntie; she didn't look anything like my Auntie Viola, who was a red-skinned black woman. This day was the start of three years of hell, which echoed for a lifetime.

Auntie Viola and Auntie Toni lived together. The only problem with their union was that they fought like cat and dog. Arguing and cussing was like breathing air to them. Auntie Toni's favourite word was 'fucking'; it was fucking this and fucking that from sun up to sun down.

Observing them shed no light on why they were together. It didn't seem to be the love for each other or the usual spellbound adoration unless they just loved to argue and cuss each other.

Life with the 'happy couple' was far from happy. Life was so vicious, I had never known such hate and horror. I became the perfect target for their anger; it was like day and night compared to what I had been used to. I was now an eight-year-old slave! I cried silently, hoping my suffering would stop.

Every day, I prayed I was having a nightmare and I would wake up in my bed, in my room at Nanny's, but reality returned every time I opened my eyes. So in desperation I wished for magic. I wished, I was Cinderella.

Cinderella didn't suffer. She had a brief spell of misery. It was nothing compared to the nightmare I was living. My life was truly wretched. I wished for my suffering to be over, to be rescued by someone who loved me; to live happily ever after! Instead, I had no magic, I was in hell.

The day after I arrived, I was in the room at Auntie Viola's, just sitting there trying to make sense of it all. Why couldn't I live with my granddad? He was all alone. He must be crying, missing Nanny and me. Maybe Granddad will come and get me. Why do they hate me? The thoughts were just going around and around in my mind and suddenly Auntie Viola burst open the door.

"Wait… you think you're on holiday? Man, nuff work out there for you. Get your ass in da kitchen."

I walked towards the door.

"Wait… there must be something wrong with she. She walking like a wind gonna blow she down. Move like you got life, or I'll make you."

I ran past her and into the kitchen before the blow could land. Once in the kitchen, I just stood there. I didn't know what to do. As Auntie Viola approached I felt a sickly feeling come over me; I didn't know what to do or what she was going to do. Before I had a chance to think, she grabbed me and pushed me in front of the sink.

"Don't just stand there, wash da damn chicken."

I looked in the sink and there was a bowl with a chicken in some water. I was too small. I could barely reach the sink. Auntie Viola was towering over my shoulder. She took each of my hands and stuffed them into the water; the water splashed over me as I struggled to reach the chicken and stand on my tiptoes at the same time.

"You is an idiot?" she screamed into my ear.

"Wash da damn chicken!" She tried to make my hands do something; frustrated, she just pushed me out of the way and she stood over the sink and began to pick the feathers from the chicken.

"Man, this girl is worse than useless. She can't even wash she underneath, never mind a chicken."

She turned to me with the knife pointing in my face.

"You had better watch good cos I won't show you again."

So I watched intensely, tears running down my face, painstakingly so, I didn't feel the wee run down my leg. All of a sudden, there was a puddle beneath my feet. I didn't get a chance to move before she punched me in the stomach.

"You little bitch! So, cos I trying to teach she something she gonna stand up there and piss she self! Well, you gonna stand up there till d-dinner done, I ain't give one shite."

So said, so done. I watched her clean the guts out of the chicken, wash the chicken under the tap, season the chicken and put it in the oven. Afterwards she put the peas on to boil, she cut up some vegetables and washed them in the pot. Next she put the pot on the fire with some butter and a pinch of salt. I watched without moving or blinking, so attentive I forgot I was soaking wet and standing in a puddle of my own urine.

"Toni come 'n' pick some rice for mah, I woulda let she do it but she ain't got no use."

Auntie Toni came and stood behind me.

"Viola, what is this?"

She stared at the puddle around my feet.

"Man, that stupid little bitch piss she self. She think, she's going to be a princess in here, well she lie."

"Viola, let the child wash she self, man."

She ushered me towards the bathroom.

Auntie Viola snapped back with pause.

"Left she, she's got nothing to do with you, I teaching she something."

Auntie Toni backed away, muttering under her breath, leaving me just as she had found me. I stood in the middle of world war five!

Auntie Toni with her thick Scottish accent shouts against Auntie Viola's strong Barbadian accent!

"Yuck, fuck off! She's as much my niece as she is yours!"

"She mother is my niece, I raise she."

"Everything you say got to have a fucking in it. You can't curse without that word in it. An' lie, you can't talk without lying! That child hasn't got nothing to do with you, she isn't no family to you. She is my niece's child, an' you ain't raise she; she mother raise she. You talking bare shite. You must be drunk or pon drugs! Toni just piss off an' mind your own business."

So Auntie Toni retreated back to the settee in front of the telly which she turned up loud. I was left to stand in my own urine until Auntie Viola had finished cooking the dinner, at which time I was dismissed and ordered to wash my clothes in the basin and hang them on the line. I disappeared into the bathroom and locked the door. I peeled my dress and knickers off. I put them in the bowl and turned on the taps. I didn't really know how to wash clothes, so I moved them around in the water. Suddenly somebody turned the door handle and began banging on the door. Auntie Viola began shouting through the door.

"Waaaaaaait, she lock da door." She continued banging and shouting, "You aren't no woman in here. Open this door, open this door."

I opened the door and instinctively jumped back, but she still managed to slap me across the face and as I landed, I hit my side on the sink. It really hurt, my side and my face.

"Don't you lock no door in here you aren't neither woman."

I didn't speak. She grabbed my face.

"You hear me talking to you?"

I tried to nod, but she still had my face in her hand.

"Then answer, yes please or yes Auntie or something. You aren't an animal; you got a mouth!"

I turned back to my clothes without speaking, I began swirling them around in the water.

"What de ass you doing? This ain't no play time. Wash da nasty clothes. Stoop down, bend your back and wash the clothes." I didn't know what she meant so I just drooped my hands in the water. Boof, she punched my back.

"Mooove."

I slid down the side of the bath to my knees, as she stood over the bath.

"Watch me and learn something. Man, you really are no use. No wonder nobody wants you. You are good for nothing, can't even wash out a few clothes. Stuuupse!"

Auntie Viola rubbed the clothes in her hands and then shouted, "This idiot ain't even got soap in the water, oh lord, how she expect de clothes to wash? Stuuupse."

She took the pink carbolic soap and washed the dress and my knickers. I learnt by watching, through tear-filled eyes as I knelt naked beside her. I realised it was learn or die!

Despite the horrors the dinner tasted nice, except for me flinching, every time Auntie Viola moved or shouted I jumped, otherwise the Sunday dinner was lovely.

From the day of baptism by beating, I realised I needed to hit the ground running or die trying. I listened painstakingly to every command, and I even tried to pre-empt her every need, so they didn't kill me.

The 'happy couple' left the house at 6am every morning to go to their factory job packing books for schools.

I'd get myself up at 7.30 and get washed. I didn't know how to wash myself when I arrived, another fact which caused my Auntie Viola to have a fit of anger. She burst into the bathroom the morning after I arrived and stood watching me try to wash my face.

I missed my nanny so much, she used to wash and dress me every day. She was so gentle. I had not paid attention to what she did or how it was done.

Nanny would hum and smile at me and then I would be ready. Suddenly, Auntie Viola was screaming like the house was on fire.

"What de rass dem people do to she? Eight years old and dem ain't even teach she to wash she crutch. She touching de facecloth on she face like she going to break! Look take de facecloth and wash your face hard, you're not made of glass. Dem do you a disservice. Now you ain't use for self or ornament."

I rubbed the cloth on my face, hoping I had done it right. I pulled the plug and watched the water run down the hole. I went to leave the bathroom, but she blocked my path.

"This nasty bitch, she give she self a cat wash, and she done. No water hasn't touch she crutch an' she done."

Boof, Boof! She started to rain blows down my torso. In between blows, she dragged me around like a rag doll. As I slumped to the floor she lathered the facecloth with soap and forced my body to stoop down over the basin, with a leg on either side. She forced my hand and the soapy facecloth between my legs so roughly, I lost my balance and fell over, knocking the basin, spilling the water, which made her lose her mind.

"You aren't no good. Can't even wash between your legs, well you better learn, or I'll make you," she yelled, while standing over me. I tried to regain the pose, stooped over the basin. But I just couldn't seem to make the cloth do what she wanted it to do. She grabbed the facecloth and lashed me across my bare back. The pain resonated down my legs. My head was spinning, and I was aching from all the blows; tears were streaming down my face but I didn't make a sound. That would have only made things worse. So I silently sobbed.

"Girl you aren't special; you is just another little black bitch, and you better learn to be of some use, cos I am not gonna let you kill me!"

As she spoke, she scrubbed my vagina. When she had finished washing it, my vagina burned and throbbed. It was an experience I never wanted to endure ever again, so I learned how to wash myself stooped over the basin.

So from that day on, every morning I washed myself; washed my panty (as Auntie Viola called them) in the basin and then hung it out on the washing line. I would get dressed; I hated every item of clothing, everything I wore added to the tramp look and smell, including some ugly boy's boots. I don't know what happened to all my beautiful clothes. I had such pretty clothes, dresses, with ribbons to match, girl's patent shoes, but they must have disappeared with my old life!

Looking and smelling like a Victorian orphan was vicious but the final straw was my hair. Oh, how I missed Mrs Green, who every Sunday would cream my skin and plait my hair. Every week I had pretty new ribbons to go with each hairstyle.

But in my nightmare life, I had a choice; either let Auntie Viola put three 'cow' plaits in my head or learn to do my hair myself. So I taught myself how to take care of my hair; how to wash, comb, part and plait my hair. This was a real accomplishment. I was proud of myself, and I felt quite grown. But my best hair triumph took me about a year to master.

I learnt how to cornrow my hair. I remember doing my first cornrow; I thought I had invented something new. I was so proud of myself. I kept looking at the plait-come-cornrow. It was fantastic, except I didn't have anyone to share my triumph with. I had to wait until I went to school.

However, before I could leave the house, I had chores to do; empty the 'happy couple's' piss pot (pail)! Next, I would make and eat my porridge. After, I would have to feed the animals. The 'happy couple' had a menagerie of pets! Three dogs, three cats, four rabbits, gerbils! I used to love the animals at first until I had to clean up their shit!

I would feed them and sweep up all their shit, dogs, cats, rabbits, and so on! It was the same routine five days a week, shit and then leave. With the smell of shit and disinfectant in my nose and clinging to my clothes I left the dingy dungeon/flat.

I walked by myself down the street and around the corner to the Grinches' house. I had been introduced to the Grinches and their mum a few days after I arrived at hell. Initially I was happy at the prospect of having friends.

I thought, yippee, friends, an escape. Unfortunately, they definitely were not friends. On the first morning of going to a new school, Auntie Toni walked me around the corner to the Grinches' flat. She pushed me in front of the communal front door, stretching over me to ring the middle bell as she barked, "Be good and fucking learn, for Christ's sake."

With that, she was gone.

At first, I thought the Grinches' mum would take us all to school but that only lasted my first day.

Walking with them should have been fun, had it not been for the fact that the children were horrible. Real bullies because they had a big brother.

But he was actually really nice, I wish I could have walked to school with him, but he was about five years older than me and went to a different school.

So I would have to knock for his sisters, who were never ready. I'd have to go in and wait for them. I hated going in their house. It was so dirty. The flat smelt like body sweat and as if they never opened a window. Which wasn't true because they used to open the window to tell me to come up.

There was dirt around and on every light switch and on every wall. The place used to make me cringe. I used to dread going in.

I was made to wait in the front room, which always had music playing, and they had the biggest speakers I had ever seen. The speakers towered up to the ceiling. Their dad was a soundman. He used to play music at parties. Their mum was lovely. She had a really sweet smile with a gold tooth on either side of her front teeth. She always greeted me with warm hugs and gave me half a pack of Polo mints and she gave her children a pack to share.

But 'The Grinch' sisters, Pamela and Jenny, were cold. They didn't know kindness! Every day Pamela would make me give my Polo mints to Jenny, so she didn't have to share hers with her.

At first, I used to give them my Polos, but then I realised they wouldn't even give me one. So I stopped. The Grinch sisters sent me to Coventry. They wouldn't speak to me for the whole day, which meant nobody else in our class could speak to me either as they were all frightened of them.

From that day, I didn't bother to resist. I just gave them my Polos. I was already in hell at home; I couldn't be in hell at school as well.

Unfortunately, the Grinch sisters tried to ruin school for me too. As soon as we arrived at school Pamela insisted I played with them, which I hated because it always involved doing something horrible to somebody.

And because everyone was scared of them, they got away with their bullying ways. Pamela would push past or take somebody's pencil and every day she would drink at least two bottles of milk. And every day somebody would be crying because there was no more milk left. She was just vile.

After school I would go home to a smelly, cold, dark, empty house. I hated not having anyone to welcome me, but it was better than them being there. The 'happy couple' got home from work at about 6pm. They worked really far away.

We lived in Paddington and they worked in Wandsworth. Every day the 'happy couple' cussed the two journeys.

I was partly glad they weren't home, but I hated the dark flat, it made me feel so lonely. I was not used to being home alone. At

Nanny and Granddad's, Nanny used to collect me from school every day. But in hell I was either alone or being persecuted.

After school, slavery recommenced. I would take off and hang up my school clothes and put on my house clothes (second-hand rags).

Then I would have to dust the 500 ornaments and sweep the floor on my hands and knees with a dustpan and brush. Next, I would cook dinner. I was eight years old and I didn't know a thing about cooking. Why would I? When I lived with Nanny and Granddad I didn't even know where the kitchen was, never mind where the stove was or what it was for.

A fact that caused my Auntie Viola to go off like a rocket, regularly. To ensure I learnt, every time she cooked, I had to stand and watch, and learn because she would only show me once and the next time I would have to cook it by myself.

Luckily for me I learnt quickly. The fear of a beating or punch to the face will do that for you.

Auntie Viola had a meal rota which was the same every week. On Mondays I warmed up Sunday's leftovers. Tuesday, I made chow mein using the left-over chicken from Sunday's dinner. Wednesday was either soup or salad. She cooked her own soup, with me as her whipping girl. Or I would make the salad.

Thursday was runny macaroni cheese. One day I tried to speed up the cooking process by soaking the macaroni before I went to school. That's how I learnt that you do not soak pasta. A punch in the face also helped.

Friday was fish and chips day. Luckily, I didn't have to cook it. I would go with Auntie Toni to get it from the fish and chips shop.

On Saturdays we usually ate at my Auntie Gwen's house after a day of shopping, not in the shops like normal people, no, in Portobello Market. The 'happy couple' did not like the high street shops, no, they loved to go rummaging through the things that nobody else wanted, things people had thrown out or had donated to charity.

The 'happy couple' would walk from the start of the market on Great Western Road to the end, Old Saints Road, stopping at every second-hand stall. Some things didn't even make it to a stall; they were on a sheet on the side of the road.

It used to make me feel sick. What did I know about second-hand clothes and markets? Nothing.

Nanny and Granddad used to buy my clothes from the high street shops, Marks and Spencer's and British Home Stores. I used to feel so embarrassed when the 'happy couple' used to hold up some little girl's or boy's unwanted clothes against me to see if it would fit. I prayed no one saw me, or worse, a friend from school.

But they didn't care! They didn't even care if it was nice or ugly or if it was for a girl or a boy. If it was for 10p or 20p it was a bargain. Then, to add insult to injury, they would make me carry the bags, which were bigger and heavier than me. My arms would be dragging down – I looked like an orangutan.

But if Auntie Viola saw the bags dragging she would bark at me like a dog or just hit me on the back of my neck.

The only thing that was nice about Saturdays was that we went to Auntie Gwen's house. She used to keep the 'happy couple' off my back. Auntie Gwen wasn't really my auntie but she had been friends with, and even went to school with, my Auntie Viola in Barbados.

They were really close, so we saw her and her family every Saturday. Auntie Gwen had a big but gentle personality. Every Saturday she would welcome us as if she hadn't seen us for years, hugs and kisses for everybody.

The wonderful smell of steamed fish and cou-cou (which I hated, the cou-cou I mean) or soup would engulf us at the door. Then she would laugh, looking at the bags, and say, "Viola, you bought up the whole market again."

And then they'd be engrossed in what horrible deals they had got. Errrr! While I sat quietly in the corner trying to make the most of the moment when I wasn't on duty.

Auntie Gwen lived with one of her daughters, Grace, and her niece, Trisha. Trisha was about eight years older than me. She was about sixteen but she always had time for me. Sometimes she would call me into her room. She was also hiding from the adults.

Occasionally the aunts talked about Trisha. Now that's an understatement. The aunts routinely talked about all of the kids in the family, and then they talked about our parents, the neighbours, people at work, people back home, they loved to chat, period.

Auntie Gwen said Trisha was too womanish and was too busy running after man. I don't know how much of that was true, because to me Trisha was always home in her room playing music on the stereo. Her favourite record and mine was 'Police and Thieves'. Man, I loved that song. It had a wicked beat. It was called reggae music and I had never heard it before.

We used to just listen to it in silence and occasionally Trisha would dance to it. She showed me how to whine. The music and cool vibe was a lovely sanctuary from the world, until dinner.

Trisha had ended up living with her aunt when her parents had gone back to Barbados to live. She didn't want to go back with them, but living with her aunt was proving to be equally as unpleasant. Therefore, Trisha had time for me.

Trisha's parents were the talk of the Bajan community because of a rumour. Out of the blue her parents decided to go back home to Barbados. On hearing the news, a friend of the family had quizzed her dad about the move, but his nonchalant response left him to come to his own conclusion.

"You must of win de Pools."

"I must have."

Those few words became a matter of public record. Auntie Gwen talked about it over dinner. She said she didn't know anything about it, but she definitely hadn't seen any money, and laughed.

I loved Auntie Gwen. Her sense of humour brightened the grey, until she wanted to know how I was getting on. Every Saturday she would ask me about school. I always knew it was coming and I used to will her with my eyes not to ask me, but every week without fail she would open the hornets' nest.

I wouldn't even get a chance to open my mouth before one of the 'happy couple' would start up.

"Man, she, she is too hard ears to learn. Man, she, she ain't got no sense. She can't learn anything. She give bare trouble."

Auntie Gwen would look at me with compassion in her eyes and say, "Is that true, Dominiquè?" I'd start to protest my innocence but all I would get out is, "No."

And then Auntie Toni would jump in.

"All she's got to do is learn, but she's too fucking stubborn."

"Toni, why can't you say something without having to swear? Man, I can't understand why she got to curse for every word."

And Auntie Gwen, seeing a storm ahead, would try to break it up.

"Viola, you know that is Toni! Man, don't worry bout she, man. Toni, how's work?"

Phew! I was off the hook for another week.

Sundays I would have to go to church. Very occasionally, Auntie Viola would come with me but otherwise I was on my own. I liked to go to church, it gave me a break from the horror I was living. I loved to sing the hymns.

My favourite was 'I danced in the morning when the world was begun' and 'Sing Hosanna'. I used to love to pray. I prayed so hard at church, I thought if anyone could help me God would. But every Sunday I willed Father Peter to help me, but he just said, "God bless you."

How was that supposed to help me? After church, I went home to spend the rest of the day ironing. The 'happy couple's' overalls for work. Every sheet, pillowcase, shirt and dress which needed ironing, I had to do it.

They used to line up huge black bags full of clothes which had been washed at the laundry. The bags were bigger than me and I had to iron about eight bags full. The only time I got a break was to have my dinner and then go right back to it.

Of course, my first ironing day was an ordeal because I had no ironing experience. I had never even seen an iron up close, never mind used it.

Naturally, I had to have a brutal tutorial from Auntie Viola and Auntie Toni, which began and ended with cursing and blows raining down on me.

So, like all the other miseducation by the 'happy couple' I learnt to iron, very well. I learnt to put pleats in skirts and seams in trousers. It was gruelling because the iron was so heavy. I usually burnt myself at least once a week. I quietly absorbed the pain because if either of the 'happy couple' found out they would just add a blow to the injury and start cussing me. I sucked it up and endured.

After my day's slaving was done, I would retreat to the/my room. I hated it, but I had no other escape. I was so completely sad, the pain overwhelmed me. I felt so abandoned and unwanted.

I used to sit on the bed hoping a fairy godmother would appear to save me. I wasn't sure of the criteria for getting one, so I wondered.

I wasn't pretty as such, the thick blue glasses didn't help, but I had 'good' hair, milk chocolate skin, only a few chicken pox marks on my legs, good teeth and a nice smile. And I was definitely more destitute than Cinderella.

My fairy godmother would have to really work some good magic, but I was sure with the right colour dress, maybe powder pink with gold sequins, and hot-combed hair and ringlets, I would be as beautiful as Cinderella.

But despite being more in need than Cinderella, my fairy godmother never appeared. No matter how hard I wished and prayed for her or somebody with magical powers to rescue me, nobody came.

I even gave up wishing and praying Granddad would come and get me. Well, it was pointless. None of my prayers were answered. No matter how hard I prayed or how good I was, nothing worked. Heartbroken and in despair, I faced the truth. I would never see Granddad again. There would be no magic and definitely no happily ever after.

As my hope faded, so did my interest in fairy tales. I stopped reading them. My life was way too real to be bothered with fairy tales.

Instead of reading, I started to keep a diary. I decided to make little notes about my day. I enjoyed writing. Reading it back was the hardest, but then I realised I could write whatever I wanted in my diary.

I started writing about my feelings, about my life and the 'happy couple'. I found it so therapeutic. I had somewhere to take my feelings. I could say exactly what I liked. It was fantastic until Auntie Viola found it while snooping in the/my room.

The 'happy couple' tag-teamed me that day. Both of them screaming about how ungrateful I was, when nobody else wanted me. How wonderful they were to take me in and feed and clothe me.

But even as they spoke it was clear in my mind; they were the only ones benefiting from the deal, they had a slave, who obeyed their every command. Who cooked, cleaned up their shitty stinking place, endured their abuse and had no one.

But of course, I said nothing. I just had to stand there and take their insults and a beating. By then I was used to it. I had gone from being a loved and cared for little girl with loving nanny and granddad to an unloved and unwanted slave within a blink of an eye.

I had learnt to interpret Auntie Viola's mood and movements. I learnt when a punch was coming, but somehow I wasn't able to escape it. I knew she would kill me if I tried to run, so instead I flinched and jumped in fear. She'd say, "What u jumping for? Something wrong with you? You got nerves?"

But what could I say? I know you're going to punch or slap me at some point so I'm ready?

But sense prevailed, I knew better. It was safer to keep my thoughts to myself and stay alert, on my guard.

It was only a matter of time before a blow would land from out of the blue. The impact always sent pain rushing to my head as she always hit or punched me in the face first.

And no matter how much I braced myself, the pain would ring in my head and I would feel a bit light-headed. I would jump to attention regardless of what I was doing.

"Yes Auntie?" I would say, trying to ward off any more blows. Like I had some control over her beatings, which of course I didn't.

Auntie Viola was temperamental. She was unpredictable. Even if I had done all my chores as best I could she would find a reason to beat me. It didn't matter how hard I tried, she would always find an excuse to hurt me.

I had even tried buying them little gifts, out of what little money people had given me which I had saved up.

Auntie Viola would take the gift, open the wrapping paper and stare at the gift. It was usually a little box with a glass ornament inside.

"You teef this? I am not gonna get lock up for you, you better take it back."

"No Auntie, I didn't steal it. I bought it with my money."

"Nobody ain't give you any money. What money you talking bout?"

I would have to account for every penny before she would grunt, "Mmmmm."

I would even try to pre-empt her by saying, "I have done all my housework and I did my best."

Peace would last less than five minutes before she would start screaming, "You call this clean? Come here to me, look at this thing."

I would be looking painstakingly, yet I could never see a single thing wrong, but she would be going off like a rocket. I'd quickly try to re-sweep the floor or wipe down something but she would punch me in the face and then rain blows down on me.

But like a soldier, I fought on regardless. I kept trying my best despite the foregone conclusion.

I started inspecting my own work. Doing things two, three times and still no credit or appreciation.

Exhausted and dejected, I resigned myself to the fact, I was damned no matter what I did.

My response was to start drinking. I'm not sure what prompted me. But I found myself having a little shot of either gin or Bosca wine.

Auntie Viola and Auntie Toni always had a well-stocked bar and the cutest little shot glasses. I'd pour myself a little shot of something while I was cleaning.

I loved Bosca wine, it was a sort of sweet sherry. Just a few sips would make me feel warm inside; but I didn't like gin. It burnt my throat and tasted awful, which put me off. I only drank that if there wasn't anything else I liked.

At first, they didn't seem to notice the drink going down, probably because they both liked a drink and they always had people over.

They were like different people when they had company. They were the hostesses with the mostessess! They would entertain in the guest sitting room, which was only used for certain company.

Everything in the guest sitting room was like new because it was only used for guests. Only the best for the guests; the best leather chairs, glass coffee table, best curtains; you name it, it was in there. But with guests the place would come alive.

The 'happy couple' would entertain, play music, wine and dine the visitors. I was the maid, so I would spend my time fetching and carrying until the company left. But the whole time they entertained you didn't see anything of the usual viciousness, nothing but teeth skinning and laughing.

Looking in, the couple looked like lovely fun people until near the end of the night, when the 'happy couple' would start cussing and fighting. The air would be blue with cussing. This was usually the cue for the guests to leave.

To be fair, Auntie Toni usually started the trouble by getting drunk and talking some kind of slackness and then Auntie Viola would try to get her to stop but that would just light the fuse and the ugly drunk would take full effect.

'Effing this and effing that' would be the beginning and the end.

Before the front door shut to goodbye, I would be in the room praying they didn't notice my absence and call me out. Their relationship was so strange. For people who had been together so long there was never any sign of love or affection, just raw aggression.

They were always screaming and shouting. Auntie Viola was always telling Auntie Toni off for something she had done. It was either she was swearing too much, or she had gambled away the rent money or she had been out all night with her druggy friends. But the cussing didn't bother Auntie Toni. She just did what she wanted to do and was prepared to cuss it out, wrong and strong. I can't tell you the amount of times she gambled away the rent or bill money. But it was the same white noise, different day.

That didn't really bother me once it became the norm. I would have been more disturbed if there was silence. But what really affected me was when she was drunk. Auntie Toni became really aggressive and belligerent. She used to frighten the life out of me. I was never sure what she would do or what she was capable of.

This person was Toni; no aunt of mine would behave so. I'd have to clean up her vomit. I hated it so much. The smell and the look of it made me feel sick to my stomach. I couldn't shake the vision or the smell. As a result, I wouldn't be able to eat for the whole day.

Auntie Viola couldn't stand drunk Toni, she'd lock her out of the bedroom and banish her to sleep on the settee, and the vomit basin would be placed beside her. Arrgh, disgusting!

Their relationship was a mystery to me. If they hated each other so much why live together? I just couldn't make sense of it. That is probably why I didn't think they were a couple. I thought they were just good friends who lived together. That reality only dawned later, when I was older.

3

HALF-SIBLINGS!

I had never considered the notion of siblings. There had only ever been Nanny and Granddad and me. And occasionally Audrey, but I knew she wasn't my sister. I don't know why, probably because she wasn't black like me. She was white. I don't think this had ever been discussed with me, I just knew.

So it came as a great surprise when one Friday evening my so-called mother turned up with two children. They came in smelling of money, love and care! They sat looking at me and I smiled at them. I was so happy to have children to play with. There was no formal introduction, so I started to talk to them.

I introduced myself.

"Hello! My name is Dominiquè."

They in turn said their names, Keres and Jamie, and carried on playing with the dogs. I was struck by how sweet they smelled and how nicely they were dressed. Keres was wearing a lovely cream argyle cardigan over a pastel peach dress with a bow at the back and pretty peach patent shoes and lace-topped ankle socks. She had lovely long thick hair, which was filled with lovely pink bobbles.

Jamie was wearing a cream argyle jumper and navy blue trousers and navy blue loafers. I looked down at myself and I felt self-conscious and sorry for myself. I was wearing an old second-hand tartan skirt and a blue holey jumper, some old odd chewing gum-coloured white socks. And I knew there was nothing sweet about how I smelt. I smelt like dog and cat shit, disinfectant and dust.

I tried to forget about it and focus on the fact that my so-called mother had brought children for me to play with. Auntie Viola was playing hostess, and this was the only time you saw her sickly gold tooth smile in the house.

"Would you all like something to drink?" she asked.

"Dominiquè go and get them a cream soda," she barked, before they could answer.

I jumped up and went to get the drinks, but my so-called mother spoke.

"Bring Jamie a Coca-Cola because he doesn't like cream soda."

I changed the drink and went back and handed them the little bottles.

I felt so embarrassed when Keres picked a hair off the bottle of cream soda. She held it up with a look of disgust and showed it to my so-called mother, who tried to hide her disdain as she spoke.

"Oh Keres, don't be silly, just wipe it off your fingers."

Auntie Viola chimed in, "Man, it ain't gonna kill she, it's just a bit of hair! Stuuupse."

I shouldn't have been surprised Keres found a hair; everything always came with a side order of cat or dog hair.

I asked Keres how old she was and she said she was five and Jamie was three.

"I am eight."

I was pleased as punch that I had something over her, I was the oldest. Just as I was getting to know her Auntie Viola ordered me to go and get a bowl and put some peanuts in it, which I did quickly. I didn't want to miss playing with the children. As I carried out the order, I heard Keres call out, "Mummy, Mummy." Then she whispered, "I need to go to the toilet."

My so-called mother got up and took Keres to the toilet. I just stared at the space they left on the settee. I kept replaying it over and over again. Mummy, mummy, she said. But she's my so-called mother but she called her mummy. And as reality dawned, I smiled as I realised that they were my brother and sister.

My joy was short-lived as my Auntie Viola barked at me, "What you skinning your teeth for?"

Just then Keres and my so-called mother came back into the room, to hear Auntie Viola barking at me, "You, you hear me talking to you?"

I quickly took the smile off my face as I answered her, "Nothing, Auntie."

"There is something wrong with she, I telling you!"

My so-called mother shot me a look that was quite clear and meant don't make me have to talk to you. But luckily the non-verbal reprimand was interrupted by Jamie, who said he wanted to go to the toilet. Thankfully I was able to play with Keres, who seemed sweet.

"Let's go and play with your toys," she said.

I felt so embarrassed; I didn't have any toys anymore. All my toys were at Nanny and Granddad's house. If we were there, playing would have been fun.

We'd have played with my favourite toys, like my perfect white dolls' house. It was fantastic because I had furniture in every room. I even had a dining table with plates and cutlery and a candlestick and everything. And best of all it had real lights that switched on and off. It was fabulous. Oh, how I longed to be back at Nanny and Granddad's house playing in my playroom under the stairs.

I could have given Keres a cup of tea out of my real china tea set. But it was all gone now.

I was just about to explain to Keres that I had nothing to play with, when my so-called mother and Jamie came back in the room for only a brief minute, because they had to go. I watched my so-called mother get my brother and sister ready to leave.

I watched her take care and really gently put their coats and hats on. Suddenly, I felt a pang of fear; I didn't want them to go. I wanted the sweet-smelling children to stay and play with me. But before I could think about it they were gone. And it was just me again, the three cats and three dogs, three rabbits, gerbils, the stink of piss, shit, disinfectant and dust.

The front door had barely connected to the lock before she, Auntie Viola, started. I'm not sure what had caused it, but she was good and mad.

"You, you tidy up the place and wash them dishes!" Auntie Viola shouted.

"That girl ain't gonna change, man she lie, everything that comes out of she mouth is a lie!"

Auntie Toni, who had just come in as my so-called mother was leaving, chimed in, "Uck, Viola, that is the way she is. You don't have to get on so, man."

"Toni, shut your ass an' listen, I talking! She going to come an' see the chile, soon, soon my ass, she ain't coming! She don't want that chile, if she did, when she get married she would have kept she."

Auntie Toni stared at Auntie Viola.

"You know she couldn't do that after she lie to that man."

Well, that's when I learnt about the backdrop to my existence. Apparently, my so-called mother, Sidero, had her first child at the age of eighteen, with a guy called William.

He had loved her so much that he wanted to make a life with her, so when their child, Dev, was about six months old he had gone to England to make a life for them and then send for Sidero.

But while he was away, she had been partying hard and had another child, Hyacinth. No one was sure who Hyacinth's father was, but it wasn't William. But my Auntie Viola had heard that Hyacinth's father was my so-called mother's best friend's man.

Apparently, they had all gone out to a fete and afterwards he had dropped her friend home and then took Sidero home but not before they fooled around. But Sidero didn't let this little indiscretion stop her from taking the opportunity to start a new life in England.

When Dev was two and Hyacinth was three months old Sidero went to England, leaving behind both children with her mother.

She didn't go to live with William, the man who had sent her a plane ticket, and who loved her despite her indiscretion. She decided he was too boring, he didn't like to party. So instead she went to live with Auntie Viola and Auntie Toni.

But the aunts couldn't stand her living with them because she told so many lies. They didn't know what she was up to. Sidero was never home and never came in at the agreed time. Instead she was out all times of the day and night.

So eventually they put 'the dirty stop-out' out. Sidero returned eighteen months later to introduce her fiancé, a light-skinned Grenadian man, who loved to drink.

Soon after the introductions Sidero had a child for 'the Grenadian' and when she was expecting her second child with him, they got married. Auntie Viola and Auntie Toni went to the wedding. The reception was held back at the new Mr and Mrs' flat.

And that is where my Auntie Viola saw a small child playing with Keres who looked familiar. When she enquired of another guest who the child was, she was told, that's Sidero's daughter, Dominiquè. Auntie Viola and Auntie Toni were so mad they left the wedding reception without saying a word.

About a year after the wedding, 'the Grenadian' unexpectedly turned up at Auntie Viola and Auntie Toni's doorstep. Apparently, while on holiday in Barbados with Sidero, he had hung out at the local rum shop at the bottom of Palm Road, where they were staying with his in-laws.

He got talking and drinking with some local guys. While the rum was flowing, they celebrated his marriage to Sidero, while filling him in on her past, including her other children.

'The Grenadian' refused to believe them and chose to defend the honour of his new bride. The night ended in a big fight.

'The Grenadian' had confronted his wife with the allegations, but she had denied everything without reservation. So, determined to get to the truth, he turned up at Auntie Viola's. But when he arrived Auntie Viola was out and only Auntie Toni was at home.

She didn't bat an eyelid as she gave 'the Grenadian' chapter and verse. Arriving too late, Auntie Viola was furious with Auntie Toni for spilling the tea.

But it was too late, the truth was out, and 'the Grenadian' was stinking mad and drunk. But before he left Auntie Viola, he proclaimed his intention; he would stay with his wife until his daughter, Keres, turned twenty-one and then he would be gone.

Auntie Viola turned to me when she caught herself and remembered I was still there. She pulled my face close to hers as she spoke.

"Better a thief than a liar, because a liar will get you lock up!"

And that is how I came to find out I had four siblings, two brothers and two sisters, and I was in the middle.

4

Summertime and the Living Isn't Easy!

What is a half-sibling? I remember hearing the term, half-sibling, and wondered what it really meant. I was offended by the suggestion that the sibling tie was below par with whole siblings. I loved my brother and sister in full, well, the siblings I knew, that is. There was nothing half about it. I loved my brother and sister as much as someone who loved their brother and sister who shared the same mother and father. But the older I got the more I came to understand what a half-sibling meant.

Unfortunately, my so-called mother did not visit very often so I rarely got to see my brother and sister except in the summer holidays, when I went to stay at their house.

The first time I went to stay at their house was something else. It wasn't really a house. They lived in a two-bedroom flat on the second floor of a low-rise block of flats in St Albans.

The area was leafy and less congested than the buzzing streets of

Paddington where I lived with Auntie Viola. It reminded me more of the area around Nanny and Granddad's house in Barnet.

The flat was brighter than Auntie Viola's house. I guess, because it was on the second floor, it got more light than that dingy basement flat, which the light and sun ignored. The flat had a lovely sweet smell, like how Keres and Jamie smelt when they came to visit.

Keres and Jamie shared a bedroom and a big bed, so I slept with them. We used to play nicely together most days, as long as we played school and Keres could be the schoolteacher. It was boring after a while, day after day playing school, but that's all Keres wanted to play.

She was such a strict schoolteacher, always putting me or Jamie to sit in the corner. Jamie would usually run out of patience first. He would let a dinosaur in to wreck the classroom or he would say he had to go to the toilet and never come back. The next time we'd see him he'd be on his bike outside.

My escape from Keres wasn't as easy as Jamie's. If I tried to leave or play something else. Keres would cry and my so-called mother would come in and slap me round the face or push or punch me!

My so-called mother picked up where the 'happy couple' Auntie Viola and Auntie Toni left off. She was just as horrible as them, but 'the Grenadian' was worse. I dreaded him coming home from work. He was always drunk but never a happy drunk.

His presence was announced like a bear in the wild, with the boom of his voice. As he opened the door he would shout "Keres!" in a strong Grenadian accent.

Keres would run to him. "Daddy, Daddy," she would shriek. He'd pick her up and give her a big kiss and a squeezy hug. He never greeted Jamie, or his wife, just Keres.

"Did you get your tidy (bath)?" he barked.

"Yes, Daddy," Keres would reply, squeezing his cheeks.

"Did you play all day?" he'd always growl and shout. Keres couldn't just smile and keep quiet. No, she had to put me in it.

"I was playing school, but Dominiquè and Jamie wouldn't play with me."

I couldn't even get a chance to run and hide. No time to explain, he grabbed me and slapped my legs about ten times, but it didn't seem to have the desired effect. I guess because I refused to cry. So he dragged me to the kitchen and beat me with the washing machine cord.

With the first lash, I think I stopped breathing and then the pain ran up my legs to my head and I started screaming. That seemed to fuel the flame.

I think he gave me four or five lashes. I lost count. The room was spinning, or I was. I don't know how I made it to bed but the next thing I knew it was morning.

Everything hurt. I had welts across the back of my legs and bum. The message was clear, do/play whatever Keres wanted. After that beating I would play with the traffic if she wanted me to, and she knew it.

Powerless, I became the perfect playmate. I played whatever they wanted, watched whatever TV shows they wanted, without any resistance or a choice. Being the best playmate was better than being a slave; at least there wasn't any shit involved.

I hoped I would never see 'the Grenadian' or the washing machine cord again. I learnt to be as invisible as possible, which wasn't hard; as long as Keres and Jamie didn't cry no one cared if I was there or not.

My so-called mother worked nights as a carer in an elderly care home. She slept in the day. She ran her home like clockwork. We were fed and watered and in bed before she left for work. This ensured 'the Grenadian' didn't have to be bothered with us. He wasn't home anyway, he usually went down the pub for most of the evening.

When she came in from work in the morning, my so-called mother would give us breakfast and then go to bed. My job was simple. Keep Keres and Jamie quiet. And that was the rub, because they knew if my so-called mother was woken, she was going to beat me and not them, even if it was them who had made the noise. So, every so often Jamie would refuse to play school, or would eat Keres's Penguin, or drink her ginger beer, and Keres would scream the house down.

My so-called mother would jump up from her sleep, run into the bedroom and beat me with the slipper and tell Keres to stop crying. I would be ordered to replace whatever it was that had been taken and we would all be told to keep quiet. The beating cycle became part of the routine.

I tried hard to be invisible while staying at my so-called mother's. I generally kept out of sight of the adults, except when there was company. For some reason the presence of visitors seemed to cause great tension in the house. After seating her guests, my so-called mother would find me and whisper in my ear, "You call me Auntie, you hear?"

This was very odd as I never called her anything, and definitely not mum. But her command or the presence of visitors had an odd effect on me. I deliberately called her mum. Hearing the word 'mum' from me visibly moved her, but she grimaced with a fake laugh, trying to blow off the scent.

"Oh, that's my niece! She likes to call me mum."

But as soon as the visitor left, I'd get a good beating, but I didn't care. It was worth it to see her squirm and lie. I just couldn't understand why she was trying to hide our relationship. She didn't tell Keres and Jamie to call her aunt, so why me?

For the most part my summer holiday was spent being the perfect playmate or getting a beating, but then there were the lovely family days out to the seaside. Except, 'the Grenadian' didn't want to take me. Nope, I had to stay at home by myself or with my so-called mother who was sleeping in the next room, which was basically the same thing.

While I was alone, I would try to take my mind off how sad I felt for myself, by dreaming about the lovely holidays I had had with Nanny and Granddad.

Oh, how I loved our holidays to Penzance in Cornwall. We used to go for three weeks every summer. We stayed in a hotel by the sea which had the most beautiful views of the sea, every window view was awesome. I just loved staring out into the deep blue sea.

Every day Granddad would take us on trips to the beach or to the funfair. Nanny didn't like the rides, but Granddad would always get on with me. We used to eat lovely Cornish ice cream cones or have apple pie with clotted cream or have a cream tea with lots of cream cakes. We had such wonderful times.

The memories felt so lovely and special, until I awoke and remembered where I was, alone in a place where nobody wanted me. It hurt to be so unwanted when I had been so loved. Why was I being punished? What did I do wrong? I had no answers, and no one to ask.

Keres and Jamie would return late in the night, from a lovely day at the seaside or a family outing with their dad. They would tell me every little detail about their day, playing in the sea, building sand castles and eating fish and chips by the sea.

And then they would show me their sticks of rock and candy floss. There was never any for me and they wouldn't even offer me some. Jamie would add insult to injury by taunting me with his sweets and even singing a 'you ain't got none' song.

Keres would come to my defence.

"Leave her, it's not her fault she didn't get any."

But the way she'd say it, always sounded as if it was my fault.

It seemed to escape them that I had never been invited along and it didn't seem to bother them either. I never heard them ask their dad if I could come. They just accepted it like it was normal.

Most children love the summer holidays, as it means the end of school days and is time to have fun, but for me the end of the school year posed an interesting dilemma; to either spend my summer with my half-siblings, my so-called mother and 'the Grenadian', in the flat which smelt so sweet but was so cruel, or spend it with Auntie Viola and Auntie Toni in the horrible dingy house that smelt like piss, and shit, disinfectant and dust, bursting with misery. It was like choosing between the devil and the deep blue sea.

Except there was no choice at the beginning or end of the six weeks' holiday. I had to go there, and I had to go back to the misery place which smelt like piss and shit, disinfectant and dust, the place where the sun didn't shine.

I could feel the impending doom, but I was powerless to stop the cycle.

5

Making a Run for It!

Once my despair had reached its limit and I realised no one was going to rescue me I began plotting my escape.

The enormity of being caught between the devil (the 'happy couple') and the deep blue sea (my so-called mother and 'the Grenadian') was too much.

I must have been about nine when I made my first real attempt to run away. One morning, before school; I packed a few things in a black plastic bag. I dragged it round to my friend Gemma's house. Gemma's family were really lovely. They reminded me of Nanny and Granddad, not just because they were white too but because Gemma's mum was so warm and caring.

I knocked on the door and Gemma opened it.

"I've come to stay."

No hello or such-like. The pressure of the escape had made me forget my manners.

I walked in, dragging my bag behind me. Gemma ran to her mum with excitement.

"Dominiqè's come to stay."

Gemma's mum suddenly didn't appear caring and loving anymore.

"You can't stay here! You have to go home!"

And with that she ushered me out of the door, with my bag dragging behind me. I was so shocked and devastated. I couldn't believe how ruthless Gemma's mum had been to me. She didn't even let me come in for a minute. She didn't even try to find out why I wanted to stay. She just threw me out into the cold.

The rejection was swift, like the guillotine. As I stood outside, I was stumped. What was I to do? I had no choice but to return to the place of misery.

Unwanted yet again, I walked quickly in the rain back to the house. Feeling shaken and discombobulated, I put my few belongings back in their place. Everything was back to normal. Or so I thought, except I had overlooked one key detail in my escape plan.

Gemma lived opposite the Grinch sisters, and their mum had seen the whole escape attempt. And with no consideration for the consequences to me she told the 'happy couple'. I don't know when.

The brutal response was as expected. I really got my ass bust. The pair were equally incredulous at my attempt to escape.

"Ungrateful bitch! We working every hour God sends to keep she and this is the thanks we get! You are an ungrateful good-for-nothing black bitch. You think dem want you? Nobody wants you!"

The verbal abuse was coupled with blows, which started with hands and ended with a bamboo stick. The pain was a great silencer. I could no longer hear the vicious words but the lashes were enough to provide the knockout.

Their persuasive might did not convince me to change my plan, in fact it only made me more determined, but next time I tried to escape, I would make sure the people who I ran to actually wanted me.

Strangely, a few months later life gave me even more misery and reasons which fuelled my determination to escape. The first thing was my so-called mother's child, her first-born, Dev, came to live with us.

His father had paid for him to come to England to live with his mother. Apparently, his behaviour was getting out of control. He was getting into too much trouble while living with his grandmother in Barbados. The decision was made to send him to his mother in England. The only problem was that his mother didn't want him either. So he ended up with me and the 'happy couple'.

Initially, I was so happy to have my big brother living with me, until I realised that he was the devil's child. He was so wicked and spiteful.

A few days after he arrived, he ordered me to make his breakfast and because I refused to do it he poured boiling water over my leg as I tried to run away from him.

Auntie Toni's initial response was to defend him and everything he did. But when he drowned some newborn puppies, she agreed there was something wrong with him.

To give them some credit, before giving up on him the 'happy couple' tried a psychiatrist, for the boy, not for them. Lol. But when even that failed they gave him to his mother. She only had him for about six months before she got rid of him too. She put him in a hostel.

Even with the devil's spawn gone, I was still in hell. I realised the cycle of slavery, shouting, arguing, verbal abuse and beatings had no limit or end.

I felt numb. What was the point of feeling hurt, wounded, unwanted, unloved or helpless? There was no end to my despair.

Time had proven there was no hope of happiness with the 'happy couple'. They were pure evil and two halves of the same coin.

Exhausted and tired of silently crying, I couldn't bear to see myself in the mirror or look at my scarred skin. Both actions triggered internal and external sobbing. I wanted to die.

In the midst of all that greyness occasionally a ray would shine. Auntie Viola loved jewellery, particularly gold, and she shared her passion with me.

For Christmas one year she bought me a silver ring with my name on it. I loved it, particularly as it was new, not second-hand like everything else I owned.

As per usual the gift came with a command. Peering into my eyes, she barked, "Don't let anyone take it off, you hear?"

I got the message loud and clear, but that instruction wasn't necessary. I loved my ring, so I definitely wouldn't let anyone take it anyway.

Jewellery was the furthest thought from my mind on sports day. There I was sitting on the grass, having a laugh with my friends, when Mrs Barker, the strictest teacher in the whole school, comes over to me.

"Stand up!" she barked.

She really didn't have cause to bother me but as I stood up she looked me up and down.

"Take that off!" She pointed at my ring.

"No!"

I stared into her eyes as she slapped me across my face. My face was stinging with the print of her hand.

Well the next thing I knew the woman was clutching her face. I had slapped her back, right across her face. I heard a loud gasp from the kids.

I felt weird. A rush of fear raced through me. It was like time froze and suddenly everything speeded up. I had no time to process what I had done. One minute I was back sitting down watching the races at sports day, with kids coming over to fish for details, and the next minute I was at home.

Auntie Viola arrived home in a tizz. The school had called her demanding she meet with the headmaster. She was cursing as usual but then she turned to me.

"You haven't cause no trouble, have you? Man, I will kill you, if you have!"

I looked at her as she ranted. What was I to say? If I told her what had happened, she was going to kill me.

If the school tell her, she's going to kill me. I was dead either way. I decided to take the delayed route. I said nothing. And she went off to the school.

While I waited, I nearly had a heart attack. Again time stood still but then it speeded up and she was back. At first there was an eerie silence and then she just went mad.

She dragged me into the bedroom and dragged my clothes off, while she's screaming, "I, I ask she, did she cause trouble, she ain't answer me yet. An' I gone down de school and what dem say, she hit de teacher. She, she hit de teacher cross she face. De woman got a red handprint cross she face, an' I ask she…"

My heart had stopped until the bamboo stick came striking down on my naked body. I tried to speak but she was in a frenzy, just railing me with blows until my skin bled. Somehow, I managed to get a few words out.

"You told me not to let anyone take my ring off!"

As the tears raced down my face, I lay curled up on the floor with her towering over me. I don't know if she heard me or not, she didn't say another word. She just left the room. It was right then I decided I had had enough. I swore by the grace of God that I would run away. I didn't know how or when, but I had to get out.

It's strange how a sequence of events becomes apparent after the fact. And how the hole you're in can turn into the escape tunnel.

Apparently, hitting a teacher in self-defence was a big deal, because a few days later a social worker appeared at the dirty dingy place that smelt like shit, piss, disinfectant and dust.

The social worker sat in the room as if she had lost all sense of smell. Her face gave no signs of disdain, she looked kind and spoke gently. I'm not sure why I couldn't make sense out of her words, but it seemed that she was there to speak to me. She wanted to know how I was feeling and if I was happy.

Now, how was I supposed to answer her? How was I supposed to tell her about the hell I was living, with the Grim Reaper staring me down?

Auntie Viola did not speak to me, but she etched the words in my head telepathically.

"Keep your ass quiet! Tell her anything and you're dead!"

I heard her loud and clear, even though no words were spoken out loud, to the extent that when the social worker looked at me intently and asked me how I was, I couldn't speak. I was mute. It was so bad, at one point I thought I was speaking but no sound was heard. I coughed to see if that would clear the blockage but still nothing came out.

The social worker tried to help.

"Maybe she needs a drink."

Auntie Viola reluctantly went to get me a drink, trying to impress the social worker. She returned and gave me a bottle of cream soda, which only ever used to come out when we had company.

The cream soda tasted delicious. I loved cream soda. It was so sweet and creamy. But even that didn't help bring my voice back, which frustrated Auntie Viola.

"Well I can't understand what happen to she. She's always talking or singing bout here."

Singing? I don't think I had sung a single note since the day I arrived there. I think the only thing I had sung was happy birthday to myself, or to them if forced to.

Not like when I was living with Nanny and Granddad. I used to sing all day and all night. I had loved to sing. Singing made me feel special. I had even learnt some bits of the songs from the 70s group The Three Degrees; they sang 'When will I see you again' on *Top Of The Pops*.

I loved them, mainly because I thought my so-called mother was in the group. I tried to sing to her, but she didn't want to hear me. She couldn't be bothered with me and definitely didn't want to do anything which meant she spent a minute over her fleeting visit.

"Maybe Dominiquè's shy?" the social worker enquired, looking at me sweetly. "Never mind, I'll visit again and hopefully next time Dominiquè will feel more comfortable to talk to me."

Auntie Viola was vexed, but she tried to hide it.

"You coming again? What for? You can see she got a roof over her head and is fed. What more you want?"

The social worker tried to reassure Auntie Viola but she was still mad as arse, to the extent that she ushered the woman out. But not before the social worker gave me a little card with her name and address on it.

Quick as a flash I memorised the address on the card; Social Services, 550 Harrow Road, London W10.

As I was memorising W10, Auntie Viola snatched the card out of my hand as she twirled past in a hurricane of rage, shouting as she went.

"Man, I take she in when nobody don't want she, give she a roof over she head, feed she, well I don't know what more dem could want! Man, she couldn't even wash sheself, but now she can do for sheself. So, I ain't know what more dem want!"

Auntie Viola continued to rage but I drowned out her voice by repeating the address over and over in my mind.

Once I was sure I knew the address by heart I worked on my escape plan. It was easy; on Monday after school I would go to the social worker's office. I just had to last the weekend.

But something was different. I don't know what it was, but my Auntie Viola tried to be nice to me. I didn't have to clean the yard. I could just go out to play. If Auntie Toni started shouting at me, Auntie Viola would jump in and defend me. It was odd. I don't know if it was the fact that I now had someone watching out for me or what, but I didn't care. I just counted down the days until Monday.

Monday was a lovely day. Everything happened as it should. I felt doubly excited. While being famous or infamous had its charm, my focus was the end of the day. Luckily, the school day sailed by.

After school, I began my escape down the Harrow Road. I followed the same route as my class took to go swimming every Friday. We'd walk down the Harrow Road and go over the Ha'penny Steps and turn left and there were the swimming baths.

But today I didn't have to go over the Ha'penny Steps, I just had to keep walking down the Harrow Road until I came to number 550. Which is exactly what I did.

When I reached the big white building, I felt a pang of fear. What if they don't do anything? What if I have to go back? I didn't care. I just pushed the door and went up to the reception. A kind lady asked me who I had come to see. I had nothing.

After all of that memorising the address I had forgotten to memorise the social worker's name. That's when I panicked. I began crying and screaming, "I can't go back! I can't!"

The kind lady ran around from her desk and began to comfort me. She wiped my tears and put me on a chair to sit down. She asked me for my address, which I gave her. I sat waiting for a while before another lady came out to see me.

She took me to a room and before she had shut the door, I started to spill my horror.

I told her about the piss and shit, jumble sale clothes, beatings with bamboo sticks and Auntie Toni being a heroin and gambling addict. The poor woman's eyes nearly burst out of their sockets as she stared at me intently, visibly disturbed. The lady was very caring. She wiped away my tears and told me not to worry.

I couldn't stop the fear when she left me alone. What if she didn't believe me or she sent me back? But she returned with kindness and to my relief I didn't have to go back to the 'happy couple' or the piss and shit.

I was taken to a children's home that very day. I was free.

6

A Home Without Abuse, Please

Once your parents don't want you it's hard to find a home with people who do. But after escaping from the hell of the 'happy couple' I didn't have any expectations or requirements.

My first children's home was refreshing. It was on Lisson Grove Estate, off the Edgware Road. The home was clean, and the staff seemed really nice and kind.

The home was run by a middle-aged white lady called Audrey, and she had a mixed race adopted daughter called Tina, who was about twenty. Tina was very sometime-ish. Audrey and Tina lived in the flat attached to the children's home, so the children's home was run like an extension of her home.

The home was for children aged eleven to sixteen. I was the youngest. I was eleven. But the home only had three children including me, so the staff were really caring.

The home felt warm and cosy, but it was weird having a cook and set meal times and set bedtimes depending on your age. The food was really nice, and I didn't have any chores. I had freedom and new clothes.

When I arrived at the home I only had the clothes I stood up in, so Audrey took me to John Lewis and bought me everything I needed, all brand new. And it got better. I had a clothing allowance, so I could get new clothes whenever I needed them and I also got pocket money, every Friday. I think it was about £3.

I had never had pocket money before. I was rich. Every Friday I'd go to the sweet shop and buy anything I wanted, it was fantastic.

But better still we had sweets, crisps and snacks in the children's home, so I didn't really have to spend my pocket money.

And I could go out to play or go anywhere I liked. I didn't though. I stayed close to the home.

Every Saturday, I loved to go shopping in Church Street market. It was a great market which seemed to sell a bit of everything. I enjoyed wandering through the market looking at all the stuff I could buy. I was good at saving up my pocket money and then I'd go to the market and buy what I wanted, it was liberating.

I remember saving up to buy a pair of sandals I had seen in the shoe shop window. After a few weeks I finally had enough money to buy them. I felt so grown up buying what I wanted, what I had saved for.

I loved the way my new sandals looked and felt on my feet. I had bought them with my own money. It was fantastic.

Initially, I had asked Audrey to buy sandals for me, but the home could only shop with a purchase order which could only be used in John Lewis or Marks and Spencer's. I didn't care, I was happy to save my pocket money to buy them for myself!

For the first time in three years I felt peace and I wasn't frightened. I had just started to feel settled, so much so I didn't look ahead.

One of the staff who worked at the children's home, called Arlene, really liked me. Arlene was from Barbados. She used to look after me like I was family. She didn't like to see a black child living in a children's home.

Every day I had to go to school with Arlene's daughter, Jacqui, who was a loudmouth, pot stirrer. It was so shocking, because when you looked at her she looked so beautiful.

She had the most amazing eyes, they changed colour with the seasons. In the summer they turned orangey hazel. In the winter they turned green, in the spring they were turquoise.

Her European features and clear caramel complexion reflected her mixed-race heritage. Her beauty flowed down her tall slender body and the only imperfection was her feet. She had the biggest feet I had ever seen on a girl. But no one ever seemed to notice her man-size feet. They were captivated by the wonder of her eyes.

Unfortunately, her eyes and beauty could not block out sound. She was such a loudmouth and boy, could she swear. There wasn't a swear word she didn't know or use. She was only eleven.

And to make matters worse her dad was from St Lucia, so she could also swear in Patois. She taught me all she knew, well, it was the only defence. I needed to be ready if she came for me. Well, that and the fact that it couldn't hurt to know how to cuss in another language.

Jacqui compounded her vulgarity with her disdain for dark-skinned people. To her, the darker the skin tone, the more it repulsed her. She actually used to look at me like I was diarrhoea.

But luckily, I graduated with honours from the 'happy couple's' cursing university. My Teflon armour and foul mouth ensured she directed her bullshit elsewhere. Her passion for cursing ran head to head with her family loyalty. She would defend me and cuss me in the same breath.

After about six months of being in the Lisson Grove home, I was introduced to Arlene's Auntie Jeannette, who fostered children.

Auntie Jeannette was married to Uncle Wilson and they had an adopted son called Nicholas, who was five years old.

Auntie Jeannette and Uncle Wilson wanted to foster me. The idea of fostering was a new concept to me and plain blind-sided me. I hadn't considered leaving the children's home before. I had mixed feelings about it, but they seemed like nice people.

Apparently, the home was only a temporary place because the council did not believe that children of my age should grow up in a children's home. So I didn't really have a choice.

Auntie Jeanette, Uncle Wilson and Nicholas lived in Essex, in a lovely three-bedroom house. The leafy countryside was a far cry from the urban inner city, Lisson Grove estate. My new life also included a new school. I guess my new home was considered to be too far from my old school, but the decision was made without my voice or view.

Living with Auntie Jeanette and Uncle Wilson was a real trip. Daily life bore no resemblance to the previous teatime visits. On the two visits Auntie Jeannette gave me the most beautiful cakes, which she had baked herself. She served the tea in beautiful china cups and saucers and the cakes were displayed on a real teacake stand with doilies.

But now, somehow the same cakes tasted completely bland which was heartbreaking because they still looked so delicious.

The cakes were symbolic of living with Auntie Jeannette, Uncle Wilson and Nicholas. The family looked lovely on the surface, but my experience of living with them was really unpleasant on many different levels.

Auntie Jeannette was unable to have children of her own and adopted Nicholas as a baby. A year before I arrived they had adopted a baby girl called Elizabeth. She died when she was nine months old.

I only became aware of this when I put my things in the bedroom and saw a photo of a baby on the wall. The bedroom was a far cry from the one at the 'happy couple's' but it was equally devoid of love and felt empty.

It was Nicholas who told me what had happened to the baby. But neither Auntie Jeannette or Uncle Wilson ever mentioned it to me.

✆

Another layer of unpleasantness was Auntie Jeannette. She had a violent temper. However, unlike the 'happy couple' there was not any verbal abuse. Shouting, yes, but not swearing. She was a Christian, you see.

Auntie Jeannette liked everything done right now. And I mean right now. Delay would start the hurricane. She didn't like 'stupidness' as she called it, which was asking her a question or giving her reasons why something couldn't happen immediately.

Any of these responses would result in a violent outburst of anger. She'd throw whatever was in her hand, be it a bottle or a knife. You name it, she would send whatever came to hand first sailing through the air; items would whistle past your ear and land beside you or behind you, or on the wall, whichever they reached first.

Her aim was army regulation perfect. She only missed you because she wanted to, or because God was on your side.

Auntie Jeannette used to work, usually two jobs, as well as being a foster parent. She was a nurse and worked at night and slept during the day. And if you valued your life you would not wake her up.

But Nicholas liked to see her roar, so he would usually do some 'foolishness'. Bang something, turn up the radio loud or start singing at the top of his voice. Then he would turn and run like a Tasmanian devil. Being five years old he could always find somewhere to hide, but me being eleven made me a great target for her wrath.

I'd get a good beating with the slipper and then she'd storm back to bed. I wanted to kill Nicholas for unleashing the dragon, but there was no point. Any retaliation would trigger a repeat beating from Auntie Jeannette. I learnt to stay away from Nicholas.

The whole scene reminded me of summers with my so-called mother. I hated it.

Uncle Wilson added his own dynamic. He loved Auntie Jeannette dearly, but he was so frightened of her, he too would avoid her wrath by disengaging himself. So Uncle Wilson was never the port in the storm I hoped for.

Far from it. He only spoke to me if he really had to. Like if he needed me to pass him the newspaper, or if he made us all a cup of tea. I would say, "Thank you," and that was it.

To me, it seemed he didn't like fostering children. He didn't really want other people's children in his home, or near his precious son, and he made sure I knew it. I attempted to stay out of his way. It was easier to be invisible.

⌘

Another thing I hated was that Auntie Jeannette did not believe in confidentiality. Your business was everybody's business, within the confines of the family and close friends.

Well, that's how she treated my business. She was by no means a gossip, and never started any trouble by chatting inappropriately about people, but my business was never my own.

She told everyone in her circle about my so-called mother and how she had lied to her husband about her children, and she told everyone about the 'happy couple' and the pissy, shitty, dusty and disinfectant-smelling house, and about the abuse.

I really hated to hear anyone talk about my family business unless it was me talking, which Auntie Jeannette refused to understand.

And God help me if I got into trouble at school! Then there would be a 'family council' meeting with all the aunts and uncles. The meetings were usually held after Sunday dinner. The elders would sit in a line; I would have to stand in front of them and account for myself to each and every one of them. I hated it.

Don't get me wrong, the 'family council' meetings were not just held for me, oh no, it would be for any of the kids in the family. We all hated them. It burns me to admit it, but they were a great deterrent, as we all tried to keep out of trouble to avoid them.

Auntie Jeannette liked to call me Jacky. "My name is Dominiquè," I'd proclaim, which only made her laugh. It was months before I realised that she was calling me a jackass…

Despite all the negatives about living with Auntie Jeanette, thankfully there were some positives. It was while living with Auntie Jeannette that I met my best friend, Jewel.

She was so like me. She was mature and understood the world like I did but hadn't had any of the traumas or horrible life experiences I had. She liked me for who I was even though she would always tell me I was mad.

Jewel was six weeks older than me, and our standing joke was that she would get her pension six weeks before me and she would feel sick when it happened or that's how I twisted her age advantage.

We were very similar in appearance and both had a Cadbury's milk chocolate complexion. We were five feet tall, exactly the same height, although she always maintained she had longer legs.

We both wore glasses, although mine were thicker, and we both had wisdom beyond our years. Best of all we both had a wicked sense of humour.

Jewel's mum, Auntie Kay, and Auntie Jeannette were sisters. They were also best friends.

They would be together all day Sunday and then spend all night talking on the phone. Luckily the sisters' closeness ensured that Jewel and I got to spend a lot of time together. Maybe I had a guardian after all.

Auntie Jeannette was so fond of Jewel, and she was her favourite of all her nieces. She would always say, "Man, she got nuff sense!"

Jewel was usual left in charge of all the kids unless Karen, Jewel's big sister, was there. Karen was six years older than us.

Karen was so stern, and she looked at me as if I was insignificant. She hardly ever smiled, and she was extremely studious. Karen was always studying or reading a book. If she was left in charge of us, she ruled with an iron pen and a stern eye. At six feet tall and built like a linebacker, nobody was gonna mess with her. No way!

Then there was Chrystal, Jewel's little sister. Chrystal was five years younger than us and the same age as Nicholas, and they were really close. Chrystal was also a mini-rhino and a force to be reckoned with.

One Sunday, we were having dinner together and Chrystal refused to eat the kidney beans that were in her rice. All through the dinner, and after a considerable amount of coaxing, she still refused to eat the beans.

When all the kids went off to play I thought she'd cave in, but no, she still refused to eat those beans. Her mother was equally stubborn and told her she could not leave the table until she had eaten them.

Chrystal sat at the table all afternoon and all evening. Right up until it was time for them to go home, she still refused to eat those damn beans. That's when I realised that although she was 'talawa', her might was like a small rhino.

The two families spent a lot of time together. In fact, most weekends and every school holiday. Auntie Jeannette really liked to be active. She would take us swimming or on Bajan excursions coach trips.

The coach trips were a great opportunity for the extended family to get together and have fun. The excursions were usually to the seaside. A different one each time.

The coach trips were organised by Auntie Jeannette and Auntie Kay's cousin, Stout. His real name was Brian, but everyone called him Stout because that's all he drank, and he was little and stout.

Now Stout was something else. He had a light-hearted fun personality and consequently he always drew a crowd, so he had no problems filling two or three coaches with people from all across London.

The funny thing about Stout was he had two families. One with his wife, with whom he had two children. And the other with his outside woman with whom he also had two children. It was clearly no secret as both families would go on the excursions.

To keep the peace, each of Stout's families travelled on different coaches, and Stout divided his time equally between the coaches. The onlookers marvelled at his peace-keeping skills and his ability to have his cake and eat it.

Stout's coach trips were legendary. The coaches always arrived late to pick up the people and they were ridiculously overcrowded with three people squeezed into seats for two. And those who couldn't find a seat stood for the entire journey, and I'm talking about three or four-hour trips or more (i.e. London to Blackpool).

The coaches were the equivalent of a modern-day party bus. Soca music boomed from every speaker. There was food 'til food can't done! Everyone shared what they brought with everyone.

Homemade Bajan corned beef or cheese paste sandwiches, fishcakes, pudding and souse, cakes and conkies (a sweet cornmeal-based cake), drops (grated coconut sweet) and the obligatory rum and coke flowed all the way there, and all the way back.

While at the seaside, we would all go sightseeing, queue endlessly for fairground rides and often long after all of that we ended the day with a big DJ dance, with music blaring, until the coaches left.

∽

Auntie Jeanette took me on my first holiday to Barbados and I was thrilled, as Jewel came with us. The timing couldn't have been better because my so-called mother was also going to be in Barbados for her nephew's wedding.

My whole family was going to be there, and I would finally get to meet them. I was so excited.

The thought of meeting my big sister, grandmother, aunts, uncles and cousins; it was going to be fantastic.

But before all of that we had to make it through the journey to Barbados. For some travelling is considered a stressful event which involves keeping track of luggage, passports, children, etc.

But stressful does not even begin to describe travelling with Auntie Jeannette. With no concept of travelling light, she opted for the opposite approach of 'bring everything' including the whole of Shepherd's Bush Market!

I had to carry a five-gallon can of cooking oil in my hand. Jewel had to carry a five-pound bag of rice in hers. I lost count of the number of suitcases, but we needed two cars just for the cases, which looked like trunks.

Auntie Jeannette was close to combusting for the whole trip. She didn't want to pay any excess for the extra luggage, despite all the suitcases being severely overweight. Then she was worrying about the rice bag bursting, or the oil spilling, or Nicholas running up and down the aisle of the plane.

The best thing about the trip was that Auntie Jeannette was so focused on other things she had less time to bother with me. I could focus on having fun with Jewel and seeing my family.

What I loved most about the flight was when we landed in Barbados, the whole plane sang the song, 'Barbados'. It was a lovely soundtrack and welcome.

I felt so proud of my country, Barbados. We had our own song. I hadn't really thought about what it would be like in Barbados but the first thing that hit me was the heat.

As I exited the plane the heat hit me right in the face. I struggled to breathe for a while. It was so hot, I wanted to strip my clothes off right there, but I didn't have a hand free to do it because of all the hand luggage that was weighing me down.

I loved the airport. The design was so tropical. It didn't have any walls or doors, the roof looked like the inside of a white giant circus tent, and the interior was light, airy and open plan.

Once outside the airport I was struck by the landscape and the houses. I hadn't given the island much thought. But if I had, I don't think my imagination could have done the designs of the homes justice.

There were so many different types of houses, from little board and shingle houses, known as chattel houses, to huge mansions.

Luckily for us we were staying with Auntie Jeannette's sister, Patricia. Auntie Pat lived in St Michael and she had a lovely big wall house, with five bedrooms, all with en-suite bathrooms.

Jewel and I had a huge bedroom with an en-suite bathroom which included a bidet. We had no idea what the bidet was for during the first week stay, but it came in handy for washing our dusty feet. That was, until we figured out what it was really used for and then we were horrified!

Once we got used to the concept of the bidet, we loved that bidet. It was so refreshing, it cooled my whole body down, by just spraying my v'jj with that little jet of cold water. I vowed I'd have one in my own home one day.

Jewel and I were free to roam close to home. Auntie Pat's son lived near her and I had a thirteen-year-old crush on him. I'd find any excuse to visit him. Jewel and I would go exploring the 'jungle' between the two houses. It was wicked.

I had never seen so many different exotic fruits growing wild. Mangoes, sugar apples, ackees, which looked like gooseberries but tasted lovely (but stained your clothes), and guavas. That's when I developed my passion for guavas.

Jewel and I picked and ate so many fruits we got high from the sugar, or the sun, or both. Life in the tropics was wonderful.

The downside to staying with Auntie Pat was that she was deeply religious. Being Seventh Day Adventist meant we couldn't play outside, play cards or watch any television on Friday or Saturday, which was when the best television was on.

On Saturdays we all had to go to church. Although I was initially sceptical due to all the rules, I quite liked her church. Everyone was so friendly and on the first Saturday that we went we all had to stand up and be welcomed by the church, who were so happy to have family visiting from England. I felt like royalty, looking at the smiling faces as they applauded us; it felt warm and welcoming.

The holiday was going really well except I couldn't find my family. It took a few days for me to get the courage to sneak the Barbados phone book into our room.

I spent ages looking through that phone book searching for my family. First, I looked for people with the surname Moore. Luckily the name Moore was in the phone book, but there were thousands of them.

Then I realised I didn't know what my grandmother's first name was. I thought it was Baa, but there was no one listed in the phone book called Baa.

I became frustrated when I didn't know where in Barbados my family lived. I realised that even if I got someone with the right name I didn't know if they were living in the right place; so I couldn't be sure that they were really my people. The search was so arduous. The more

I searched, the harder it hit me. I had none of the key information necessary to find my family.

After days of scouring through the phone book, it suddenly dawned on me; my so-called mother didn't want me at the wedding. Nor did she want me to meet my family.

Refusing to be deterred, I spent many hours just staring at the names in the phone book. I would go over and over all the Moores, hoping and praying a number would jump out at me.

A few times I got brave and actually called a phone number in the phone book but when the person answered the phone I got scared. A man barked at me in a thick Barbadian accent, "Hello, hello, who would you like to speak to?"

I stuttered, "Baa Moore."

"There is nobody here by that name."

Before he could say anything else, I blammed down the phone, tears streaming down my face. The reality that nobody cared whether I was there or not, and that I was so near but yet so far, was too hurtful to bear.

I asked myself, why would my so-called mother tell Auntie Jeannette about the wedding if she didn't want me to be there? Then I remembered, how could I forget, because she hated me. But I refused to be dissuaded.

About a week into the search, after I had all but given up all hope, I had an idea. What about my dad's family? Maybe I could find them. Maybe they would want me. But I needed to remember my father's surname.

There was only one occasion, many years before, when I was about nine, I heard Auntie Viola mention my father. It was after I had had a moment of madness, on a rare visit by my so-called mother. She had come to beat me for something or other.

After she had finished beating me with the heel of one of my school shoes, while the tears ran down my face, I dared.

"Who is my father?"

I don't know what had possessed me to ask her. I think I figured, she's beating me anyway so what is the worst that can happen? She would just beat me some more.

"What father? You haven't got a father. Your father is dead!"

She spoke without pause, spitting the words out as if they were nothing as she marched out of the bedroom door.

I remember feeling weird. I had mixed emotions. I felt happy and sad at the same time. On the upside, at least I had a dad. That was more than I had before. As tears trickled down my face, I sobbed deeply for my father.

The real downer came as I realised with my dad dead, who would rescue me from this horrible dingy, piss, shit, disinfectant and dust-smelling place with the 'happy couple' who are never happy and who use me as a punch dummy?

The realness and loneliness of my situation was so painful. I just sobbed and sobbed, so hard and obviously too loudly because Auntie Toni came into the room. She asked me what was wrong. I told her, my dad was dead.

"Uck, man, that's nothing to cry for! It ain't gonna bring him."

As she stumbled back out of the room, drunk or high or both, I overheard her tell Auntie Viola that I was crying about my dad, but Auntie Viola then said something like, "Them Browns ain't no good."

I couldn't hear all of what they were saying clearly and was unsure of what she meant or who the 'Browns' were. Was this my dad's name? I didn't dare to ask the 'happy couple' any questions about my dad. I couldn't face another beating.

As I looked at the names in the Barbados telephone book I wasn't sure if Brown was a first name or a surname. It was so frustrating. Needless to say, the search was futile.

The hunt made me feel unwanted and alone in the world. I felt totally pathetic. Why did I keep thinking that there was going to be a happy ending? I desperately wanted to be loved; to feel special, to feel wanted; but all roads led back to the same hell!

Happiness had left me when Nanny died. Every time there appeared to be a ray of hope it was snatched away like I was cursed. Nobody wanted me, and I just needed to accept that my life was not a fairy tale and I was going to live a life of misery.

I had had my life's happiness with Nanny and Granddad. From then on, I have been condemned to living a life of misery. There was not going to be a happy ever after. Well, that's what I told myself. I put my family and the wedding out of my mind. Well, as much as I could.

Being on an island full of black people didn't help. Every time I saw someone who looked like me, or who looked kind, or who showed me kindness, I wondered if they were my family. Was that lovely lady my grandmother or my auntie? It was pitiful.

We spent about two weeks with Auntie Pat and then we went to stay with Auntie Christine, Auntie Jeannette's oldest sister, and her husband, Uncle Howard.

They lived in the parish of St John, which was very rural compared to St Michael. We took the bus from St Michael to St John, and boy, what a journey that was! It was hard going. The chairs didn't have any cushioning or padding, and my bum got numb very quickly.

The sides of the bus were not enclosed, and I could see the road when I looked down by my feet. I had to hold on tight to stop myself from falling out of the side of the bus, as my little body could easily slip under the guard rail.

The bus was perfect for sightseeing. We saw monkeys and parrots in the trees. We saw so many gorgeous beaches and endless sugar cane fields.

Barbados looked so beautiful as we drove by. It smelled so sweet. A mixture of sugar cane, vegetation, tropical fruits, coconuts and flowers.

Staying at Auntie Christine's and Uncle Howard's was so different to staying with Auntie Pat. The house was a board and shingle house with a corrugated iron fence. The house had older period architecture and décor.

There were no en suites. In fact, going to the toilet the first time was a complete shock. The toilet was outside, but luckily someone was using it. I was offered a hole in the ground to wee. Bemused, I shook my head.

"No thanks, I'll wait."

And I did. I waited until the next day; the memory of the hole in the ground made my wee retreat. The toilet in the wooden box wasn't much better but at least there was an actual toilet.

Jewel and I had a really small room, which looked worn and tired. To make matters worse there where ants everywhere. In the bed, in the chest of drawers, on the curtains. Everywhere. The ants and the room made my skin crawl. I had to sleep with my face in my hands and one eye open.

The rest of the house wasn't much better. The kitchen was overrun with flies during the day and 'mahogany birds', which are giant flying cockroaches, that come out at night.

The roaches were as big as my hand. They used to scare the life out of me, and Jewel, who usually loved all creatures big and small, but the big people didn't pay them any mind. In fact, Auntie Jeannette used to say, "I wonder who has come to visit us. It must be a friend or family member who has passed away."

Was that supposed to help the situation? It just made me feel as though the place was haunted.

Now if all that wasn't bad enough, on top of all this there was Granny Baker, well, that's what I called her. She was Auntie Jeannette's elderly mum.

Unfortunately, Granny Baker, who was eighty, had Alzheimer's really badly, so they had to keep her locked in the bedroom, otherwise she would run off; and for an elderly lady she could run fast and far!

Apparently, the last time she ran away she made it to Bridgetown, which was about fifteen miles away from the house.

While she was there she accosted a policeman, and that's how they found her because the policeman called them. From then, she was under lock and key.

Granny Baker was quite funny. She used to curse stink if they bothered her. It was really funny to hear her swearing.

Well, that's what I thought until one day she caught me laughing and she chased me out of the house with a broom. She wouldn't let me back in and all attempts to rescue me was met with a verbal assault. I was outside for hours. After that I kept my laughter to myself and kept out of her way.

Jewel thought it was hilarious, she nearly wet herself laughing so hard. Afterwards, anytime Granny Baker came near me, I would cower, and Jewel would try to reassure me.

"She won't trouble you," with a cheeky grin on her face.

What was nice about the stay was sitting in the gallery with Jewel just watching the day go by. We used to talk to the neighbours as they passed the house, ran errands for the aunts, or just sat and enjoyed the sun on our face and the cool breeze. It was lovely, but I couldn't wait to leave the place; it made my skin crawl.

꿈

Soon after we got back from Barbados, I overheard my so-called mother tell Auntie Jeannette that her sister Gloria had cursed her for not telling anyone I was in Barbados.

Aunt Gloria had demanded to know from my so-called mother where I was staying. It was the day I was leaving Barbados. Aunt Gloria had made her way to the airport to see me, but it was too late. We had already gone through to the departure lounge.

Aunt Gloria was so distressed by the missed opportunity. She wanted me to know that the family loved me. When she got back home from the airport, she cursed out my so-called mother again.

I found it comforting to know that someone in my family had wanted to meet me. It made me feel warm inside. I used to imagine meeting her, but it was never to be.

A few months later my Auntie Gloria was murdered by her boyfriend, right in front of my grandmother's house. Apparently, she was seeing a man with a terrible temper.

Somebody warned her not to see him because he had killed a woman. Auntie Gloria got scared, she tried to ease out of the relationship, but the man wouldn't let her go.

While he was killing her, he was heard saying, if he couldn't have her then no one could. He cut her up with a cutlass. There wasn't a place on her body that didn't have a cut, the police said.

The murdering man went on the run. The police gave the family a chance to deliver their own justice, but the man had friends who hid him until the police found him.

He was sentenced to ten years' jail time which, to me, just didn't seem like justice, particularly as he had already served ten years for killing his first victim. Clearly a ten-year jail sentence wasn't a sufficient deterrent.

When Gloria was killed I realised hoping for love was hopeless. Every time there was a ray of hope it would be snatched away, leaving me further down in the depths of despair.

I only had Auntie Gloria's love in my life for a few months before it was snatched away in the worst way possible. I needed to forget hope.

My life was real. I was not living a fairy tale. My nightmare would not end with a happily ever after. No, it seemed I was going to be tortured for the rest of my wretched life. And the sooner I accepted it the better I would be. So said, so done.

The effects of the holiday had soon worn off and Auntie Jeannette was back in fighting form. Being in Barbados had had a calming effect on her. She hadn't really hit me for the duration of the holiday, just the odd bark or command.

It was a shame she couldn't maintain the composure because there were so many things I liked about living with Auntie Jeannette.

I loved her relationship with her sisters, particularly Auntie Kay. Their bond was so close, and they shared everything. They bought everything in twos, so they could give one to the other.

They were also close with their niece, Auntie Arlene. They rotated festive holidays between them so that each family would host the festive holiday. I loved how the families lived, it loved, shared and cared.

Unlike my experience of family life there weren't any lies, or secrets or fighting.

I loved to watch them all together. The family was pure united family. I admired it.

But unfortunately, family life alone couldn't hold me. In between Auntie Jeannette was set to kill me. Things were getting too much, the beatings, the arguing.

She was driving me mad. I couldn't bear the tension in the house. Nicholas could do no wrong, despite him being in league with Medusa for causing trouble and lies; I think he was taking lessons. He could win the world championship for lying.

But his father, Uncle Wilson, refused to believe his prince could do any wrong. As a consequence, I had to take the blows for everything.

Auntie Jeannette didn't care who the culprit was, she just wanted to beat somebody. Even the family dog, Maxi, had had enough. She used to get some good licks too.

One day she just didn't come back from her walk. I shared Maxi's view. The situation was becoming unbearable.

One morning I got myself ready for school. Auntie Jeannette had bought me some school shoes from Marks and Spencer's. They were nice enough but were far too high and dressy for school. She refused to get my point, so I had hidden my trainers in my school bag to change into on the way to school.

I left the house as usual with the school shoes on my feet. I bid her farewell and left the house. I waited until I was around the corner before I put my trainers on and then went to my friend's house, because we walked to school together.

Just as I arrived at my friend's house I realised I had forgotten my homework. I had to run back home. I ran into my room and picked up my homework off the bed and just as I turned to leave, I saw Auntie Jeannette standing in the doorway.

Man, she started yelling about the school shoes. I looked down and realised that I had forgotten to swap my trainers for my school shoes.

Next thing I knew, she started chasing me around the bed trying to hit me with one of my school shoes which I bent down to put on.

And that was it for me, I had had it.

I was not going to allow another person to beat me. It was bad enough when my so-called mother or my Auntie Viola did beat me, but I was not going to be abused by people who weren't even related to me. It was a step too far. So I left Auntie Jeannette's family that very day.

I didn't even have a plan. I just knew I couldn't take living there anymore.

Instead of going to school I travelled from Essex to Paddington, back down the Harrow Road.

I went to see my social worker and I told her the whole brutal story, from start to finish. Luckily the council was not paying foster parents to beat other people's children, so my revelations meant an immediate end to the foster placement.

Where I would end up, I didn't know. I hadn't given it any thought, but I knew I was done with families, mine or anyone else's. DONE!

7

No More
Families Please, a
Children's Home
Will Do

Well that's what I thought until I ended up at an assessment centre.

Up until that point I thought I'd been to hell, so things should be on the way up. An assessment centre is exactly what it says on the label. It is a centre where teenage children were sent to assess their behaviour and needs. It was more like a secure unit or borstal (young offenders' jail). It was so horrible.

A social worker I didn't know drove me to the centre. As I looked at the rough concrete building I felt as though I had committed a crime, and this was my jail.

Getting into the building was like going into a maximum security prison. There were untold security doors and keys. It frightened me.

Once inside, the place looked institutional, with graffitied walls,

fully because she could be vicious when she was ready, and she took no prisoners.

But for some reason, which neither she nor I understood, I wasn't frightened of her, so she knew bullying wasn't going to work with me and, despite her rough edges, she could be very protective. She wouldn't let me go out late, or go out raving with her and the others, as, at thirteen, she thought I was too young to be 'pon road', as she put it.

Amanda Rose even warned the other kids off me and told me to tell her if anyone troubled me. I felt safe with her around, but I hated the place, the staff and the kids. All those kids were true delinquents, hardcore juveniles, just waiting for their next crime or drug.

I counted down the days to freedom, but I still didn't know where I wanted to go next. Amanda Rose advised me to decide quickly, before the social worker decided for me.

The only thing I knew for sure was I couldn't go to another foster family. I had had enough of families to last me a lifetime. I was only a child, I had no clue what to choose and just didn't know what else was on offer.

Amanda Rose was going to live in Zen House children's home, but you had to be fourteen to live there and I was only thirteen. Amanda Rose encouraged me to try to get in to Zen House.

And that is exactly what I did. I had to have an interview with the manager of the home, Leo Hope. He explained that he ran his children's home differently to most other children's homes because he wanted young people to be responsible and actively involved in their own care plan. All residents had to sign a contract, which listed the goals to be achieved while living in Zen House.

I must have interviewed well because I got in. Luckily for me, I didn't have to stay at that horrible assessment centre for the full six weeks. Leo said I could move in straight away, so I only ended up doing four weeks, which felt like a lifetime.

I was so grateful for Amanda Rose. If it hadn't been for her, I wouldn't have made it. She kept the horrible kids away from me and found me a great new home.

Life at Zen House children's home was better than the assessment centre, Auntie Jeannette's and the 'happy couple' but it's not easy. Living in an institution is not a substitute for a loving family.

I had to learn how to live with a rota of staff and a rotation of challenging young people. Nothing prepares you for it because it's not like anything you have ever experienced before.

The difference between Lisson Grove estate children's home and Zen House was stark. Lisson Grove home was nestled in a little house, with a small staff team and a few kids; Zen House had a large staff team of twelve so it didn't feel like my home. I didn't have a home.

The staff team at Zen House was divided between caring and loving staff who respected the fact that we lived there and horrible staff who just did the job to get paid with no care or compassion.

Zen House was a six-bed unit, for fourteen to eighteen-year-olds, with a 'move on' flat for semi-independent living.

I was the youngest resident. Zen House had a mixture of personalities, behaviours, needs and energy. There was Kenneth, who was into jazz music. He was very chilled and laid-back. He was in there because his mum had mental health problems and he had been in and out of care all his life. He never showed signs of damage; instead he was very cool.

With his long green parka with a target on the back and a quiff, Gary was a 'mod' (England sub-culture), barely spoke and never socialised in the house. He was always in his room. He didn't even eat with us or watch TV or anything with us. I don't know why he was in there, but he had an air of mystery.

Sophia was a white girl who thought she was black. She even had a gold tooth and her nose pierced. She used to listen to reggae music and wore pleated skirts, Gabicci's and crocs (crocodile skin shoes). She really was a black girl; her hair was really curly like an afro. And of course, she had a black boyfriend. He was everything to her and a great distraction from an alcoholic mother and absent father.

Maxine was Amanda Rose's sidekick. They were as thick as thieves. Maxine's mum was an alcoholic too. Amanda's mum was also an alcoholic. I guess that's what they had in common.

Except Amanda Rose was a daddy's girl. She wanted to go and live with him, but his new wife wouldn't agree so he used to buy her anything she wanted to make up for not being there. The sky was the limit.

Once he bought her a Burberry outfit, a reversible cape with a matching skirt. It was wicked. But the high from every gift was always short-lived because no sooner than she had it, she would be calling him for something else. She really didn't want things, she just wanted to be with her dad.

Amanda Rose basically ruled the home, and Maxine and Sophia used to follow her. They all had boyfriends who were criminals, so there would be Visiting Orders and prison visits and raving.

Usually stirred up by Amanda Rose, the kids in the home tried to pick on me sometimes, but I didn't care. I would argue with whoever wanted to come for me.

I only remember her trying to attack me once. I had refused to turn the TV over. The staff were frightened of her and wanted me to leave the room to avoid things escalating, but I refused. I had had enough of her calling the shots, so I stood firm.

I carried on watching my programme. Man, she went mad, but I didn't care. She screamed and shouted but I still refused to comply. It took three staff to get her out of the room. They had to take her in the office to cool her down. She threatened to get me, but I didn't care.

That was a turning point. I was tired of being abused and bullied. I had already been to hell and survived. I wasn't frightened of her and I had no intention of putting up with being abused anymore. Not by her, or by anyone else. Those days were done. I had survived others, I had no doubt I would survive her too. I had a fire roaring inside me.

Ex-residents visited the home regularly, and one in particular, Scott, introduced me to the torment of what it was like to be a gay man who wanted to be a woman. Scott, from Scotland, had fair skin, stood tall, model-thin, with really thick blond curly hair.

After he moved out, Zen House remained his family and support because we were all he had. Every Friday Scott turned up in his usual super-skinny jeans, white blouse or tight cotton V-neck jumper and a racy pink scarf.

His hair was always blown out, but the curls made it a soft large curly afro. And he would wear pink lip gloss and big movie star rimmed sunglasses.

His favourite topic was always his latest love affair. Scott spoke very softly about his lovers. He loved black men, but they were a bit rough with him.

Every week he'd have his heart broken and a new love to dream over. But he suffered with periods of depression. Living as a man distressed him. He wanted to be a woman, but he was trapped in a man's body. It seemed to haunt him.

A few weeks went by when we realised we hadn't seen or heard Scott, which was weird because on the odd occasion he didn't come on a Friday, he would always be there for Sunday dinner, which was his fallback day.

The staff referred their concerns to the police, who broke into his flat. They found Scott hanging from his favourite pink scarf. Unfortunately, the significance and sadness of his passing just blended into the usual children's home madness and drama. Maybe the melee deflected our pain. I think we all felt glad he wasn't being tormented anymore. In a strange way, he had found his peace.

The best part of being in Zen House was actually having a say in my life. I had agreed my personal goals when I first moved in and I was focusing on reaching them.

I kept myself to myself. I focused on getting through school and stepping towards a better life. I avoided all youthful temptation.

I didn't want prison visits to a criminal boyfriend like the other girls. I wanted to leave school with qualifications and a nice caring lover, not a bully or gangster, nor a liar or a thief.

To me it was more important to be admired and praised like Karen, my best friend Jewel's sister. Karen left school with about ten O Levels and was studying law at Oxford.

After leaving my foster family I initially kept my distance, but after a year or so I occasionally visited Jewel; we were still close. Somehow our friendship had bypassed the awkwardness of my reasons for leaving her aunt's home.

Despite living very different lives we still had so much in common. She was also my conscience. I could hear her in my ear if I even considered doing something dodgy, like bunking school or telling a lie.

I tried my best to keep out of trouble. I didn't hang around with the other kids in the home. I only ate meals with them and maybe watched a bit of TV with them but that was it.

Luckily, I loved my own company, so I spent a lot of time in my room reading. Being in my room got easier when I got my record player.

For some unknown reason my so-called mother gave me her old record player. She even gave me Bob Marley's *Revolution* album. The whole album was wicked.

I loved Bob Marley, especially 'So Much Trouble in the World' and 'Three Little Birds', they had such a wicked bass. Thus, my love of music was born. Every week I'd buy my new favourite record from Blue Birds record shop on the Edgware Road or from Woolworths, if the song was top of the music charts.

Singles were so cheap, £1.50. The new sound would fill my room for the whole week until I bought another hit. Music became my therapy.

When I wasn't playing records, I listened to Radio Luxembourg. They used to play all the latest reggae and soul music. Listening to music made me feel happiness when nothing else did. Music was a great escape from the madness and loudness of the home.

With music I became self-sufficient. I took care of me. I kept my room clean. I washed my clothes. I wasn't like the other kids in the house. I didn't need to be told to clean my room or wash my clothes, I had my own routine.

I hated dirt. There was something about dirt and bad odours that reminded me of living with the 'happy couple' and just the thought of that stinking hellhole kept me on track to cleanliness.

Amanda Rose, on the other hand, was a whole other story. She didn't do anything she was supposed to do. Her keyworker, Jo, a lovely gentle soul, tried her very best to keep her in line, but the mismatched battles were constant.

She refused to wash herself, her clothes or clean her room, or comply with a curfew. She did things in her own time, which meant it rarely happened.

The environment in the home became toxic as every day was filled with Amanda Rose battling, undermining and threatening the staff.

When the staff tried to wake her up for school, Amanda Rose responded with violence. She'd throw whatever she could reach at them, alarm clocks, mugs of tea; you name it, she threw it.

She never complied with bedtime. She went to bed when she was ready and if the staff even tried to get her out of the TV room she'd start a riot.

Amanda Rose was a force to be reckoned with, and at an early age she had learnt how to control other people. She used all her assets. She could be as sweet as sugar but if that didn't work, she would be as mean as a gunslinger, with or without a weapon.

She could argue for England, like an earworm song on auto-repeat. She'd keep going and going until she wore down her opponent and she got what she wanted. She was a master manipulator. I watched and learned.

The staff took us on a number of holidays. We usually went to Newquay in Cornwall, where we stayed in a holiday cottage.

One year we went camping in Brittany, France. I really didn't want to go. Just the thought of it made me itch.

I hated the idea of sleeping in a tent and sharing bathroom facilities and all that mud. Eeek, it was my worst nightmare.

But at the same time, I didn't want to miss out and get left behind, so I went begrudgingly and moaning the whole way.

Our main mode of transport was the home's ten-seater van and a long ferry ride, which was awful. Under normal circumstances I love the sea. I find the vision so calming and tranquil, but this sea was different. Instead of being calming it was rough as rass.

We started the ferry trip joyfully. The other residents split up into a little clique. Amanda Rose, Maxine and I just hung with the staff. We all ended up down below watching a film but as the sea whipped up, one by one, people began running out of the cinema room.

All I remember is my stomach began to rock me. I felt so sick. My instinct took me up to the top deck, where I couldn't feel the boat's motion as bad. I sat on a chair and prayed for the nightmare trip to be over. I slept until my wish was granted.

On the drive to the campsite we stopped for a toilet and snack break. Unfortunately we picked an unwelcoming pub.

Initially the bar staff were friendly to the staff, who were all white, but when they saw four black young people they became really nasty. The pub owners' kids led the attack, swearing and calling us black this and black that.

Well luckily my foster cousin Toni had taught me Patois and I knew some good swear words. Amanda Rose and co also knew a good few choice words in English and French. Needless to say, we didn't stay for snacks or a drink.

And that was the general tone of our French experience. I don't think the staff had considered or were prepared for the racial abuse we encountered everywhere we went.

The abuse was awful and had a negative effect on us kids. It doesn't take much to fuel six young people in care, whose parents are unfit or unwilling to care for them.

We were walking time bombs and racism was the perfect ignition. The racial taunts started from the moment we set up camp on the campsite. The staff tried their best to defuse the situation, but it was futile.

There was no way we were going to allow people to racially abuse us without defending ourselves. But it was clear by the end of the first day we just weren't welcome.

⁓

After dark some of the kids went to do some washing but instead of doing their own, they 'helped' other people with theirs. They took washing off one washing line and switched it with another around the campsite.

The next morning the staff were awoken by screaming people, so we left the campsite and went home.

I felt overjoyed. I didn't have to stay and experience the cold and muddy wash huts. I left as I arrived. I took my dirt home with me. And that's where my camping experience began and ended. I just had to endure the horrid ferry trip to get home!

Back home Amanda Rose resumed fighting the staff for control. She disrupted everything the staff tried to enforce, bedtime, dinnertime, curfews, what we had for snacks or dinner; you name it, she disrupted it.

She even prevented the staff from having staff meetings or handovers, which the staff held daily to manage the home.

But the final straw came one night when some agency staff were on shift and they lost control of the house. Amanda Rose staged a riot.

She stole a set of staff keys and locked all us kids in the TV room. After a three-hour stand-off, the rioters got hungry. They raided the food storeroom and emptied it of its contents. The riot ended with a fire hose and fire extinguisher attack on the staff.

The staff had to call the police to regain control of the house. But the staff had had enough. They got Amanda Rose good, they put her in a secure unit in Kent for six months.

Poor Amanda Rose was never the same again. Well, you wouldn't be, secure units are no joke. It is worse than prison. They drug you at will and keep you locked up all day. No visitors or contact from the outside world. It is serious, particularly when you are only fifteen.

Zen House changed after that. When Amanda returned, they kept her under manners and as a result the place became less tumultuous.

❧

But I now had a social life, so I wasn't home much. I started hanging round with Pamela and Jenny, the Grinch sisters, who lived around the corner from the 'happy couple'. It was strange how it happened.

One afternoon I was strolling down the Harrow Road when who should I see but Pamela and Jenny. They had grown up some and seemed nice.

They invited me to go with them to steel pan practice at the Factory, a local community centre, so I did. And that's where I fell in love for the first time.

8

WHAT IS LOVE?

It's funny how life leads you down certain paths and you go without knowing where they will lead you.

The day Pam and Jenny took me to the Factory was so strange. I had gone with them out of curiosity and boredom rather than anything else.

The Factory was like a hub in the community for culture and music. It had music and art studios and all the local kids used to hang out there, but it also used to have raves every weekend. But that day Pam and Jenny were going to a steel pan practice.

As we turned into the Factory, we bumped into some of their school friends, Ronald, Cameron and Anthony. They had come to get some studio time. Anthony and Cameron were singers.

The moment I saw Anthony I had butterflies. He had the most beautiful eyes I had ever seen, and he looked at me with such intensity and sincerity. His gaze was magnetic. It was so hard to look anywhere but into his eyes.

He had the gentlest voice. It was a bit like listening to Michael Jackson. He had a similar smooth gentle tone. I remember feeling giddy. There was so much going on. The guys were telling us about their music session.

Anthony had just recorded a music video for Sony. It was exciting. I don't know what made me do it, but I broke off a single rose from a nearby rose bush and gave it to Anthony. He took it and put it in the rim of his trilby and gave me a kiss on the cheek. I was in love.

I had had a few boyfriends before. My first boyfriend was Chris. I met Chris at the church I used to go to with Auntie Jeannette and family. Chris was my friend Cheryl's brother, he was white.

Well, in Essex, it was either white boys or be a lesbian and that wasn't my flavour.

The church youth club was a great escape; it was the best excuse to get out of the house in the week, particularly as Auntie Jeanette was a devout Christian and active member of the church.

I loved the Lord too but I'm not sure what went on at youth club, except Chris and I would spend our time kissing. We'd sneak off into one of the side rooms, off the main hall.

Chris kissed my face off and touched me between my legs. Our chemistry was cosmic. We French kissed, only stopping to draw breath. Chris had A+ skills, maybe because he was older, about fifteen to my twelve.

Every Wednesday we would meet and do the same thing. No talking or hanging out, nothing else, just kissing and feeling each other up.

I don't know how long Chris and I were together, but it was brought to an abrupt end when foster cousin Jacqui came to youth club with me one week and went home and told Auntie Jeannette all about me kissing a boy and that was the end of that. I got a good cussing and beating. And to make matters worse, I was not allowed to go to the church youth club anymore, and that was the end of my passion.

But my feelings for Anthony were different. I loved everything about him. He was gentle. He liked me and then grew to love me. He was different to other guys his age. He was more mature, probably because he had had an unconventional childhood too.

He was raised by his grandmother because his mum had gone to work in America when he was a baby. Anthony understood what it was like to be abandoned.

Our relationship quickly became intense. We used to see each other every day and, when we weren't together, we would spend hours talking on the pay phone (yes it was all about phone booths in those days) or the staff's phone when I ran out of money.

I felt so special being with Anthony. He was very popular but at the same time he was very shy and reserved. I started to spoil him, buying him records, clothes, you name it. If he wanted it, I bought it for him. I even got him a special microphone. It was about £50, but he wanted it for his music and I would do anything to make him happy. It made me feel happy too. I loved to see him smile. He had dimples and those beautiful brown mesmerising eyes.

Anthony's and my love started with a spark which grew as we got to know each other but we made a conscious decision to abstain from sex until we were sure it was real love.

After about six months we couldn't fight our love and burning passion. We planned my visit to the family planning clinic together. I had decided to get the pill.

The doctor examined me and basically chucked the pills at me as if he was handing out Smarties. He had clearly been in the job too long because he treated me as if I was in there every week. He left me feeling very embarrassed, but I didn't care. I was fifteen going on thirty! And I was in love with Anthony and he loved me, and we were going to make love. The damn doctor could kiss my ass.

It's weird, when you think you are ready for something, you think you are prepared but when it happens you realise your preparation didn't do anything to prepare you for the reality.

The first time we made love was so intense. I would like to say it was my first time ever, but it wasn't. My first time was with a guy who lived in the home, about six months before I met Anthony.

For some crazy reason I had become really curious about sex. I think it was the fact that the other kids in the home didn't seem to talk about much else. I felt like the odd one out. The kids used to mock me and tease me about my lack of sexual experience.

But that wasn't really my deciding factor. I didn't suffer fools or bullies lightly, but curiosity was another beast. I just wanted to know what all the fuss was about.

So, on impulse one night, I let Steven in my room. He was older than me and he had been flirting with me for weeks.

Well, I must say I found the whole sex thing very overrated. It was over in a flash. I just couldn't believe what all the fuss was about. All that puffing and panting for a few minutes and it was done. And so too was my virginity.

I had no regrets. And despite Steven's persistent knocking at my bedroom door every night I was content in my new-found knowledge and saw no reason to repeat the experience with him.

My first time with Anthony was very different. It felt like love, and we made love to Steve Arrington's album. We put it on repeat and kissed for what seemed like hours. And the actual sex was nice, gentle and passionate. Our connection felt like euphoria, it was real love.

The more we made love, the closer we got; I felt wonderful, I had someone who loved me. We were inseparable. We spent so much time together just gazing into each other's eyes, hugging and kissing and making love.

The love affair was fun but every now and then we would have interference from the Grinch sisters or Cameron and Ronald. I guess because we had all started out as one big group, they didn't like it when we didn't hang out with them, so they would start some 'he said, she said' mess.

Anthony and I decided to ease out of the group. I started hanging out with Roxanne, his brother's girlfriend, who had two kids. I really liked Roxanne. She used to let me hang out at her flat and she let me and Anthony spend time alone together in her bedroom. Roxanne's flat was such a fun house. Roxanne was young, only twenty-two. She used to play music all day and I would play with her children. It was a place of very few rules, so I could just chill.

Anthony and I would be at Roxanne's all day and all night if we could, but I had a curfew. Anthony would walk me home about 10pm and then I would walk him back and then he would walk me back home and we would end up doing this for hours. So I was always home late, after my curfew, but I didn't care, I was in love and somebody loved me.

But then things started to change for Roxanne. She and her boyfriend, Martin, broke up, over nonsense really. Roxanne wanted Martin to move in with her, but he wouldn't, he liked living at home with his mum and visiting her. He wanted her to stop raving and having so many men friends. Roxanne was young and wanted to live her life the way she wanted, so they broke up.

From then on things started to go downhill for Roxanne. She stopped taking care of the house. She started raving and playing bingo every day. Roxanne was a lot of fun. Even if we were both broke, somehow Roxanne used to find a way to get some money for us to go raving.

She would either sell or pawn her records, at Honest Johns Records in Portobello Market, or beg or borrow or do 'magic'. I'm not sure how she got the money and I didn't ask any questions, but she would leave the flat broke and come back with enough for both of us to go raving. Raving with Roxanne was hardcore. She used to take me to all the top clubs, like Oasis, Three Trees, but All Nations was her favourite.

She was practically a member because she used to go every week. What she loved about All Nations was the fact it was like three clubs in one. It had soul music on the top floor, mixed party music on the middle floor and lovers rock in the basement. The sound called Salvadors used to play the wickedest lovers rock. By the end of the night the basement used to be so rammed that sweat used to run down the walls.

It was wicked. We never left before the club closed at 6am. Then we went to the bakery in Rigley Road market for bagels. But in the afternoons Roxanne left me to take care of her kids and clean the house.

If I didn't stay with the kids, she would leave them on their own and go to bingo anyway.

Then she started dating these horrible guys. She couldn't see them the way I did, so she never understood why I didn't like them. But

I could see that they were just using her because she was so kind-hearted. She would give you her last pound if you asked. The guys just abused her kind nature.

Then Roxanne met Jeffrey. He wasn't really her type, but he really liked her; but by then she was so caught up in her raving and nightlife, she didn't really give the relationship her time.

One day, out of the blue she became pregnant for Jeffrey. He practically moved in with Roxanne, and with him he brought his cousin Clinton, who had just come over from Grenada and didn't have anywhere to stay, so he crashed at Roxanne's for a while.

I hadn't been hanging out there much anymore as I didn't like the new vibe but one afternoon I went to visit Roxanne. After banging on the door for a while Clinton opened it and told me that Roxanne had popped to the shops, but she should be back soon.

I was walking away but he encouraged me to come in, saying that Roxanne shouldn't be long. I went upstairs and waited in the front room. Clinton and I were watching television. I was sitting in the armchair and Clinton was sitting on the sofa.

Everything seemed fine. We were watching the news and there was a story about a woman being raped on her way home from work.

Clinton quizzed me.

"What would you do if you was raped?"

I didn't really want to talk about rape.

"It's hard to say because you never know what your reaction would be."

Clinton walked across the room. He reached towards the top of the wooden curtain pelmet. I wasn't paying attention to what he was doing and started watching the TV again. Before I could blink, he grabbed me by the back of my neck and held a kitchen knife to my throat. He forced me to the ground and raped me, all the time with the knife held to my throat.

Tears rolled down my face. I couldn't speak, and as I tried to swallow, I could feel the knife pressing against my throat. When he was done, he said, "If you tell anyone I will kill you!"

He got up, and coolly and calmly put the knife back on top of the curtain pelmet. I pulled down my skirt and walked slowly down the stairs, out of the front door.

I didn't dare run, just in case he ran after me. I made my way home as fast as I could. I was terrified. I didn't know what to do but I knew I couldn't tell anyone because he was going to kill me. The walk home took forever. It usually took about ten minutes, but today, even though I was walking as fast as I could, I just couldn't seem to get there. I kept thinking he may come after me to silence me. I walked faster, sometimes running but still my progress was slow. I eventually reached home. I flew into the house past the staff who opened the door for me. I didn't speak.

I just ran upstairs, down the hall and into my bedroom. I lay on my bed hugging my pillow, and silently sobbed uncontrollably.

I decided to stay quiet and say nothing. If I told Anthony, he would go to jail for murder or Clinton would kill him. I couldn't win. I decided that the best thing to do was to say nothing and put it out of my mind. But it was easier said than done.

Why did horrible things always have to happen to me? I didn't do anything wrong. I was a nice person, caring and considerate, but yet something horrific was always waiting around the corner for me. I sobbed for ages until I didn't have any tears or energy left.

I went to have a shower to wash him off me. I scrubbed between my legs, but I could still feel him inside me. I realised it didn't matter how hard I scrubbed, the feeling would not go and neither did the flashbacks.

I decided to file the memory with all the other horrible memories and push it to the back of my mind. I had to pretend it didn't happen because thinking about it didn't change the fact that I had been raped.

No one noticed anything different about me, not Anthony or the staff or my friends. Somehow, I managed to get away with the charade, until a few months later.

Roxanne called and summoned me to her flat. I hadn't been there since the day of the nightmare and she was desperate to see me. I told her I would only come if Clinton wasn't going to be there. She assured me that he wouldn't.

When I got to her house Roxanne looked a mess, she looked frightened, the place was a wreck. Then she told me Clinton had raped her too. She had told Jeffrey and he had thrown Clinton out.

But a few weeks later Clinton had killed a girl in Ladbroke Grove and he was on the run. Apparently, he had tried to rape the girl. She had screamed so he stabbed her to death right outside a nightclub.

I broke down, telling Roxanne that he had raped me too. Roxanne was distraught. She hugged me and cried, but I felt numb and shocked. I couldn't shake the thought that he could have killed me.

My life could have ended just like the girl's. I didn't scream. The knife digging into my neck kept me silent. Now it was out, I had to tell Anthony; well, we both had to. It was awful. I wanted to file it away again, but I had no choice, I had to tell him.

The words hit Anthony. It was brutal. He had so many emotions, but most of all he was broken, crushed. As I cried, so did he. Anthony was very compassionate; he tried to kiss me better and was distraught that I hadn't told him. He wanted to kill Clinton but there was no way he was going to win against a murderer.

Luckily, after three months on the run the police caught Clinton and he was eventually sentenced to 'Her Majesty's Pleasure'. The police contacted me during the investigation because Clinton had confessed to raping me, but I refused to give them a statement. I wanted nothing to do with it. I refused to relive the nightmare. It was best buried.

Unfortunately, the effect wasn't. I'm not sure who was troubled more, Anthony or me, but our relationship was different.

We began arguing. He accused me of being too possessive. I wanted to know what he was doing every minute of every day and I was actually with him for most of the time. He said I was suffocating him. I acted like before, but it didn't erase the reality. We were different. The pressure grew until Anthony broke up with me and our two-year love affair was over.

I was devastated. I couldn't imagine living without his love. The feeling was unbearable. I just wasn't prepared to live without love again, it hurt too much. My life was empty. I didn't have anyone else in my life, nobody loved me. I had nothing to live for.

The answer to my problem was obvious, I had to end my suffering. As I developed my plan, I dropped a few hints to Anthony but instead of him being caring, he was cold. He said he would never speak to me again if I did something so silly.

I didn't think it was silly. I was deadly serious. I didn't want to live anymore, and it was clear he no longer cared. I left Anthony more determined.

I arrived home. I said brief unassuming goodbyes to the staff and went to my room. I wrote a long goodbye note to Anthony, then I took fifty penicillin tablets, which was no mean feat. The taste of each pill made me gag, and once down I had to fight against the urge to throw up.

I tried to sleep but I couldn't. I felt so sick. The taste of the pills kept repeating on me. It was awful.

Suddenly, one of the staff was banging on my door, insisting that I open the door. But I couldn't get out of bed. So she used her key and as she peered at me from the doorway, she caught sight of the empty medicine bottle on the floor.

"Oh Dominiqè, why did you do such a silly thing?" she said, as she ran from the door. The next thing I knew I was in an ambulance.

You would think that the doctors and nurses would be caring and compassionate when faced with a suicidal sixteen-year-old; but they were not. In fact, they were quite rough and abrupt, barking questions at me.

"How many pills did you take?" "What made you do a silly thing like that then?" "Luckily for you, you didn't take enough to kill yourself but you're not going to like what happens next!"

And he was right. I didn't like the tubes being rammed down my throat or my stomach being flushed out. I felt so sick. And up until that point I had never vomited. I prided myself on being able to prevent myself from being sick. The whole idea of vomiting made me want to vomit. I just couldn't bear the thought of it.

But now I had no choice. I had been forced to be sick and even when the tubes had been removed, I was still vomiting. It was awful, a horrible torturous experience.

I decided then and there that if I had to commit suicide again I would have to find another method, because an overdose was out of the question.

The whole situation made me feel even worse than before my suicide attempt, which I thought was impossible. I hid my distress under my bed sheet. My tears flowed silently. I had no reason to ever stop crying. Everything had gone so wrong. I was still alive.

And then things spiralled out of control when Anthony refused to visit me. I felt even more suicidal. Then, as if to compound my despair, for some ungodly reason my so-called mother turned up at the hospital.

Well, that was the final straw. I was livid. How dare she come to visit me? Why was she there? To check if I was dead? Why did she care? She wanted me dead as much as I wanted to be. So what did she want? She didn't bring me so much as a grape, but there she sat, next to my bed.

Why did I do it, she wanted to know. Well, I went mad.

"Why do you want to know? Don't pretend that you care. What do you want? Why are you here? Did you want to check if I was dead?"

She couldn't take it, she left abruptly without uttering a single word. But she confirmed my suspicions. She didn't even try to challenge my assertion.

Oddly enough, her visit evoked something within me which empowered me to live. I decided not to kill myself, just to spite her. I refused to give her what she wanted.

Her presence had crystallised one crucial fact; if I didn't love me, no one else would. So what if no one loved me. I loved me. And that's when I learned to love myself for the very first time.

When I got out of hospital, I spent time learning to love me. I started by looking at myself in the mirror, something I had avoided doing for years. When I looked at myself in the mirror it made me want to cry. I felt so sorry for myself, I couldn't even see myself.

But now I was actually looking at myself, really looking, and I liked what I saw. I was beautiful. I had lovely thick long black hair, which was rare for a dark-skinned black girl. I had big eyes, which could barely see without glasses or contact lenses. I had a straight cute nose and big lips with a full 'perfect teeth' smile. I had beautiful milk chocolate skin and a figure to die for. I had the perfect hourglass shape. I had big breasts, a tiny waist and a big bum. I looked fabulous!

Well, that's what I told myself every time I looked in the mirror. And day by day I grew stronger and I felt loved because I loved me.

A few months after my suicide attempt, I decided to call Anthony. I thanked him for not coming and informed him that I understood why he couldn't love me. I knew it was because I didn't love myself, but that had changed because I had learnt to love myself.

Anthony was relieved. I think the burden of loving me had been overwhelming for him. He liked the new me, and after a few months we got back together.

This time our relationship was different. I no longer focused only on Anthony, I put myself first. I had developed a more mature understanding of love. I knew I couldn't rely on anyone's love because all love is conditional except my love for myself.

9

UNCONDITIONAL LOVE

About one year after the big suicide attempt, I suddenly found myself pregnant. I don't know what had gone wrong with the pill but somehow, I was having a baby. I was so excited. I was going to have a baby to love, and the baby would love me. It was wonderful.

But Anthony didn't share my joy. He was horrified. He said the shock of him having a baby would kill his grandmother. I wasn't bothered. It sounded cruel, but he was not focused on what I needed.

It was hard for me to consider Anthony's family. He hadn't really introduced me to his family, so I didn't really have any feelings for them.

Anthony's family was like a big secret. I used to go to his house to meet him. I could count the times I went inside on one hand, and I wouldn't need all the fingers.

When I knocked on the door, his grandma spoke to me through the letterbox. I would hear her call Anthony. He would come outside, and we would leave.

Anthony had been living with his grandma since he was born. His mum had gone off to start her nursing career in America and she never came back for him.

So Anthony grew up with his grandma, his Uncle Martin and Auntie Ruth, except he called them his brother and sister. I didn't really get to know either of them.

The only thing I knew was that his sister didn't like me calling the house. She was so frosty on the phone. But I didn't let her chill bother me. I loved Anthony whether she liked me or not. I really didn't have time to worry about his family, I wanted to have my baby.

Anthony continued to stress; if it wasn't about his family he found some other reason. He worried that the baby would have the same birth defect that he had.

Anthony's right foot hadn't grown properly, so he only had a heel and deformed toes. But I didn't care, I wanted my baby and nothing and no one was going to change my mind.

The staff in the home were on Anthony's team, they tried to talk me into having an abortion, but my mind was made up.

But ugly fate had other ideas. When I was sixteen weeks pregnant, I began to bleed. I rushed to St Mary's Hospital on the Harrow Road and they transferred me by ambulance to the Elizabeth Garret Anderson Hospital in Euston. It was a specialist women's hospital.

For me there wasn't anything special in the way I was treated. When I arrived, the staff treated me like a naughty schoolgirl. They just ushered me into a room to have an ultrasound. There weren't any smiles or compassion.

The nurse scanned my belly and barked, "There is no heartbeat. The baby is dead! But never mind, you're young! You can have another one!"

I was stunned. The nurse didn't even look at me. She just ushered me out of the room and a porter took me to a bed on a ward.

My tears just gushed down my face as I replayed the words over and over again. I was all alone. I don't know where Anthony was. I had called him from the first hospital and he said he would come but he never arrived. The nurse gave me a tablet to start my labour.

The pain was unbearable. I don't remember doing anything else but cry. My baby was dead. What had I done wrong? I was healthy. I had been to all my antenatal appointments, and everything had been fine. So why was my baby dead?

After a few hours I went to the toilet and a huge orange-sized form of blood plopped into the toilet. I remember staring at it for ages. With tears streaming, I called the nurse. I expected her to rescue my baby out of the toilet, but she just peered into the toilet and just flushed my baby away.

Oh, how I sobbed. For about a whole month after I lost my baby I was still just crying and clinging to the few baby clothes I had bought.

Anthony was very supportive once I was home from the hospital, which was a relief, because he hadn't visited me once while I was in there. I had called him repeatedly, asking him to come. I needed him, but he chose to focus on what people would think about him getting me pregnant.

It wasn't easy in hospital. He was right, people were very judgemental, and the service was definitely better for the married women than for the single black girls!

But I wanted him there with me. I wanted him to comfort me and tell me I'd be okay but instead I had to go through it all on my own.

Luckily when I got home he was a great comfort. He wiped my tears. He kissed me and caressed me, and it did help. His love made me feel better. The only thing which made me feel empty is when he said, "It's probably for the best, we are too young, we weren't ready for a baby. But when we're older and married we can have a house full of kids."

I didn't bother to respond. I didn't have the energy to dissuade him. But I had a better idea. Let's make another baby, now! I used every opportunity to make love. At first, he was reluctant, he didn't seem to trust me. I convinced him that I was taking the pill and it was highly unlikely that I would be able to conceive again for at least a year.

This seemed to reassure him, and he stopped resisting my body. Well, I had to say whatever it took to make him comfortable to make love to me without him using a condom.

It took a couple of months, but eventually I got pregnant again. I was, of course, over the moon, but Anthony was really disappointed. But what could he do? He had seen how devastated I was when our first baby died. He did not want to see me like that again. He couldn't bring himself to tell me not to have the baby, so he reluctantly went along with it.

This time, I kept my pregnancy a secret from the staff and my friends until I had had my first scan, which showed that the baby was fine.

When I eventually revealed I was pregnant, of course, there were the naysayers, the doubters, in fact no one supported my pregnancy. Auntie Jeannette and Auntie Kay both lectured me about the responsibility of having a child.

But I just blocked most of what they said out and told them I knew what I was doing, which I did. I knew I was mature enough to have a baby. I would love the baby, unconditionally, which was more than I had had. I knew I would do a better job than my so-called mother.

Luckily my pregnancy was smooth, really. No morning sickness or vomiting. The only issue I had was in my mind. I was so fearful something would go wrong because I had lost the first baby. I was frightened for the whole nine months' pregnancy.

I demanded so many scans to check the baby was fine. The process gave me comfort for a day or so and then I would start worrying again. I so desperately wanted my baby. I couldn't bear the idea that something could go wrong again.

It was a long pregnancy. It felt like it was for at least a year due to my stressing, but actually it was the normal nine months gestation plus two weeks, according to my dates.

Any patience I had left was completely diminished when my due date came. And went. To make matters worse, Anthony's friend Michael's girlfriend Susan was pregnant at the same time as me and her baby came early. My baby didn't come for another two weeks after hers, chuuuups!

I was so vexed. I was pregnant before Susan, and my baby was due first.

Oh, but when my baby arrived, she was worth the extra wait. I had a beautiful baby girl. The labour was ten and a half hours. I didn't scream or make a whole heap of drama, like I had heard some girls did, no, my labour was very dignified.

I had a bit of pethidine in the last couple of hours, and no stitches. When the midwife told me I had a baby girl, I couldn't believe it. I made her show me her v'jj. I had been so desperate for a girl that I had convinced myself it was a boy, so I wouldn't be disappointed if I really had a boy.

My baby girl was so sweet. She had Anthony's beautiful full brown eyes and a full head of silky black hair, a perfect button nose and cute pursed lips.

I couldn't stop looking at her and kissing her. She was perfect. Of course, Anthony was nowhere to be found. I called him when I first went into labour and he said he was coming, but he never turned up.

Luckily, my keyworker from the home, Beverley, was with me during the labour, otherwise I would have had to do it alone. But I didn't care, I had my baby girl. I held her so tight. The nurses kept telling me to put her in the cot, but I wouldn't let them take her.

They moved us from the labour suite to a ward and I lay in bed cuddling my baby girl. I must have fallen asleep, and the next thing I knew I woke up in a panic. I thought I must have dropped her when I fell asleep as I hadn't put her in the cot and she was not in my arms.

I peeped over the side of the bed, dreading seeing her on the floor, but she wasn't there either. I searched frantically around the bed with my eyes, and then I saw her, snuggled in a blanket in the cot. Phew, I nearly had a heart attack! The nurse must have taken her from me as I slept.

We stayed in hospital for five days. The ward was hard work, as it was full of baby boys who cried constantly.

But my baby girl slept peacefully from the day she was born. I was so irritated as I didn't want them to disturb my baby girl.

I didn't have many visitors, only staff really, with the exception of Ronald, Anthony's friend, who came to see his sister, Annemarie. She had had her baby the day after me.

So he popped in to see me. He was really happy to see my baby girl, and he brought so many gifts, it was lovely. He made me feel cared for, which was nice as Anthony still hadn't turned up to see his baby girl or me.

Ronald was furious that Anthony hadn't been there for me. He visited me every day until I was discharged. Even when I went home, he was a great support, much to the irritation of Anthony.

Anthony finally turned up on the discharge day. He came to take me home. Hey, better late than never! But the love in his eyes when he saw his baby girl for the first time made up for everything at the time. He looked like he had fallen in love. He kept kissing her and snuggled her to his neck. I felt so relieved. I had been worried that he was going to abandon us but right then I knew he would never leave us.

He carried her out of the ward. As we approached the hospital doors, I can still remember the feeling of fear that struck me as we left the hospital with our baby girl wrapped in her white shawl with her little bonnet peeping out. She slept through the departure, but I felt a sense of panic.

As the morning sun shone down on us as we went down the steps of St Mary's Hospital, Praed Street, I realised the sheer burden of responsibility that was on my shoulders. The same steps that Princess Diana would walk down some years later. I wondered if she felt the same fear and panic? Anthony ushered me into the waiting minicab, so I didn't really have time to run back in.

We went to the mother and baby's home in Earls Court. Initially I had been really reluctant to live in such a place. I was prepared and ready to take care of my baby. Due to the exuberance of youth, I felt I didn't need any support. But my keyworker Beverley convinced me it was for the best.

I'm glad I listened to her advice and changed my mind. The place was nothing like I had expected. The support on offer was minimal and not mandatory. The home was a large Victorian house, which was divided into self-contained apartments.

My bedsit was on the first floor. It contained a separate kitchen, bathroom and a large living room/bedroom. I had a large bay window, which kept the room looking bright. We shared the laundry facilities and a large sitting room in the basement for socialising and meetings.

When I first moved in I kept myself to myself but once I realised that the other women were the same as me and not 'head cases', as had been my experience in previous homes, I let my guard down and began to mix with the residents.

But still a little guarded, I kept it really casual. Living in Earl's Court was out of my comfort zone. I had never lived in that part of London before, but it was an okay area for the most part, full of tourists and, after dark, prostitutes and 'Johns'.

The staff in the children's home had given me money to buy things for the baby and I also got a maternity grant from social security. I had everything I needed for my baby girl.

Anthony didn't give me a bean. But luckily I found some lovely bargain wholesale shops in Petticoat Lane Market, which sold baby clothes for next to nothing. I bought loads of Babygros and sailor suits in neutral colours.

The first days at home with 'baby girl' were hard work. She didn't want to sleep in her cot. I'd rock her to sleep and as soon as I put her in the cot she'd lift her head up and look up at me, which was shocking as she was a newborn baby and I didn't know they could do so much, so soon.

But despite my best efforts 'baby girl' wouldn't sleep in the cot. I tried different ends, I tried putting her down on her belly, on her back, on her side. It didn't matter what I did. As soon as she realised she was in the cot she'd open her beautiful little eyes and look around for me.

By the end of the first month I was done. It didn't help that the TV channels went off promptly at 1am. I had no company, just 'baby girl,' who didn't want to sleep in her cot. I needed sleep desperately.

I reach my breaking point and decided I didn't care who judged my parenting.

My baby could sleep anywhere she wanted to! And she did. On my breasts at first and then beside me in bed.

Anthony was of little to no use during the night. He slept like the living dead. If I managed to wake him, he would fall back to sleep before I could hand him the bottle of expressed milk.

But he loved his baby girl bad and when he was awake, he used to cradle her, sing to her and rock her to sleep. He even named her Antoinette, which was as close to calling her Anthony as he could get. The only problem I had with him was that he hadn't told his family about his baby girl.

Well, I gave him six months to tell them about her or I would. Those six months came around real quick, and he was still too chicken to tell them. Fed up, I took Antoinette round to his grandma's house, the place he called home.

I knocked on the door. Anthony wasn't home. His grandmother spoke in a gentle Grenadian accent through the letterbox.

"Anthony isn't here."

"That's fine, I didn't come to see him, I need to speak to you."

She reluctantly opened the door and let me push the buggy in. Once inside, I introduced her to her great-grand-baby Antoinette. She looked at Antoinette, puzzled. Even though the baby looked just like her and Anthony, she didn't say congratulations, or pleased to meet you, or anything.

No! Instead she shouted for her daughter Sheila, who came running down the stairs like there was a fire. Sheila didn't say hello or anything pleasant. Nope, instead she said, "We can't be sure it's Anthony's baby!"

Well, I thought I was going to commit a murder! Now before she acts right, and says congratulations or aww, she's so cute, she's going to come and call me a whore to my face?

Well I looked her dead in her face and I cussed her good and proper.

"You might be a whore, but I've only been with one man for the past four years and he's your brother/nephew," and laughed in her face.

"Go and get a man and then you can chat to me, otherwise, keep your opinions to yourself. Don't worry about my baby, you won't see her again until you learn some manners!" And with that I left.

I don't think I ever went back. Anthony was furious. But not because his sister had insulted me, as you might have expected, but because I had done his 'dirty work' for him.

We ended up in a big argument. And that was the first day he hit me. Of course, I hit him back, as I had been schooled by too many abusers. We ended up in a big fight but, at the time, I never considered it domestic violence. I didn't feel abused. I just thought of it more like wrestling.

10

MONEY, MONEY, MONEY!

I was determined to give my baby girl the best family life a child could ever want. The responsibility for giving it to her was all mine.

I had connived to have her, so I was determined to give her everything she needed, with or without her daddy's help.

Unfortunately, his contribution was limited. Don't get me wrong. He loved his baby girl. He fed, bathed, dressed and played with her. He read her stories, he took her to the park, but his shortfall was money.

He never had any cash. He was following his dream of being a pop idol. To give him his due, he put in the grind, spending every hour trying to make the dream a reality. But at the end of it all he still had no money. He always sang me the same song.

"I'm working on spec, I'm doing backing singing for somebody..."

I tried to be supportive, but it was hard going, with a toddler who was eating and growing out of her clothes every day.

I grew weary, and then it came to me.

"Honey, maybe you should get a regular job and do your music in your spare time?"

Well, who told me to suggest such a thing. It was tantamount to treason. He went off like a rocket.

"You say you love me and want me to be a star but then you say that. How can I do music if I've got to go to work every day? I thought you understood what my dream means to me. Music is everything to me. I have to have time to create music. It takes time and I need time. I thought you understood. Music is like food or water to me. I have to live music."

I tried to bring the discussion back down to earth but it just made his anger grow and boil over. He started shouting and screaming in my face. Then he grabbed me by my neck and used his body to press me into the wall. He spat his words.

"I don't care what you say, I'm not getting a job. I'm going to make music, and when I'm a star I'll be rich, and we'll have all the money we need. You just need to give me time!"

I felt powerless and that I just had to take it. Antoinette was watching and crying. She had seen and heard everything. From the look of terror in her eyes I knew I had to make sure she never saw or heard anything like that again.

From that day I avoided all issues with Anthony that could be contentious when she was present. Well I tried, but it wasn't easy.

My temperament is naturally fiery, and my natural instinct is to defend my point of view, and myself. But it got harder and harder to do either because Anthony had a bit of a split personality. His look of sincerity could melt butter but inside he harboured uncontrollable rage.

Don't get me wrong, he wanted the best for us, but he could see only one way of getting it. So our view of the world was continents apart.

This contention was the cause of most of our arguments. We lacked the ability to agree on anything. Whether it was something small, or something big, it would result in an argument or blows.

I decided to take full responsibility for financing my life. When Antoinette was five months old, I was offered a maisonette by the council. I really didn't want it as it was on the notorious Mozart Estate in North Kensington. The estate had a seriously bad reputation for robberies, rapes and murders.

But it was a nice maisonette, with large rooms and a garden. It had everything going for it except the location. Luckily it wasn't on the thirtieth floor of Trellick Towers or in a part of London I didn't know. The offer was the best of a bad deal.

I kitted out the place mainly by myself, with a little bit of help from Jack, my keyworker from the children's home. He even gave me a shag pile carpet for the front room.

The rest of my furniture I bought with my housing grant. Nothing from Anthony, but that was no surprise.

I decorated Antoinette's room in a lovely pink wallpaper which had a day of the week poem and lovely little children playing on it. It was so cute and reminded me of my bedroom at Nanny and Granddad's.

I bought her a single divan bed, a chest of drawers and a wardrobe. She had all her toys in there and I bought her a television, so she could watch her kids programmes in bed. Her room was complete.

I painted my bedroom a lovely ocean blue colour and I bought a beautiful luxurious navy blue carpet. And I managed to get a great deal for a double bed and wardrobe set, from a place in Hammersmith.

A few days after they were delivered, the shop I bought the furniture from went bankrupt and ran off with people's money. I felt so blessed that I got my stuff just in time; I would have been in a mess if they had run off with my money too.

My flat was just how I wanted it. Once I was behind closed doors, I loved it. I decided the safest way to live on the estate was to keep myself to myself, so that's what I did.

Don't get me wrong, my neighbours were quite nice and they kept themselves to themselves too, only knocking on my door in an emergency.

I settled in quite nicely. Despite the fact we were still together, Anthony didn't move in. Instead, he just slept over about three or four times a week. This was fine with me, as it was hard enough feeding and clothing Antoinette and me, without having to feed and clothe him too.

I loved having my own place. I felt secure for the first time since living with Nanny and Granddad. I had a tenancy in my own name and my social workers to support me until I turned eighteen. I was finally home. I felt all grown up. The only rules and regulations I had to follow were my own, created by me.

Now I had control over my life, and I was more than ready for the responsibility. I was determined to do a better job of looking after me than any of the adults, except Nanny and Granddad, who had no concept of loving and caring for me.

Adult life brought new challenges every day, but somehow I felt equipped to meet them. Having my own flat was a magnet for my friends. I had kept my location a secret, and only told my closest friends, but even they were too much.

They'd come around to 'cotch' and 'block'. I didn't mind the company at first but without staff to tell them to leave, they didn't know when to go home. One of my cousins, Claudette, came for a visit and didn't leave for three months! But I didn't mind, as she had a baby boy nearly the same age as Antoinette and they played together.

Eventually I took control of my space and learnt how to tell people to leave. I wasn't about to let my home become a youth club. No way!

Having my flat made me feel settled and I decided it was time to go to college to learn secretarial skills. I didn't want to be a secretary, but I decided if I had secretarial skills, it was probably the easiest way to get a job.

But my real career choice involved being either a journalist or a social worker. Writing had always been a passion of mine. Throughout my childhood I loved to write and had kept a diary, until my Auntie Viola found, read it and busted my ass for expressing my thoughts.

Writing had been my only way to escape. I wrote about my day or wrote stories or poetry.

I could leave the room in my head and enter the pages; it felt like I was leaving the hell behind.

In the words and pages I wrote I could travel to happiness. As I got older, I found escape in other people's words. I used to read lots of books and loved Enid Blyton's work. When I was a teenager, I read the *Sweet Dreams* books, which depicted young love, and I found them truly addictive. I wanted to live some of those dreams.

I read for hours. Book after book. They were fantastic, much better than real life. My reading and writing skills meant that school was a breeze, sort of. I liked school. I liked learning, but I was too mature and had experienced far more than most schoolchildren and even most adults. I was misunderstood by the teachers.

It didn't help that I had experienced multiple changes of primary and secondary schools over the years, two primary and two secondary. (It would have been three secondary schools, but I went back to one I had left previously.)

At eleven I went to St Augustine's Secondary School. It was a Church of England school. Auntie Viola had worked hard to get me in there because she said I had sense, and could learn. That is the only compliment I ever remember my aunt giving me.

When I went to live with Auntie Jeannette I went to Manor Hill, in Essex. And when I ran back to Paddington, I went back to St Augustine's.

Unfortunately, back then, schools did not acknowledge the challenges a child in care experienced so there was no support available. Consequently, I became a bit of a rebel.

I coped at school by keeping quiet and trying to fly under the radar until I went to Manor Hill School, where there were only five or six black children in the whole school, which was a real culture shock for me, coming from an urban melting pot of cultures in London W9. I was militant to begin with, and after seeing *Roots* (a film about slavery in America) we took control and practically ran the school.

The white kids were so scared of us they did whatever we told them to. The Asian kids were timid anyway, so they just kept out of our way for the most part. Despite my militant ways I still managed to have a mixture of friends.

Coming from my background, I was able to manoeuvre and adapt to playground politics. I learnt well. I was in the top stream for Maths and English and didn't really get into trouble with the teachers. I quite liked the school. It had a tuck shop, which was a new concept for me. Being an Inner London girl, we didn't have such a thing.

I also loved the school buildings, which were so different to Inner London schools. I liked the Victorian architecture, and the main school building was only two storeys high and the rest of the school was spread out over a number of little outbuildings.

But best of all was the view from the science lab. You could see Ally Pally (Alexandra Palace), which was miles away. It was a lovely view.

I enjoyed going to that school. By the time I got back to St Augustine's in Maida Vale, my former school, I was a rebel with a cause and that cause was me. I was a free spirit and I was not about to be controlled by anyone. I wanted to learn but I didn't want them to kill my spirit to do it.

It was strange going back to my old school. The teachers were the same, but the kids had formed into army camps, or at least that's how it felt. All the kids were in little cliques, which I found restrictive.

When I had originally been at the school I had hung around with my best friend Kathy. We had been best friends since primary school. Our friendship blossomed when the 'happy couple' organised closer supervision after my runaway attempt. Much to my delight they chose Kathy's mum to look after me every day after school.

I loved going to Kathy's house. It wasn't really a house, she lived in a flat in Salters Point, which was right across the road from our school.

I thought Kathy had the best mum in the world. She was so relaxed. I don't think I ever heard her shout at Kathy. Kathy didn't have any chores. Her mum was warm and caring. She always asked us how our day was, and made us a snack, which we ate while we watched TV or played in Kathy's room.

Kathy's mum was modern. She smoked and wasn't strict at all. Kathy used to comb her hair in the kitchen and her mum never said a word. I was incredulous. My Auntie Viola would have killed me if I put my hair in the kitchen bin, let alone comb my hair in the kitchen.

It was great going there after school. It was a fantastic escape from my hell, the three dogs, three cats, three rabbits and five budgies, the piss, shit, disinfectant and dust and of course the 'happy couple'.

Kathy and I were great friends. We walked to school together and hung out at breaks. On the way to school one morning Kathy told me a secret. Her mum was having a baby. I couldn't believe it. Her mum was really old. I think Kathy read my mind because she told me her mum was forty-nine years old! It was a miracle. Well that's what the doctors told her mum.

Kathy and I remained friends until one day I swore at her. Well, not really at Kathy, just in a sentence, but she took offence and refused to speak to me. I tried to apologise, even though I didn't think I had done anything wrong, but it was no use, she wouldn't speak to me.

Years later Kathy and I met at a gathering. She remarked, "You was a lot back then, I couldn't keep up." I appreciated her honesty as I had often wondered where our friendship had gone wrong. It's clear our friendship had been a casualty of my difficult childhood which rendered me too grown and mature for regular kids.

When I returned to the school after leaving Manor Hill I had to start from scratch. I was put in a different tutor group and I didn't really see much of Kathy. The tutor group was more like little army squads. On my first day it was made clear that I couldn't sit just anywhere. I had to sit where the leader of the squad told me to sit.

At first, I tried to play the game, but it stuck in my craw. The thought that someone was going to dictate where I could sit just didn't resonate. So by the second week I was done. I went and sat exactly where I wanted to.

Some fool called Lorna, the squad leader, tried to direct me to sit somewhere else but I was having none of it.

"That's Betsy's seat!"

I looked her straight in the eyes.

"I don't give a fuck whose seat it is, I'm sitting here!"

Well, the girl lost her mind, jumped up and tried to move me. Well, let me tell you, I gave her a beating she will never forget. Our form teacher tried to break it up but she got turfed out of the way.

When I was finished beating Lorna, I sat back in the seat. But not for too long. The teacher picked herself up off the floor and frogmarched Lorna and me to the headmistress's office.

But I didn't care, my point had been made. The next day I sat where I liked. In fact, I sat in Lorna's seat, just for kicks, and she couldn't say a word.

Word soon spread around the school, "don't mess with her… she beat Lorna up!" I guess she had been the 'bad girl' until I arrived.

After that, school days were pretty easy going. I studied hard in the classes I liked and I played the fool in the classes I didn't. I loved English Language and English Literature, Sociology, French, History, Geography, but I didn't like Maths so, needless to say, that's the class where I had the most fun.

It's not that I didn't like maths really. It was that I didn't like the way maths was taught. All we ever did was complete worksheets. It was so boring. It would have been more stimulating if they worked sums out on the board and asked us to try solving them.

But no, just worksheets. So, maths class was my opportunity to start some mess, or wind the teacher up. I would occasionally go too far and end up with a visit to the headmistress's office, but it didn't faze me. It wasn't as if I was going to get into trouble at home.

Now if I was still living with the 'happy couple' I would have kept my ass quiet. But living in the children's home there was never any real consequence for my bad behaviour.

I don't think the lack of compassion by the headmistress did much to help either. She didn't care that I was in a children's home and had had the childhood from people's worst nightmares. She just didn't care at all. All she wanted was for me to behave.

Unfortunately for her, that approach actually made me feel like being more disruptive. I tried hard to get the balance right and knew I had to learn and that it was important to me to do well at school. I wanted to leave school with lots of qualifications because it was against the norm.

People didn't expect me to do well, not even the staff in the home. Don't get me wrong, they were supportive to a point, but they didn't seem as though they really believed the 'rallying' speech they gave us. This inspired me to do well despite my past.

I guess they did have a point, as so many of the kids in the home had dropped out of school without getting any qualifications.

So I tried to keep my head down. One morning, I was running up the stairs as I was running late for my French class.

Just as I hit the last flight of stairs, I literally bumped into a boy called Philip Paul. Before I could apologise, he started cussing me.

"What's wrong with you? You blind or something? Open your eyes, they're fucking big enough, you fucking bitch!"

"Bitch, your mother's a fucking bitch!" I shouted in his face.

"What, what did you say?"

He glared right in my face. Our faces were so close together we could have kissed.

"You heard me. I didn't stutter, your mother's a fucking bitch."

His face went crimson, I thought he was going to combust. He was no longer white; his skin had given way to the reddest of faces I had ever seen.

He looked so angry, but yet confused. Before he could decide his next move a teacher appeared, shouting and ordering us to class. Philip walked down the steps slowly and mouthed, "You're gonna get it after school!"

I was in a mess! Philip Paul was at least 6ft to my 5ft 2 and was built like a boxer! I was a good fighter, but even I had to admit I was no match for Philip. One punch and I would be unconscious.

At break everyone was talking about my bust-up with Philip and people were getting hyped up about the prospect of seeing a fight after school. What was making it really juicy was the fact that it was going to be boy versus girl.

There was such a buzz, it's a wonder they weren't selling tickets or taking bets on who was going to win, and in what round!

The morning was moving at a lightning pace. Before I could blink, I was in second period. I couldn't tell you what subjects I had or what I learnt that day, all I could think about was my impending doom.

Then, as if by magic, it came to me. I would have to bunk school, run home and then change school... again! I was no chicken and even though I usually enjoyed a good fight, that was usually if I liked my odds, and only if I was hit first.

This wasn't going to be like that. I had never been knocked out before and I wasn't about to start now. So without looking back, at lunch break, I beat a hasty retreat. I walked calmly out of the school, hoping nobody noticed me. I kept my eyes straight ahead, so they wouldn't make four with anyone else's.

Before I knew it, I was on the bus and then I was walking down the road around the corner from my house. As I crossed the road, I looked down the street and who do you think I saw walking up the street? My heart nearly missed a beat! It was Philip! He saw me, and before I could escape, he smiled and waved at me as he turned the corner.

Wow, it was such a shock and a relief, I couldn't believe my luck. He had bunked off too and he clearly didn't want to fight me either. That's when I knew God loved me! I had cussed the boy's mum and had lived to tell the tale. It was amazing!

Unfortunately, my luck did not last long. The next day at school my maths teacher sent me to the headmistress for a minor infringement. She kept barking at me for homework which I hadn't done. Why would I? It was just another worksheet which I could do in class.

She kept yelling in my face and finally I lost my rag, I told her to move herself, and when she continued on barking in my face, I told her to fuck off! She was so shocked, but what did she expect, shouting in my face like that?

To make matters worse, the headmistress must have been on her period or something. She went mad. She started shouting about protecting her staff from abuse and bad behaviour. Apparently, she wasn't going to tolerate them being sworn at.

But what she didn't know was that I wasn't going to tolerate her shouting at me either. Who did she think she was? She wasn't my so-called mother. I told her to go and find something soft to suck and walked out of her office. I was done with her and her fucking school.

Pure madness! I had lost my mind. I don't know what I was thinking. I only had a few months to finish school and I was hoping to do well in my exams. I don't know why I was unable to keep my big mouth shut. But I had done it now, and there was no going back. I was never going to apologise, and I knew the headmistress wouldn't have accepted it even if I had.

My regular school life was done! I ended up going to a pupil referral unit, only returning to school to sit my exams. Turned out the pupil referral unit was actually quite nice. I had initially dreaded going there, as I thought it was going to be full of horrible bad kids, but it wasn't.

The manager was a lovely woman called Bryony. She was so positive and motivational. She gave me exam papers to work on and all the encouragement in the world.

With her support I was able to get a few qualifications, including O Level English Language, English Literature, Sociology and CSE Grade 2 in Maths. I was really proud of myself. I had overcome so much to get those qualifications and I wasn't going to stop there. I was going to make something of myself.

Having decided to build on my qualifications, I went to Kilburn Polytechnic to study a secretarial skills course, one day a week. Kathy's mum looked after Antoinette for me. She was very encouraging.

"Having a baby young is no reason to give up on life and a career."

Funnily enough I had never given the notion that having a baby would stop me doing anything a second thought. In fact, having a baby was my beginning, not my end.

Unfortunately, in contrast to the other girls, who appeared to be enjoying it, I really hated the secretarial course. I felt the course was beneath me. It was merely a means to an end; I was going to be a journalist or a social worker. I did the course so I could take care of Antoinette.

A baby is a great motivator, well at least she was for me. I focused on my studies and I didn't bother to socialise with the other people on my course. I had a one-track mind.

I finished the course and I learnt to type forty-five words per minute. And I do Teeline shorthand. With my new office skills in hand and a reference I got a part-time job as a personal assistant, working for a social care charity called Wellness.

The charity provided social services to people in need, including single parents and old people. The manager was an old lady who had five dogs, which she took everywhere she went. If you saw her, you saw the dogs too.

Because of my experience living with the 'happy couple' at the petting zoo, I actually hated little dogs. I hated the way they smelt, the way they licked you and the damn hair, which was always all over me when they left.

But to get along I had to pretend I loved the lady's dogs to keep her happy and I quickly realised that the dogs were like her children. Well, that's what she told me.

I did my best to be a good assistant. My manager used me for everything. I would collect her dry cleaning, make restaurant reservations, and occasionally I would type a letter. I didn't really like the job, but I had no choice. Antoinette was eighteen months and was growing and needed more every day.

The highlight of the job was talking to the social workers about their cases. Their work seemed so interesting, and far more important than my tasks as an assistant. I worked there for about one year and it was an okay stopgap, except they always paid me late. The dog lady (manager) was scatty like that, and despite me reminding her well in advance she would still forget to pay me.

One week I was relying on getting paid, so I could do some shopping, as my cupboards were bare. But the dog lady didn't come in the office, so I didn't get paid. I was so fraught I didn't know what to do.

ॐ

I had had toast for dinner the night before with the last piece of bread because there wasn't enough corn beef and rice for me to have some too. I barely managed to feed Antoinette and I had to get some money.

I used the safe key to access the petty cash box and I took out £20. I wrote an IOU which I placed on top of the money in the tin and then I put the tin back in the safe and locked it. I put the key back in the dog lady's desk.

When I went to work on Monday, I chased the lady for my pay, which she gave me eventually before she left for a meeting. It had been a long morning because I was praying she wouldn't have to go in the petty cash tin. Luckily for me she didn't, and I was able to put the money back that time. This gave me a false sense of ease, because I did it a few more times after that, each time putting the money back, until the last time when I got caught.

Like a mad woman, I forgot and left the IOU in the petty cash box after I had actually put the money back. When she discovered the note, the dog lady didn't believe that I had put the money back, although after counting the cash a few times, she accepted that I had. But she was still not happy with me. I explained that she kept paying me late and I needed my money on time because I had to take care of my daughter.

Sadly, the dog lady didn't care. She gave me notice and paid me in advance and I left that day. I was glad really because I didn't want to be anyone's secretary or assistant long-term. I wanted to do something which felt like a vocation.

Luckily for me the lady gave me a good reference, which was great because I needed to get another job quickly. I went for a few interviews to be a secretary but found that I just couldn't be convincing when answering the questions. I always ended up telling them what I really wanted to do, until one interviewer said to me, "This job is not suitable for you. You clearly have bigger plans, which you should pursue."

He was being sarcastic, but it was actually true. I decided to apply for jobs that would give me experience that I could use to develop my career. I applied for, and got, the post of careers administrator in a careers guidance centre for young people.

The job was great. I gave young people job information, arranged job and college interviews, and sometimes I had to give support and advice on other personal issues such as housing or health, terminations or problems with their parents. I loved it.

Things seemed to be coming together. I was doing a job I liked while raising my daughter. Anthony was still chasing his dream.

He was still singing but he had started writing songs for people and every now and then he would sell one. His money never reached us, but apparently, he did get paid for some work.

We didn't need his money and that's the way I liked it. I dreaded the idea of being dependent on him, I never wanted Anthony to have that kind of control over my life. I refused to ask him for money and, if he gave me some I said thank you, and kept it moving.

11

CAN HALF-SIBLINGS EVER BECOME WHOLE?

I was busy getting on with my life as a mother, employee and a girlfriend, when out of the blue Dev came to visit me. He was working in the area and wanted to see how I was doing. I hadn't seen him for about ten years!

I don't even know how he found me. But it turned out he had settled down with a girlfriend called Sinitta, who had a daughter a little bit older than Antoinette.

After the first visit he began to visit regularly. He said that family was important and even though our mother was a bitch we shouldn't let that stop us from being a family. I agreed, I still longed for a family, so I put the past behind me.

I began spending time at his house and we used to spend Sundays as a family. His girlfriend Sinitta prepared dinner and we had a fun time. Somehow he convinced me to take Antoinette to meet my so-called mother.

"She's her grandmother, she should be helping you with her. She can babysit so you can go raving. Come on, let the past go, leave it in the past, you shouldn't deny Antoinette the opportunity of having a grandmother."

"Grandmother, she couldn't even be bothered to be my mother, so how the hell is she gonna be my daughter's grandmother?"

Despite my anger and resistance, somehow he convinced me to go for a visit. He took us in his car although, for the whole drive, I was smarting.

The whole event was strange. My so-called mother and company had moved from the flat and had a house in Streatham.

The visit was brisk, as just looking at my so-called mother filled me with rage. I just couldn't bear to be in the same room as her.

It didn't help that she looked at my daughter with such disdain. It didn't take long for me to blow. I just couldn't hold in my rage. It was one thing to treat me with disrespect, but to try and treat my daughter in the same way was never gonna happen. Not while I drew breath anyway.

"What's the problem? You not interested because she's a girl? What is your problem with girls?"

I didn't give her a chance to answer. I snatched up my child and went through the door like a bullet. Dev ran after me and took me home. He tried to make light of the situation, but I was having none of it. I told him straight, blunt and clear.

"I would never leave my daughter with that woman, ever. Even if it meant I could never rave again."

He tried to calm me down and suggested that he looked after Antoinette for me.

I don't even know where this sudden urgency to go raving came from but looking back, I think the notion had been planted by him, because I hadn't really been out much since I had Antoinette, but that had been my choice.

Even when I had a babysitter, I stayed home with a Chinese and a small bottle of Canei. I had made Jewel Antoinette's godmother,

113

and it was a standing joke that whenever she had Antoinette for the weekend and asked what I had done with the time, I had always stayed in!

So I wasn't in desperate need of a break. But Dev kept offering to have her, saying "I'm her uncle, if you can't leave her with me, then who?"

Then he would paint the picture. She'd be able to play with Sinitta's daughter and Sinitta would help him look after her. So eventually I gave in. He came and picked her up and brought her back at the end of the weekend.

When she came home Antoinette told me she'd had fun. She probably only stayed with him twice, but not long after the last visit, Antoinette began to play up at the nursery.

One morning, I had taken Antoinette to nursery and, as I was running late, I forgot to kiss goodbye. When I got to work the nursery called, asking me to collect Antoinette. She had smashed up the play room. She had thrown paint and pasta all over the place, overturned tables and chairs, tornado-style. This was totally out of character for my mild-mannered little girl.

When I arrived to collect Antoinette, the nursery teacher asked me if everything was okay at home. I reassured her that everything was fine and explained that I had forgotten to kiss her goodbye, and that seemed to ease her concern.

But a few days later I got another call from the nursery, asking me to come to a meeting with the officer in charge. At the meeting I was informed that Antoinette had touched one of the children inappropriately during a toilet break.

She didn't want to alarm me, but they were concerned that Antoinette had been exposed to some sort of sexualised behaviour, either perhaps on TV, or maybe she had seen me with her father in bed. I remember feeling a sense of panic set in.

I was scared. I don't know why but I felt frightened.

I tried to remain calm on the outside while reassuring the officer in charge that I was particularly careful with Antoinette, and she had not been exposed to anything like that at home.

I prided myself on being the best mum I could be, and thought I now had to be skilled and tactful, so I could find out what had happened at nursery. I took Antoinette home in the normal way and didn't mention anything to her.

We just talked about things she liked to play with and her favourite TV programmes. We ate dinner as normal and I bathed her and put her to bed. As she lay in bed, I gently stroked her forehead and whispered, "I love you and I will protect you. I won't let anyone hurt you. Nobody has the right to touch your mini parts, only Mummy.

"You can tell me anything, and I will protect you. Has anyone touched your mini?"

She opened her eyes wide.

"Uncle Dev played hide and seek with me and when he found me, he hurt me."

This was not what I had expected at all. As her words dropped like bombs and blew me away, I did my best to remain calm. I didn't want to frighten her or stop her from telling me what happened, but I had erupted inside, and my thoughts were exploding in all different directions.

"What did Uncle Dev do?"

"He put his thing inside my mini and it hurt. I told him I didn't want to play hide and seek anymore."

Antoinette sobbed as she spoke, and I hugged and kissed her until her tears stopped.

"You are safe, he will never hurt you again. I will protect you. No one will ever hurt you again. You are safe now. Thank you for telling me."

I lay hugging her close until she fell asleep.

After tiptoeing out of Antoinette's room, I crept downstairs, entered my front room and shut the door behind me. My tears streamed silently down my face as I was mindful of Antoinette sleeping. Her words maddened me. The rage launched out of me so much that I had started screaming into a cushion.

My heart was racing. I paced up and down my living room, trying to calm down and think straight. My overwhelming desire was I wanted to go and kill him but then who would look after Antoinette?

How could I tell Anthony that my brother had sexually abused his daughter? My head was spinning, and the tears wouldn't stop falling.

After the initial mania began to pass, I called Jewel's sister, Karen, for legal advice. She had become a barrister who specialised in childcare and family law.

The only way I could get through it was to act professional and imagine I was Antoinette's social worker. I couldn't allow myself to feel because it hurt so bad and from experience, I had learnt that feeling solved nothing. Instead I focused on getting justice for Antoinette.

But right from my initial conversation with Karen, justice looked like it was going to be hard to get. Her tone was matter of fact and cool.

"A child's evidence is considered hearsay by the court."

"But Antoinette will tell them herself, in her own words, exactly what he did to her!" I shouted desperately.

Listening to the advice just compounded my feelings of helpless despair.

Karen stated, "The court will not consider the evidence as fact, but second-hand information, because a child is considered to be a poor witness."

Now if that isn't an injustice, I don't know what is. My child experienced something awful and life-changing, which she could testify to, but the court will not give her testimony credibility because she's a child. It just didn't seem right. Who can lie more than an adult? A child abuser!

Talking to Karen provided no relief from the nightmare. Her voice was devoid of comfort or compassion and she informed me with an air of being above such drama. My emotional madness gathered momentum as my anger grew.

I wanted to know why that stupid so-called mother of mine had brought that child abuser to England. She was to blame, as she had brought him into our lives. Just one more reason for me to hate her with a passion. I called her and when she answered the phone, I didn't even give her a chance to finish her greeting.

"Hel—"

I just blurted out, "Your child sexually abused my daughter!"

There was silence, which was immediately followed by the voice of my seventeen-year-old sister Keres.

"What's wrong?"

"Her son sexually abused my daughter!"

I didn't get to finish the sentence before I heard Keres's piercing high-pitched scream. The sound was jarring. It totally baffled me.

My so-called mother came back on the phone, while Keres continued screaming in the background.

"Keres will call you back." And the phone went dead.

As I hung up, I was haunted by the sound of Keres's screams. I hung up, but I could still hear the piercing scream ringing in my ears, even though the phone was down. I struggled to make sense of it. Why would Keres be screaming? If anyone should have been screaming, surely it should have been me. It was my daughter who had been abused. I just couldn't understand it.

A few days later Keres called me and filled me in. I was horrified to learn that Dev had sexually abused her too, and that's why he had been sent away by his mother to live in the children's home so quickly after he went to live with her.

Up until that moment I had no clue as to why he had been sent away. I thought it was because he had been acting up. It was like another bombshell went off in my head. I was so angry, and all because of my so-called mother's secrets and lies, my daughter had been exposed to a paedophile and she knew it, and did nothing to prevent it, or to protect my child, her grandchild.

I had always felt disdain for my so-called mother but on that day, I felt something new. It was pure, unadulterated, raw hate. I loathed that woman with every nerve in my body. I wished her dead in the most horrific way. I couldn't even continue the phone call with Keres.

I felt so much rage I didn't know what to do with myself. Killing my so-called mother became an overwhelming urge; this was the only punishment I felt fit the crime. Retribution was the only justice I wanted.

As my plan began to take shape I thought of Antoinette. Who would love and care for my daughter? My love for my daughter surpassed the hate I felt. I wouldn't let her rob my daughter of a mother, no way.

As I tried to contain the volcano of anger which was trying to consume me my thoughts turned to Keres. I wanted to support her, but I felt conflicted. She seemed equally responsible. Why hadn't she told me or warned me?

Amongst all the emotions was a motorway still to cross. I still had to tell Anthony. The thought of it was killing me.

How exactly do you tell the father of your child that your brother has sexually abused his baby girl?

After three days of praying I could keep the nightmare a secret, I succumbed to my professional self. The reality was clear. It was impossible to prevent the inevitable. I had to make the call. Anthony arrived looking anxious and we sat down. I got as close to him as I could. I wrapped my arms around him and held him tight.

I knew it would be the only way to prevent him from tearing up the place or storming out to kill Dev. As I held him, I spoke the words deliberately but gently. He sobbed and sobbed until his anger was ready to erupt.

He raged uncontrollably. I could literally feel his breath in my face. As he grabbed me he barked, "Where does he live… tell me?"

"What's his address, Dominiquè?"

I tried to hold him, but he wrestled me, pinning me to the wall.

"You will have to kill me before I'll give you the address to commit murder."

"Where is he? If you won't tell me I'll find him myself."

Anthony stared at me with pure venom. He drew back his arm and slammed his fist into the wall a hair away from my ear. I thought he had broken his hand, but he refused to go to the hospital; instead he just cried in my arms.

Luckily Antoinette was at nursery, so she didn't have to witness the anger and pain. I convinced Anthony that Antoinette had lost enough already without having to lose her father too. He didn't buy it initially, but he collected Antoinette from nursery and by the time he came back he wanted to love his daughter more than he hated the paedophile!

It wasn't an easy fight. Really, I just wanted to let him go and kill Dev, but although he resented me for it, I wasn't going to let anyone deprive my daughter of what I didn't have. A mother and a father who loved her.

Many years later, Antoinette, thirty, acknowledged she had no memory of the sexual abuse but criticised me for denying her the justice her father would have given her.

Reluctantly, I followed Karen's advice and informed social services rather than dealing out my own rough justice. A child protection investigation was carried out which included a memorandum interview carried out by the police, a social worker and a medical examination.

The only good news to come out of the whole horrid process was that Dev had not taken her virginity, just her innocence. And for this reason, the police chose not to prosecute the paedophile.

Going forward I tried my best to love up Antoinette, to make her feel special and safe. I redecorated her room because it came out in the memorandum interview that Dev had exposed himself in her room, when he was supposed to be saying goodnight. How wicked and vile.

Antoinette chose some new wallpaper and her new room made her feel better. She had art therapy once a week for about six months, which she enjoyed. They used the art therapy to help her to come to terms with what she had experienced. I also took her to a dance class because she loved music and dancing. I tried to keep her occupied. But it was also important to improve our communication, so Antoinette knew that she could tell me anything and I would keep her safe. I bought her books on being safe, so she knew how to protect herself.

Antoinette's tears turned to smiles, she got stronger as she felt safer. The experience left no visible scars but there was something different about her. Her view of the world had changed.

Something good came out of the sordid mess; it had brought my brother and sister, Keres and Jamie, back into my life. My so-called mother drove them to my home, dropped them off and picked them up.

On Keres's first visit, I made it clear to her that if she didn't want her mother dead, she needed to keep her far from me. She needed to ensure her mother's eyes and mine never made four. Thank the Lord Keres made it happen.

Keres and I were in a new space. She began to open up to me, she explained why she hadn't told me about Dev sexually abusing her before.

Firstly, her mother had told her to keep it a secret, so Keres had buried it deep inside her. That secret was unearthed on hearing he had done it to her niece, and only then was she confronted with her own unresolved sexual abuse nightmare.

She was eight when it happened to her. She had never talked to anyone about it, not even her mother. They didn't even give her therapy. She buried her feelings and memories.

For the first time ever, I felt sorry for Keres. I had always thought her life was peaches and cream, but knowing she had suffered too made her more relatable.

I even tried really hard to forgive Keres for not telling me and putting my daughter in danger.

Instead, I put the full responsibility and blame where it belonged, squarely with my so-called mother.

After so many years, out of the misery, suddenly Keres and I had a common bond. We were joined in the hatred of my so-called mother. It turned out that Keres now despised her too, and the sexual abuse was not the only reason.

Keres had come to realise that her mother only had time for Jamie. He was her heart and Keres was sick of it. It was ironic; the family didn't have the picture-perfect life I had imagined.

Her and Jamie's father was a raving alcoholic, who hated his wife and his son. Apparently, their father, 'the Grenadian', didn't give Jamie the time of day so the house was fractious.

Her mother, my so-called mother, worked from sun up to sun down. She was never home. She even worked on festive holidays, like Christmas and Easter. Her mother and father barely spoke to each other and Keres couldn't bear it. She was counting down the years until she could move out.

Hearing about her life was strange. The picture she now painted didn't look anything like what I had imagined. There was no picket fence in that picture, no swing in the garden. There were no cosy family days. Instead it sounded horrible.

Strangely enough that misery didn't bring me any comfort, it just added another layer to my hatred of my so-called mother. I couldn't believe she dashed me away to live with 'the Grenadian' all for nothing. The thought of it just increased my desire to kill her, a thought which I fought hard to suppress.

Jamie had been visiting me regularly too, but he didn't wait for his mother to bring him, he would make his own way on the Tube. He would just turn up and stay for days. Apparently, he was doing a basketball course at a local sports college. I didn't see much studying, just a lot of little girls chasing him.

He had grown up into a looker. Tall, caramel skin, wide smile with dimples either side. He thought he was a prize. He was really cute, and I loved my little brother. We got really close as he was at my house so much.

Interestingly, both Keres and Jamie had a lot of questions about our maternal family. They had gaps in their knowledge and I was only too happy to fill them in.

Jamie had a running joke that when he was little, he was scared to open the front door, for fear of letting in another brother or sister.

He said brothers and sisters he had never heard of just turned up, and no one ever explained how they were related to him.

I really enjoyed bringing my siblings up to speed. I didn't spare any details. I hated the secrets. Secrets had already done so much damage to our family. I wasn't going to be party to the deceit.

Finding out that their mother was a child-abandoning liar didn't go down too well. Keres, of course, focused more on her father. She now understood why her father was a drunk and why he treated his wife the way he did.

Jamie was just relieved that there weren't any more siblings that could come out of the woodwork. Interestingly enough, they had news for me too. They had a brother on their dad's side called Mark. He lived with his mother in America. They had only recently found out about Mark, because he had turned up to see their dad.

Again, there had been no formal introductions. They just heard Mark call their dad, Dad and he didn't correct him. Keres had tried to find out more information, but her dad just said he was her brother and that was that.

I eventually got to meet Mark about a year later when he came to England for a visit. I invited him for a family dinner, with Keres, Jamie, Antoinette and me. The minute I met him, he felt like my brother. We had so much in common. He hated his dad and so did I. He hated his mother, and I loathed mine. We were akin. It was a lovely family day. We all got along so well.

It was the first time we had all been together for a meal as siblings. We shared stories of our childhood, including the horror stories. We all agreed it wasn't our fault that our parents had kept us apart. We made a pact to be one family from then on.

It felt lovely to have a family. Antoinette had an auntie and uncles, and she loved it. Deep down I still craved for a loving family and I hoped I had finally found one. I wanted to live with my brothers and sister like Auntie Jeannette lived with her sisters. I wanted to have lovely family dinners full of laughter and fun. I really thought if we put the past behind us and worked at it, we could all be really close.

So I embraced Mark as my brother. I knew he was only my stepbrother, but I loved him like a brother, although Keres and Jamie didn't give him the time of day. He told me the only time he saw or heard from them was if he called or came to England.

And when he visited his dad, they were not very nice to him. If he asked their dad for money, they told him not to give it to him.

So Mark and I bonded together as the outside 'marriage children'. I guess being outsiders made our relationship tighter; we called each other regularly and he always came to visit me when he came to England.

But the scales of life always shift up and down as things change. As my family was coming together my relationship with Anthony began to pull apart.

Anthony was deeply involved in his music, and I was trying to make a home for Antoinette while working part-time. I was doing well at work at the careers office, but decided it was time to make my career move.

I applied for an Access to Social Work course. The minimum age to attend the course was twenty-three. I was only twenty-one, but I was determined to apply and get on the course.

My application was accepted, and I was invited for an interview. I felt this was a precursor for a face-to-face rejection. I met with the course leader and deputy course leader.

Despite never having experienced such a process before, for some reason I didn't feel intimidated or even fazed that there were two people interviewing me. I had prepared myself mentally. I intended to be professional and get on the course despite my age.

The interview went according to my plan. I used all my personal experience and work experience to wow them. And it worked. A few weeks after the interview I received an invitation to join the course in September. I felt so proud of myself. I had managed to put my past to good use and I was going to use it to get all the way to the top.

I determined I was going to be a social worker if it killed me. I wanted to use my experience to improve the lives of children in care. I knew first-hand how important social workers are to children in care and I was going to be a trailblazer who makes a real difference.

I was so happy to hand in my notice at work, although I was sad to leave the careers service, but I wanted to do more with my life.

Most of my colleagues seemed genuinely sad that I was leaving, although a few of them couldn't hide their jealousy. They tried to raise doubt in my mind, by asking me how I was going to cope with all the study while looking after Antoinette.

I didn't really have the answers, but I was confident and happy about my decision to leave. I didn't know what to expect from the course or the pressure it would put on me. But I blew them off by saying, "Where there's a will there's a way."

Funnily, Anthony raised the same doubt as my colleagues. He refused to let anything, including the needs of his family, stand in the way of his dreams, but he didn't mind standing in the way of mine. He wanted to know how I was going to be able to study and look after Antoinette.

I chose not to get into it with him. It wasn't like I relied on him to look after her anyway, so I knew he was just trying to start something.

Antoinette was older and very aware of the tension between her father and me. She would flinch if he shouted at me and she got really clingy. I refused to bring my daughter up in fear. I wanted her to feel safe at home. And I wanted to feel safe too.

I avoided that spark. Our love for each other had changed. I'm not sure if it was due to our changing roles or simply because I had Antoinette. Whatever the reason, I didn't need his love anymore. It was strange. I felt love for Antoinette, but I knew I wasn't the woman for him and he wasn't man enough for me.

I wanted a partner, who I could share my life with. I wanted someone who could stand toe to toe with me, with the same amount of effort put in to our life and love. I wanted a man who would be my knight, who could defend me and who could soothe me.

I desired a man who appreciated my passion for life and love, who understood my journey enough to carry me before I ran out of steam.

Unfortunately, Anthony did not fit that description at all. He had started to make some negative comments about my personality.

Why couldn't I be meeker or milder? Why wasn't I more like other women, be seen and not heard? Initially, I internalised his inference. I started to criticise myself. I even tried to moderate myself.

But something deep inside me said, *Why should you have to change yourself to be loved by the man who loved you before? Why should I have to change who I am, when he is not changing to meet my needs?*

Somehow, Anthony sensed me slipping away from him, so out of the blue one evening he asked me to marry him. Early on in our relationship I had toyed with the idea of being his wife. I wanted to marry him more than anything else in the world.

Now things were different. However, I wanted to give Antoinette the family I never had. I accepted his proposal. He did not give me a ring. I started to wear one of my rings on my engagement finger to make it feel real.

For a moment, I got caught up in the romance of getting married.

I wanted my bridesmaids to wear burgundy and I would wear ivory. Antoinette would be our flower girl. I could see it all, but strangely, I could see everyone in the picture except Anthony.

About a month after the proposal, Anthony and I were lying in bed together, talking about how we thought our life together would be. In Anthony's description of life together, I couldn't picture me. He seemed to be describing somebody else. If I was to be married to Anthony, I would have to become someone else.

The price was too high. I wanted to be married to somebody who wanted to be married to me, the real me, not a Stepford (robot) wife. I ended our relationship there and then.

Anthony was so shocked, but I didn't care. I knew I could never be the woman he wanted me to be and I knew he would never be man enough for me. It took him a while to get the message.

He stalked me for about three months but eventually, when he saw me dating other guys, he accepted my decision. A few months after that I heard he was dating a girl, Michelle, who was supposedly my friend.

Not a casual friend or acquaintance. No. A real friend. Michelle used to come to ladies' night at my house every Friday night. We would drink wine and order takeaway and laugh and crack jokes well into the early hours of the morning. Occasionally she stayed over.

Well, Michelle obviously liked my life and wanted it for herself. She had provided Anthony with a shoulder to cry on after we separated. I don't know if he started to see her to make me jealous, but it had no effect on me. Antoinette had been the one to spill the tea. She had seen Michelle at her dad's flat a few times.

Soon after, Michelle visited me. She wanted to be upfront about her relationship with Anthony. I wished her the best of luck. I knew she was gonna need it. I told her my only concern and focus was Antoinette and I hoped that she was going to treat her right, particularly as she had known her from the day she was born. She assured me she would be good to Antoinette.

And with that my childhood love affair was done and so was the family life I had planned for my daughter. It was sad. But I knew in the long run it was the best decision for all concerned I didn't want to raise Antoinette in a domestic violence environment or in a loveless relationship.

I remained determined that Antoinette was going to have the best that life had to offer, and I would make sure her home life was lovely.

12

THE START OF MY TRAVEL BUG: 1989

After the storm Antoinette and I needed the sun and pastures new. As I considered my options, which were non-existent, as they included gruesome ways to kill a paedophile and marrying a man who needed someone else, I had a brain wave; let's go to Florida.

My stepbrother Mark lived there. He was always bragging about his Floridian life in the sun. He was desperate for us to visit, particularly as none of his other siblings showed any interest in visiting him.

Taxiing down the runway as the aeroplane wheels gathered speed, I was struck by how fast I make decisions. As per the beat of my drum, my plan to go on holiday was executed in just four weeks, starting with an enthusiastic call to Mark.

Antoinette's four-year-old excitement had boiled like a volcano as she absorbed the news.

"Where are we going?"

"Guess."

"Are we going to Butlins?"

I shook my head. "Nope."

"I know, the seaside."

I peered into her face, with a big grin. I was distracted momentarily by her sweetness; her button nose, sparkling, captivating chestnut-brown eyes, pure white perfect teeth, thin lips and pure milk chocolate skin.

Antoinette was the image of her father. She had no trace of my genes, never had since birth. Every now and then my eyes searched hers for a trace of me, but the answer was always the same; she's her dad. Her curious smile captivated me as I teased her.

"Micky and Minnie Mouse don't live at the seaside!"

As she processed the Disney characters Antoinette shook her head.

"No way! We're not going to Disney World, to see the Magic Kingdom. You're tricking me."

She locked her eyes with mine, seeking the truth.

"Yes, we are, we are going to Florida to stay with Uncle Mark and while we are there, we are going to Disney World, so you can meet all your Disney friends."

Before I could finish giving the holiday details, Antoinette was screaming with glee and running around the room, throwing things up in the air and, hugging me. As I kissed her chubby cheeks, I searched her face for reassurance that she was going to be okay. Her elated beam melted the last sliver of hidden sadness from her smile.

Antoinette's excitement unleashed mine. I hadn't been on holiday for a few years and this was my first holiday as an adult and a mum.

My friends were so pleased for me that they all brought me going away presents. Even Amanda Rose popped by to give me some beach towels, which was totally unexpected, as I hadn't seen much of her. Even Anthony gave Antoinette some spending money.

Sitting on the plane sipping my brandy and coke, I felt like a pioneer. I was the first one in our clique to go on holiday under our own steam.

Strangely enough I hadn't given the magnitude of my plans much thought until I boarded the plane, and by then it was too late to have any doubts.

First stop, Florida for a month, then Barbados for my first family wedding and holiday with Keres and Jamie. Then it was back to Florida for two weeks and then home. My plan was pure madness. Who goes to a foreign country for six weeks on their first visit? Me.

The flight was long and uneventful. Antoinette was an absolute peach the whole flight. She just played with her toys and watched movies, unlike some of the other kids, who chose to run up and down the aisle or screamed their lungs out. I relaxed and tried to soak up the holiday vibe.

Clearing US immigration and claiming our luggage was a breeze. As we entered the arrivals lounge, Mark ran to us, all dimply smiles. He was Jamie's twin in looks and 'the Grenadian' on his best day, with tall Greek god features and caramel clear skin.

"Hey sis, how was your flight?"

"We made it... I can't believe we are really here! The flight was great."

Antoinette was tripping over her words, she was so excited.

"I, I sat by the window. I could see the engine, clouds, little houses."

Mark bear-hugged me so tight, I could barely breathe. Tickling him was the only way to get him off me. He snatched up Antoinette and rested her on his shoulders. The two of them together were at least ten feet tall; he had to stoop down to get through the doors.

As we approached the exit, my attention was drawn to a beautiful Miami Airport picture postcard scene which was framed by the floor to ceiling glass windows. But as we stepped outside, we were hit by the intense evening sunshine and sweltering heat.

Antoinette's and my eyes were glued to the new scenery. The lush palm trees and colourful bungalows suggested Caribbean, but the commercial marketing screamed American Dream.

Mark drove for about an hour on the I-95 freeway, chatting and playing L.T.D.'s greatest hits. We reached Fort Lauderdale, where he lived in an area called Plantation.

Interestingly, I hadn't given his accommodation any thought until Mark pulled up at a quaint bungalow and, instead of going in the front door, he walked round the back.

Curiously, in silence Antoinette and I followed behind Mark, dragging one of the cases. He put his key in the back door and crept in. We followed him down a small passage until he used his key to open another door.

We entered a small room, sparsely furnished; there was a double bed, a chest of drawers with a small TV on the top and that was it. No other furniture.

I didn't know what to say. All I could manage was, "Where are we going to sleep?"

Mark's tone was very matter of fact.

"You guys can share with me."

I was so flustered, all I could manage to do was to sit down on the bed. Mark must have seen the look on my face because he tried to make light of it.

"Don't worry sis, I'll 'small up' myself." He laughed while sucking in his belly.

His attempt at humour did nothing to calm the fear that was rising up in me. How could three of us share a double bed for six weeks? Mark was 6ft 2 and was built to play American football or rugby.

Antoinette giggled while trying to push in Mark's belly.

"Your bed's too small, Uncle Mark. And there's not enough room for all my teddies. Mummy can you open my suitcase, I want to show Uncle Mark my teddies."

"Hold on a minute, baby girl."

I continued sitting on the bed looking around the small room, processing the scene, as Mark explained.

"I'm renting a room, not the whole house. The lady's okay but she has a few house rules, so just stay out of her way... sis, are you listening? Antoinette, what's wrong with your mum?"

Antoinette peered into my eyes. I tried a fake smile so as not to worry her.

"Mummy, Mummy, are you tired?"

"I'm fine, baby girl, we are on holiday."

130

"Okay, we can make this work, it's only for a few weeks... I'll sleep next to Uncle Mark and you can sleep snuggled up next to me. And your teddies can take turns."

I spent the rest of the evening pretending I was happy. But inside, I was frightened to leave the room and desperate to get out of the house. I felt like a burglar.

I could only use the kitchen between certain hours. Mark had a shelf in the fridge; everything else he kept in his room in a bag on the floor.

Mark ate out most of the time, so, while the arrangement worked fine for him, it was impractical for looking after Antoinette, who loved food and, in particular, all her meals and snacks.

I wanted to go home, right then and there, but how could I? I had plans to go to Barbados, which was crucial, plus I didn't think I could afford another return ticket. I was stuck.

Every morning while in that room, I woke to the boxed-in feeling, and Mark leaving for work. Antoinette's and my days were spent watching 500 TV channels. The choice of children's shows was mind-blowing. Antoinette was in her element, dodging the prison guard of a landlord and going for walks around the neighbourhood, sightseeing.

On one of our walks we bucked up on a deserted children's play area, but it was 95–100°C in the shade and everything was roasting. Poor Antoinette could only look on, not touch, or swing or climb.

Antoinette's and my daily routine also included a trip to Sam's Club, which was like bulk-buying heaven. We'd spend hours walking round the store, not buying anything, just looking.

And every evening, Mark either took us out for dinner or he'd bring takeout home, which we ate in the room.

I only ventured into the kitchen to fix cereal for Antoinette.

I felt so uncomfortable in the woman's house and her stern manner ensured that never changed for the duration of our stay.

Luckily for us, in the second week of our stay Mark took us to meet his mum, Vivian, which came as a surprise to me because he said he despised her. It was Mark's dislike of his mother and hate for 'the Grenadian', his dad, my stepfather, which had cemented our relationship. We both understood what it was like to be unwanted by our parents.

Vivian appeared to be different from the mental picture I had etched in my mind of her. Visually, she looked very similar to my so-called mother. She was dark chocolate, with full auburn eyes, African straight nose and thick lips, ebony relaxed curly hair; medium height, with big breasts, small waist and big hips.

But unlike my so-called mother, Vivian was warm and caring. On hearing we were staying with Mark in the one room she was horrified, while also being irritated because a roommate in her spare room meant she had no room for us.

Every day after work Vivian picked us up and took us over to her apartment, which had a pool. It was a big help; Antoinette and I loved to spend time with her and loved the pool even more. We spent so much time there I taught Antoinette how to swim.

Over the next few weeks Mark's mum and I got really close. She talked about her relationship with Mark and how hurt she was by the way he treated her. Mark barely gave her the time of day.

Mark had never told me why he hated his mother, but his mum did. Vivian had been dating 'the Grenadian' for some time when she discovered she was pregnant. The relationship was rocky, but she wanted the baby, so she decided to go ahead with the pregnancy.

By the time Mark was born, the relationship with 'the Grenadian' was over. She was happy to co-parent but 'the Grenadian' didn't want to. When Mark was two years old, 'the Grenadian' kidnapped him from the childminder and took him to Grenada, where he left Mark with his parents. 'The Grenadian' turned on his heels and returned to England.

Vivian tried over the years to get her son back but 'the Grenadian' family blocked her every time. She must have tried about five times and every time she went to Grenada to get her son, she returned without him. Mark was fifteen by the time she managed to 'snatch' him back and take him to Boston.

Mark had hated her ever since. He didn't believe that she had tried hard enough to get him back when he was little. By the time she did get him back he had grown accustomed to his life in Grenada, where he lived like a prince with his grandparents.

To make matters worse, Vivian had got married and had twin boys, who were four years younger than Mark. He hated them all equally.

Vivian said she had worn herself out trying to plead her case and reassure Mark that she had never stopped loving him, but it was no use. He refused to blame his dad for the whole sordid mess, choosing instead to blame her, even though she too had been traumatised by the kidnapping of her son, to the extent that her marriage had ended after only five years. Her husband had compounded matters by establishing custody of the twins.

It was easy for me to empathise with both of them, but I thought with a bit of help I could get them reading from/singing from the same page.

I tried to get Mark to see how his mum had been affected and hurt too by his kidnapping, but he was as stubborn as an ox. He reminded me so much of his dad 'the Grenadian', both of them pig-ignorant and incapable of seeing someone else's pain.

Mark was impossible. He loved to sulk in silence, and to his credit it was a great weapon against me because I loved to talk and hated angry silence.

So I gave up championing his mum's cause and chose instead to get 'happy' Mark back, which was near impossible, and took days. It was Antoinette who got him out of the funk in the end. Every evening when Mark got home from work Antoinette jumped into his arms and he caught her, but after a few silent nights she stopped doing it. Mark couldn't bear it, he started tickling her, and normal life resumed.

Before we left to go to Barbados, Mark introduced us to Brenda, who was a family friend from England. Meeting Brenda signalled a fabulous change to our holiday.

Brenda was nuff fun. She was really popular, and her brother was a big time DJ in Florida. He played at all the best clubs.

Brenda's mum was happy to look after Antoinette, so I got to rave in Florida. It was wicked. On Wednesday nights we went to Classics, ladies' night. They had male strippers and at the end of the night we did a formation dance called the 'Electric Slide'. I hated the sleazy strippers but loved the buzz of the place.

Saturday night we went to Centrepole. It was like a saloon from the wild, wild west. It had so much wood, the place was a forest fire waiting to happen.

But Brenda's brother Ricky had the place packed every Saturday night. Usually the night would end with some gunshots outside the club and everyone would have to duck and roll to get to their cars. It was a crazy time.

After every rave we'd go to Denny's, for hot chocolate and strawberry pie. I loved it. I felt so free. I hadn't raved so much since before I had Antoinette. I was on holiday and I had childcare on tap, so I made the most of it until I went to Barbados and even when I got back.

❧

Barbados was a trip and a half. For two months I had toyed with the idea of a simple family holiday with my siblings and getting to know my family. Just a glimpse of that picture excited me.

But I failed to consider the fact my so-called mother and 'the Grenadian' would be there too. But the way I saw it, I would have my family on my side, or so I thought. Hope was always my downfall.

Again, I hadn't given the sleeping arrangements any thought until the day I arrived, which was crazy given what I had endured in Florida with Mark.

I loved being back in Barbados; I was mesmerised by the tropical smells and visions as we drove to my grandmother's house. Everything looked the same as my imagination had created from the descriptions

I had heard as a child. Cute little colourful shacks and mansions sat side by side with palm trees, fruit trees and flower-filled hedges along the various roads.

My grandmother's house was situated on acres and acres of Moore land, which had been in the family for generations, on the Palm Road, in St James. The peach-coloured house was built part board and shingle and part wall, with three bedrooms, a bathroom, kitchen and sitting room. The surrounding land was full of different palm and fruit trees, chickens and gullies.

And ten feet away from my grandmother's house was my aunt's house, which housed her family. My sister Hyacinth lived in our grandmother's house, so Antoinette and I slept in her room, with Keres.

But what I hadn't bargained on was my so-called mother and 'the Grenadian' sleeping under the same roof as me. They were too close for comfort; just hearing their voices made me shudder. I didn't want to be anywhere near them.

I hated them equally with a passion. My only defence was playing ghost while gritting my teeth and averting my eyes, so theirs didn't make four or six with mine.

Antoinette was oblivious. She loved being in Barbados, from the first day when she ran between the two houses, my grandmother's and my aunt's, without fear of her new surroundings. She bonded with her great-grandmother from the first night.

As soon as we arrived Antoinette ran through the darkness straight into my grandmother's bedroom. I had been a little more hesitant. I didn't know what to expect from old people and I feared death more.

My grandmother was far from dead. She had such a lively energy.

"Man, you feel good enough."

She spoke as she felt me up, as if she was blind. Her fingers didn't miss a bit of me. Antoinette laughed, "She did that to me too!"

Baa laughed too.

"Man, I love to feel me family."

"How ya? Man, wunna come far enough, good dear."

"We are fine, not as good as you."

Gran chuckled.

"It mussy cold enough in England?"

"It's summertime now, so the weather is warmer than usual but not as hot as here."

As I spoke I studied her closely. There was no doubt she was my grandmother. I looked just like her. It was comforting but scary too. She was the only person I had ever met who resembled me, but if she was my mirror, old age wasn't going to be kind to my beauty. Gran's features were hard to distinguish through the wrinkles but her sunken eyes, straight nose and full lips were all me.

Gran seemed distant from the family, yet she was happy. She never ate a meal with us. She had all her meals in bed. But Gran had a trail of visitors all day. If you wanted to talk to her, you had to go to her. She was about eighty, and tired, she told me. I didn't like to see her cooped up in her room all day. But that's how they lived.

The first couple of days with my family were like I had imagined. My sister Hyacinth showed Keres and me the local area and introduced us to cousins as we passed by.

Then I noticed that family members began taking out my so-called mother, 'the Grenadian', Keres and Jamie, while Antoinette and I were left at home with Hyacinth. This behaviour triggered a déjà vu feeling which I resisted, choosing to focus on having a good holiday. I guess Keres and Jamie felt the same, because neither of them mentioned it.

Bedtimes were the most fun, as we, Keres, Hyacinth and I, lay in bed chatting, telling stories and jokes. Every time at least one of us got a stitch or the hiccups laughing too much.

One night I was reminding Keres about our kids' game 'Return to Witch Mountain'. She sat up in bed, put her index fingers on each temple and screeched with laughter as she tried to speak.

"Come in Shritti! Come in Shritti! Over. Over!"

I screamed with laughter. Poor Hyacinth just stared at us.

"Man, you two are 'mad as France'… what is Shritti?"

I laughed as I remembered Shritti's face.

"Oh, she is my childhood friend. We always played the 'Return to Witch Mountain' game and when I tried to teach Keres and Jamie how to play, they couldn't get past her name."

Our ruckus caused my so-called mother to shout at us to go to sleep but whispering just made us giggle even more until we burst out laughing again.

I think the fact that we were having so much fun is what sparked the ogre to catch a fire.

One night in particular, we (Keres, Hyacinth and I) had decided to go clubbing in town. My sister Hyacinth had been raving about a club called September's. One Saturday night we were busy getting ourselves ready when 'the Grenadian' starts bellowing and shouting that Keres couldn't go out.

At first, I thought he must be joking, but when Keres came back in the room crying, I realised he was serious.

Well, I thought I was going to have a heart attack or rocket to the moon. I was so mad. Keres was nearly nineteen years old. How could he stop her from going out? It just didn't make sense.

Through the patterned breeze block in the party wall between the bedrooms we could hear growling.

"She na go nowhere… me na care what you say, she na left ere!"

Despite my so-called mother being in the room with him, I didn't hear her voice.

I was furious. I started cussing and shouting. Hyacinth tried to quieten me, but it was no use. I couldn't understand why he had to ruin everything.

He continued, snarling unchallenged, "Keres! Keres!"

Keres ran to attention.

"You hear what I say, you na leff ere, to rass!"

Keres returned to the bedroom. She threw herself on the bed, curled up like a foetus and sobbed into her blankee (as she called her baby blanket).

Looking at her just fuelled my rage. I just couldn't understand why no one would ever defend us. Why didn't the family step in?

I felt terribly isolated. Hyacinth had nothing to offer. She didn't shout or say anything. She was so submissive, she made me sick. I couldn't bear to look at her, as she resembled her mother too much. Even with their mouth closed they appeared to be smiling. I started shouting at her.

"Say something. Shout. Curse. Do something, don't just sit there."

"What do you want me to say? If she can't go, she can't go. That's her father, so dat's dat. Done!"

"That's it, done. Why aren't you angry? He's spoiling our night out, which we've been planning for years, doesn't it bother you?"

"Him, he can't do nothin' to me. He's bothering she!"

"That fucking man is always getting between me and my brother and sister and I'm sick of it. What's fucking wrong with him? Why doesn't he want us to be together? He's fucking kept us apart for years and he's still not happy. He needs to fuck off and leave us alone! Go on, fuck off!"

"She na want me to come in dere. Me will kill her to rass!" He left, slamming the sliding patio door.

"Dominiquè, easy man." Hyacinth stared at me.

Her demeanour astounded me. Why didn't she feel aggrieved? She had been abandoned by our so-called mother at three months old. She had as much right to be angry as I was, but she wasn't.

And to compound my anger and feeling of belonging there was no response from the peach-coloured house six feet away, despite it being full of witnesses who must have heard everything.

The insurmountable betrayal I felt fuelled my wrath and I determination to leave that house forthwith. As I made my exit in deafening silence, in the absence of care or compassion from any of my relatives, I threw my suitcases over the cliff, past the stone stairs, onto the road below, where my cousin was waiting for me.

I called Antoinette from next door and we were gone. She must have felt the energy or read my face, because she just hummed softly as we drove away.

The smells of the Caribbean night, sugar cane, coconut and floral mix and the gentle warm breeze, couldn't refocus my stirring anger.

My expectations of what a relative meant had finally diminished completely; beneath the warm welcoming smiles was nothing, no interest or connection, and definitely, no love.

I think the thing that struck me the most was my family's silent collusion, which had magnified how my so-called mother had got away with doing so many vicious things. I had now witnessed my family's response first-hand. In planning my reunion, it hadn't occurred to me that I would discover the root cause. I thought my so-called mother was an exception, not the rule. My family manufactured wickedness like most families integrate love.

Believing she was an anomaly is what had kept my hope alive, the dream that one day I would have a fairy-tale ending. But yet again I was knocked down by the harsh reality of my life.

⁓

In my rage I went to stay with my aunt S, she's also my so-called mother's sister. Aunt S lived about five minutes away from my grandmother, and she had a farm, well it wasn't really a farm, but she had pigs, goats and flies.

During the day the house was overrun with flies of every description. I never knew there were so many varieties of flies; big ones, small ones, they had no fear of humans, they just swarmed the place. I don't think I ate in that house the whole time I stayed there.

The flies tormented Antoinette too. She looked like a beekeeper with a towel over her head. She kept it on all day when she was in the house and even ate under it.

My aunt S was very child-friendly, so she wasn't offended or, if she was, she didn't mention it.

Aunt S had a caring face with a curious permanent frown. She rarely conversed, just the odd question. But there was no mention of my sudden arrival or talk of my so-called mother. Thus her caring appearance did not translate into action, well, she never showed me any love.

Aunt S shared the same physical appearance as her sisters, including the Moore trademark big breasts and big ass, but her thin waist had given way to a big belly.

The house was a melee of people and pre-wedding fever, as I was staying with the mother of the bride's family. This gave me the time to get to know them.

My cousin Sonia was marrying a guy who was ten years her junior, so there was a lot of gossip. I didn't care. I liked Sonia. She had a sweet smile and loved to laugh like me. We were like a double act.

e~o

Man, it was a lovely wedding. The happy couple oozed 'black' love. St James Parish Church was full to capacity. The reception was held at the Plantation, which was the number one venue in Barbados.

I was having a lovely time at the wedding with my sisters and Antoinette, until I realised no one was introducing me to my extended family. And yet, my so-called mother was gliding around the reception, grinning like she had won a new life.

Her stupid grin was driving me mad. Why was she so happy? Did she have no shame or guilt? Every time I saw the smile on her face or heard her laugh it sent up my pressure.

To distract myself I went into the kitchen to offer my help.

"Come, come, hand round this cake for muh," one of my aunts ordered, as they gave me a large tray full of sliced cake.

As I made my way around the guests with the tray of cakes, I bucked up on my so-called mother laughing with a group of ladies. The next thing I knew I had a kitchen knife in my hand. I was going to kill her. Just as I was about to plunge the knife into her back, a guy grabbed my wrist and took the knife out of my hand. I ran out of the reception hall, straight to the bar in the courtyard.

The guy who saved me from a murder sentence found me downing straight Old Gold rum. He joined me with a drink of the same.

"Hey, I'm Marvin."

"I'm not really in the mood to talk."

He looked strikingly handsome and sweet with big dimples, red chocolate skin, athletic build and diamond studs in both ears.

As we sat amongst the guests, I felt like I was in a fish bowl with everybody watching and talking about me.

"Do you want to get out of here?" I nodded emphatically.

I left Antoinette with Aunt S and I was gone.

Marvin understood my silence as he drove me away from the wedding reception. I tried to enjoy the scenery while listening to the radio. Along the way he picked up a few friends. My role as an observer continued as we arrived at a spring in St Philip. Marvin's friends had organised a picnic.

It was a beautiful night. We lay on blankets watching the clear black sky. The stars looked just a touch away.

Marvin and his friends were a few years younger than me, but I didn't care. They were friendly. I was happy just listening as they chatted amongst themselves, while eating and sipping rum.

I felt really chilled with my new friends. I must have got home about 3am. Marvin lived next door, so I didn't need him to wait while I went in.

I knocked on the door. No answer. And then I knocked on the bedroom window. No answer. I did everything I could to get someone's attention to let me in the house, but no one opened the door. After frantically knocking on every ground floor window, I realised I had been locked out.

With no way to get in the house, or a backup plan, I had to spend the night sitting on the gallery wall. I was still wearing the dress I had attended the wedding in. I didn't even have a jacket or anything. Luckily the night air was warm but every now and then there was a cool breeze that made me wish I had a cardigan or something.

There was no way I could sleep, I was too frightened. Everything seemed still or deathly silent except for the occasional breeze. I could have been murdered out there, but nobody cared enough to let me in, so I kept watch all night until 6am, when my cousin left for work.

He didn't say a word. And neither did I.

I just went into the house and went to bed. When I got up later that day, I expected somebody to say something to me, apologise for the terrible mistake of locking me out, but nobody did.

But I heard my aunt mumble something under her breath, something about people better get in before she locks her doors and that was it. I couldn't believe my long lost family could treat me like that, without warning or anything. It was clear, viciousness was a family trait.

I swore then and there I would never stay at another relative's house ever again; it would be hotels for me.

That experience killed the family reunion dead. I avoided all contact with all of them, even my sisters and brother, for the remainder of my time in Barbados. The distance was my proven method for protecting myself from unmet expectations.

Marvin was a perfect pastime; he loved 'the Rock', as he called Barbados, so he was happy to be my tour guide. We went to all 80 beaches and drove around the island making memories.

Even Antoinette liked Marvin. She came out with us a few times. He was great with her, whether it was building sand castles or water fights. And I hadn't bothered with formal introductions, there wasn't any point. Antoinette had a healthy social diary, she was spoilt for choice with cousins to play with. So it was really just me and Marvin.

Being with Marvin was easy; we just clicked, and spending every waking hour together ensured our romance flourished. Our age difference had no bearing as his maturity was captivating. Intuitively he knew how to make me feel special and our chemistry was on fire.

"All you have to do is say and I'll do whatever you want."

Marvin stared deep into my eyes, while holding me tight around my waist, as we stood toe to toe in the bandstand of the sports field.

"Yeah right, there's no way you'll do whatever I ask."

"Ask me and then you'll see, I'm a man of my word."

I laughed as I thought of an appropriate test.

"Okay, run around the field naked!"

"What da ass, I knew you was going to miss da point."

"You set the terms. You said whatever I want, that's what I want from you!"

As he toyed with the idea, he began taking off his T-shirt.

"Man, you're playing with me, you know I was talking about doing whatever you want when we are making love!"

I laughed until I nearly wet myself. He was just taking off his last trouser leg when I stopped him with a kiss.

We had so much fun together for two weeks, but fun is all it was. I had no intention of having a long distance relationship. I knew that what looks good in the sun doesn't look the same in grey England.

But saying goodbye was harder than expected. I shed a few tears and our last kiss was pure passion. Marvin had been my real knight. He had rescued me from the madness of my family. For that I would be forever grateful.

As we stood outside the departure lounge doors, I wasn't the only one crying. Antoinette had cried all the way to the airport. I was puzzled because I thought she'd be desperate to get back to all the 'mod cons' and cable television.

Instead she sobbed and sobbed. I couldn't console her.

"I don't want to go home to the white people. Why can't we stay with our family?"

Until she said it, I hadn't realised that I hadn't seen a white person for the whole trip.

"Did the ladies at the nursery treat you different to the white kids?"

I listened intently for her answer, worried I had missed something.

"Yes, the white girls always get what they want."

Antoinette's insight was mind-blowing. My little girl, who was born and raised in Paddington in London, one of the most diverse places in the world, was aware of discrimination. It was scary. It seemed that on a basic level nothing had changed for black children, even in 1989.

I took a moment to swaddle Antoinette.

"You may not always agree with someone's decision but it is against the law to treat you differently because of your colour, or because you're a girl. If this ever happens to you, tell me and I will deal with them for you... okay?"

But Antoinette, at the age of four, was aware, and what's more had an opinion about it. I was so shocked. I hugged her close.

"Awww baby girl, I know it's sad to leave your cousins, but we have to go back to see Uncle Mark and then home in two weeks. Your daddy must be missing you bad. Don't you want to go and see your daddy?"

"Yes, but can we come back after we see him?" she sobbed.

"But you're starting your new school when we get home, remember?"

Antoinette nodded as I kissed her on both cheeks. With one eye on the issue and the other on Antoinette we boarded the plane.

As the plane's engines roared and the wheels began to turn, I exhaled. I thanked God for getting me out of Barbados. Despite my brief love affair with Marvin, my holiday had been pure torture and I was desperate to get as much sea as possible between me and my so-called family.

❧

After sitting in the arrivals lounge at Miami airport for seven hours, Mark eventually picked us up.

He arrived with no apology or anything. I was baffled. For hours I had worried, thinking maybe he had had an accident or something, but his stern demeanour suggested something else.

I was perplexed. I had left for Barbados on good terms with him, but he was mute for the whole drive home and I was too pissed off to ask him why.

After a frosty couple of days, I overheard Mark chatting on the phone, telling someone he didn't want us to stay with him anymore. And that's why he'd left us waiting at the airport.

The problem was he was a coward. He didn't have the balls to just tell me how he was feeling. Instead we had to endure sulky silence, which was unbearable, especially as we had to share a room, and a bed. I started counting down the days until we could leave, again, but luckily Brenda saved us with an invite to stay with her.

I really appreciated Brenda for taking us in, particularly as she didn't really have the room. She was still living at home and we all had to share her bed. The only problem was, Brenda was a really big girl who needed the whole bed to herself. But bless her heart she shared it anyway.

Staying with Brenda was fantastic. Her family was really welcoming and for the first time in two months I felt like I was part of a family. Brenda was great fun too, we raved at least three nights a week and she also took us sightseeing.

Brenda, Antoinette and I went to Disney World. Antoinette had a ball. The look on Antoinette's face when she approached the Disney castle was magical and seeing Mickey and Minnie Mouse nearly hypnotised her. She moved like she was dreaming as we explored the park and rides, engulfed in a swarm of people and in the 102-degree heat.

After insisting we stayed to watch the evening Disney parade, Antoinette nearly passed out when the life-sized Winnie the Pooh came over to give her a hug. She took off running, which was crazy given how much she loved him. We nearly lost her in the swathes of people.

The drive home was also a trip because Brenda kept falling asleep behind the wheel.

"B… B, wake up, wake up." I tapped her arm until she opened her eyes.

"Did I fall asleep? But my eyes were open. I was looking at the road."

"Beeeeeee… wake up man!"

"Nooooooo, not again, but the road looks so real."

"Wind down your window, let the breeze hit your face. Maybe we should just pull over, so you can get a nap."

We both opened our car windows and Brenda shook her head and hands to wake herself up.

"Na man, dem alligators will eat us for a snack. It's all right, I'm awake now."

My exhale was interrupted by loud gurgling.

"Beeeeeee, Beeeeeee, you've dropped off againnnnnn!"

"Right, let's sing songs and see who's the best. I know I'm gonna win."

"You wish! Me a de badest chick."

"We'll see. First track, 'Hold on to your love', En Vogue."

I began singing and that's how we avoided death by sleep-driving. I wouldn't have minded but it was a three-hour drive home after a fifteen-hour day.

Mark remained scarce but showed up to bid us farewell on the morning of our departure. He gave a tongue in cheek apology and said goodbye.

I had had such high hopes for my first holiday under my own steam but instead of giving me the fresh start I needed it added to my misery. Once again, my so-called family had been the source of my pain.

I was still looking for love in all the wrong places. And to make matters worse, Ronald's mum's suitcases, which I had borrowed for my trip, arrived at Heathrow airport mashed up, so I'd have to buy her some new ones.

13

YOUNG, FREE AND SINGLE!

My relationship with Marvin had been a great way to get back in the dating game; I was ready to have some fun.

I started hanging round with my friend Nina. Nina was the perfect road dog, she loved men and she loved to rave.

She was also a single parent to her daughter, but you would never know because it was rare to see them together; she had childcare on tap.

So hanging out with Nina was pure fun! We raved hard and met a lot of guys. We had our party trick worked out; we used to dress in the same outfit and it worked every time. We had more attention than we knew what to do with.

But dressing the same was where our similarity ended. Nina liked to have a lot of sex and she wasn't fussy about who gave it to her; in one week she slept with seven guys. That's when I realised she was a nymphomaniac!

Nina wasn't bothered about having a relationship, she just wanted to have sex. One guy described dancing with her like dancing with someone who had just come out of jail!

Rubbing to lovers rock was her thing. I was more reserved. Don't get me wrong, I had my fair share of fun but I was respectable. I'm a one-man woman and I like a relationship.

I had a good reputation and I aimed to keep it. People kept telling me to drop Nina as a friend, but I liked her and what she did with her body had nothing to do with me.

Every year Nina and I went to Notting Hill Carnival together and this year we went dressed in Aztec outfits, with belly tops and pencil skirts. As usual we had nuff attention because we looked and danced wicked, wukking up stink!

Until the heavens opened, and the Carnival was drenched. It was the wettest Carnival on record. But we didn't let the rain spoil the fun; we joined behind a float and danced up a storm, which attracted this group of guys. But this one guy was on me like white on rice.

Calvin, mmmmm! Calvin was fine. He had a cute, cheeky smile with just the hint of a gold tooth, tall, about 6ft 2, athletic build, Nubian dark chocolate, he had a six-pack and he could whine. We danced and partied all day in the pouring rain.

As it got late, and the Carnival drew to a soggy close, Calvin's mates, Nina and I danced behind the Factory float as it made its way back to the Factory, where there was a wicked rave. The community hub was heaving ravers.

We partied together till morning. Calvin and I felt the music and each other as we danced sensually to lovers rock. We got so caught up in our feelings we began kissing.

Our chemistry was on fire by end of the night. Desperate to be together again, we arranged to meet at Queens Park Station the next day at twelve.

The next morning, I was on such a high from the Carnival rave, while feeling a little apprehensive about meeting him at the station, fearing he may not turn up.

But he was there at twelve on the dot. He kissed me tenderly, right there for everyone to see. I felt so shy it was crazy. We went back to my place.

As soon as we got through the door he was on me. I tried to be cute and fight him off, but the passion was burning hot and he was only kissing me.

"Would you like a drink?"

"You are all I need."

His sweet grin grabbed me as I stood up, so did he and he pressed himself into the top of my thigh. Damn, I was frightened, he was so hard and big. I was scared he might do me some damage.

I gave up fighting and succumbed to my desire. Calvin played my body like it was a harp, the lust, the passion, made my body pop. We couldn't get enough of each other and his maturity, being twenty-seven to my twenty-one, was evident in every move he made.

The way he kissed and caressed me, licked me and bit me made me open up to feel every part of him but nothing prepared me for what he had; he was built for depth, comfort and speed!

We made lust all day long and well into the night. When he left my body was on fire and I wanted more. Luckily for me he felt the same attraction, so we became inseparable.

Calvin moved with a Grove Estate Sound, so we raved every weekend and every Wednesday Nina and I went to visit them at Steve's house. Nina was seeing Steve, so we became a foursome.

Nina and I loved raving with the Sound, they played wicked, so the parties were always rammed, and the Sound's drink of choice was Mumm champagne. That is where I acquired my love of Mumm demi-sec champagne.

Calvin and I would rave together all night and then go back to mine and make lust all morning! Sometimes Steve and Nina would stay over too, so we used to have the weekend all together.

The relationship was going great for about five to six months, when, for some crazy reason, Nina and I decided to go to the estate on a Tuesday instead of the usual Wednesday.

From the first few steps into the urban estate things felt weird. There was an odd energy in the air.

Familiar faces appeared unwelcoming. Just as we entered Steve's block we bumped into the main Sound man.

"Hey Moth, how's things?"

"Hey, all right." Moth disappeared like a ghost.

We went to Steve's flat as usual, knocked a few times, but he appeared to be out. And it was at that moment I realised I didn't know where Calvin lived.

We stood in the dingy scarcely-lit stairwell looking lost.

"Doesn't Steve's sister live on the next floor?" Nina looked at me with a spark in her eyes.

"Oh yes, you're right, but what number?"

Nina shrugged.

"I guess we'll have to knock every door till we find her."

"Let's try the flat directly under Steve."

After the first few attempts our persistence paid off as somebody told us which flat to try. Nina was too afraid to knock so I did. Steve's sister Susan answered the door.

"Hi, we're looking for Steve."

"If he's not in I'm not sure where he is."

I was about to leave.

"Do you know where Calvin lives?"

Susan opened the door wider as she spoke.

"He lives here. I'll just get him." Susan retreated behind the front door.

A few seconds later, Calvin stood in the doorway, dressed in his dressing gown and slippers. As his eyes registered, he looked stunned.

He spoke in a low whisper, "What are you doing here? I can't talk now, go home, I'll call you later."

Before I could answer or ask a question, he shut the door. No bye or nothing. I thought it was strange but began to walk away when the front door opened.

Susan whispered too. "Why are you looking for Calvin?"

"Why do you want to know?" I looked at her intently.

"Because I have been with him for seven years." Our eyes locked as her words hit me.

I was stunned. I didn't know what to say, I was in too much shock to speak. Susan looked concerned as she watched me intensely.

"Woman to woman, have you been seeing him?"

Her words struck a chord, women need to stick together or something, because before I could think it through I answered, "Yes, I have."

Susan's silence accompanied her inside as she closed the door. Suddenly Calvin charged out of the door with a baseball bat, shouting, "What did you tell her?"

Susan grabbed him and when that didn't stop him charging towards me, she ran in front of him.

"Just go, go!"

As we made our way home, I was tranced, my thoughts were absent of the journey. I just couldn't believe what had happened. Nothing made sense. How could he have a woman, when we were together every weekend and every Wednesday?

He never left my house before twelve on Sundays, what woman would put up with that? How could something that felt so right be so wrong?

Was he really going to hit me with the baseball bat? The questions just kept going around and round in my head and back and forth with Nina.

Between us we were unable to make sense of it. For days I heard nothing from Calvin. I had a neighbour friend, Grace, who lived on the top floor of my block. For some crazy reason I confided in her.

Grace was expecting her first baby and I had been supporting her during a difficult pregnancy. I told her what had happened, and she was very consoling. She was older, so I appreciated her perspective.

About a week after everything had blown up, Calvin showed up one evening. At first, I wouldn't open the door but he begged me and wore me down.

As he entered, he looked so dejected.

"I'm sorry, don't finish with me, I want you." Calvin held me tight as he looked into my eyes, pleading.

"Yeah, I saw how much you wanted to kill me with a baseball bat!"

"I don't want to hurt you, you know I love you."

"Love, that didn't look like love to me!" He squeezed me tighter.

"I'm sorry, I shouldn't have done that, but you know I would never hurt you." I tried to break free, but he wouldn't release me.

"But you did, you really tricked me."

"I should've told you, but I wanted you so much and I knew you'd blow me out if you knew about her."

"So that's it, you'll lie to get what you want."

He began kissing my face, lips first, each eye, my eyebrows, cheeks.

"I'm sorry, I'm sorry, I won't lie to you ever again, never. Believe me, please believe me, I love you." As he kissed me, he caressed my curves, running his fingers up and down my back.

"You love me, but what about Susan?"

"Just give me time, so we can be together."

His desire was so convincing. As we kissed I suddenly had the strength of a boxer.

"Get out, I deserve better than a liar. I pushed him off me and out my front door.

My head was in a spin, but I was determined to end the relationship. I deserved better and I resented the fact he had deceived me. He should have been up front, he should have given me the choice to either be with him on the side or not but no, he tricked me.

I stayed strong for about three weeks, but he kept calling, begging, or would just turn up, begging me to stay with him. He would cling to me and run his hands all over my body as he kissed me. My head said no but on his visit my body said yes.

I just loved the way his body made me feel. It was wrong, but I just couldn't resist him. So we were back together, and he reassured me he would leave her.

❧

About four months into our undercover love affair, my period was missing. My distress felt insurmountable and every time I considered my fear, my heart rate and temperature soared.

As I braced myself for the difficult conversation with Calvin, my prep was rudely interrupted by an unexpected visit from Susan. She appeared at my front door with a girl from around the way who I couldn't stand.

Before I could compose myself or speak, the two twenty-seven-year-olds demanded to know if I was pregnant. I was baffled. My mind was a hailstorm of questions. How did they know where I lived? And how did they know about my missing period? I hadn't discussed this with anyone, not even Nina; the only exception was Grace!

The grown ass women stood menacingly in my doorway.

"Look we haven't come to play, are you pregnant?"

"Play, what have you come for?"

"I just want to know if you're pregnant for Calvin?"

"I don't know what you've heard but I've got no news. I'm definitely not pregnant, I don't think."

I tried to close the door, but Susan put her foot in the way.

"I'm not leaving till I know if you're pregnant for my man!"

My stare darted back and forth to each face. The woman I couldn't stand was clearly the aggressor, her mouth was pouted as if she were chewing a wasp, while Susan looked like a mouse pretending to be a lion.

I just wanted them to leave my yard.

"Well I don't know. I've got nothing more to say."

"How late are u? It's probably not even Calvin's, she probably sleeping with the whole Sound!" The vicious one glared at me.

Livid, I got defensive.

"I'm not a slut and it's not my fault Calvin wanted to be with me. If I am pregnant it's between me and Calvin. It has absolutely nothing to do with you and most definitely it's got nothing to do with you!"

"That's it, we're going to find out right now!"

The situation was futile, so they frogmarched me to a family planning clinic. I felt pressured, but I really needed to know too, so I went along with it.

Unfortunately, the nearest clinic was closed so we had to walk all the way to Ladbroke Grove. We must have looked odd, the three of us together but sitting rows of chairs apart.

After the green mile wait, the test was negative. I wasn't pregnant and thankfully the panic was over.

As I walked out of the clinic into the afternoon sunshine, Susan tried to fight me. As she threw a punch at my back, she shouted, "That's for sleeping with my man."

Well, I gave her the kicking of her life. I was wearing pointed gold-tip shoes, which I just kept kicking her with.

She was a rubbish fighter, all she kept doing was pulling my hair, while I was punching and kicking her.

In defeat she skulked off with her sidekick. I was so disappointed by her lack of maturity. The person she was supposed to beat was Calvin not me, but it was easier for her to attack the woman.

Luckily for her the sordid incident sealed the fate of my relationship with Calvin. I had too much class to be reduced to fighting for a man, so I let her have him.

I wanted a man I could trust, and I would never be able to trust Calvin. He cheated on her and I'm positive he would have cheated on me. I was done. Unfortunately it took Calvin years to accept it was over.

Every Carnival he would turn up at my door begging me to be with him. At first it was hard to resist him but just the memory of the fight with Susan was deterrent enough for me to keep my legs closed and after a while I just didn't answer the door to him.

In amongst the emotions was a loose, Grace meddling big mouth. As I stood at her front door feeling sore, I observed her sheepish smirk as I spoke.

"Why did you feel the need to chat my business?"

"Well, Susan had a right to know, that's her man."

I felt incredulous, not a sorry or nothing! It was clear we were far from friends, not even acquaintances. Thankfully, she moved away and without visuals or scars, I was able to file away the sordid mess.

cro

One thing to come out of the whole Calvin nightmare was my decision to get sterilised. My views on birth control were most definitely pro-choice.

I actively used the pill. I hated everything about it, but most of all, I just didn't feel protected, particularly when I heard how ineffective it could be if you drank alcohol or had a cold. I often had both.

I took the pill every morning I remembered to take it, but my memory was unreliable. The little pill resembled a multivitamin like Haliborange. I just couldn't trust that little thing to stop a 7lb baby!

The fear of getting pregnant became all-consuming, I couldn't shake it. I loved my daughter but that's where my maternal instincts began and ended.

I never wanted to be trapped by a baby again. The baby was only part of the argument; I also hated the idea of being tied to a man I didn't love or like for the rest of my life.

But above all my fears was the thought of ending up like my so-called mother, five kids from four different men. No way, that just didn't suit me.

I didn't want to have any children I didn't want and end up like her with children I have to hide or forget, no, no sireee!

Not me, I was sticking at one child if it killed me. I did some research and discovered it was easier to have a child you didn't want than it was to get sterilised.

The 'powers that be' felt it was better to encourage women to live with their bad choices than to encourage them to make considered decisions to prevent any more.

It was unbelievable. My doctor informed me I would not qualify for sterilisation on the NHS, but the NHS would give me as many terminations as my body would permit, no questions asked.

It seemed so ridiculous. I refused to be deterred. I looked into private clinics and found out that the Marie Stopes Clinic would do it for a fee, but I would have to be interviewed first to see if I was sane enough to give informed consent.

Undeterred by the £350 price tag, I went to the Marie Stopes Clinic in Euston, as arranged. It was a lovely bright summer's morning; the sky was clear blue, and the sun was beaming hard.

I felt empowered by the day and my decision. I arrived at the address, but the building just looked like a regular Georgian townhouse.

My mind briefly worried that the clinic was some back street, kill you on the table affair, but I shook my head and the thought away as I proceeded inside. The interior was clinical while having an air and soft furnishings which made you feel less formal.

The lady at reception gave everyone a fake name for confidentiality.

"Claire… Claire." The Irish voice behind a matron-looking receptionist beckoned.

I didn't pay her any mind as she continued calling. Just as the receptionist stood in front of me, I registered the name game.

"Claire, you're next, please follow this corridor down to the end and go into room 8."

"Room 8?"

As I wandered down the hall repeating the number, I tried to remember the directions.

Inside door number 8, I was greeted by a pleasant fifty-something female doctor, who, after a brief introduction, interviewed me about my decision to be sterilised.

At first, she tried to be authoritarian in her tone but when she realised I wasn't playing she softened her approach.

"Are you sure you aren't going to change your mind and want children when you're older? You're only twenty-two." Her eyes X-rayed my responses.

"Nobody asked me any questions when I wanted to have a baby at seventeen and a half! Nobody interviewed me to see if I wouldn't change my mind. How can that decision be less important than my decision to be sterilised, when this decision is about me getting sterilised and having a baby will effect somebody else's life?"

The doctor appeared impressed by the logic of my question, so much so she booked my sterilisation immediately.

My determination was evidenced in my presentation. I was twenty-two and I was beyond sure. I felt so free in the knowledge that I would be able to enjoy having sex without having to worry the whole month about unwanted pregnancies.

A few weeks later, I breezed through the procedure. As I emerged from the general anaesthetic, I was greeted by the most powerful sunbeam shining through the window in my private room. My feelings of relief were accompanied by excitement as I imagined the joy of living a sterile life.

∽

Back in the real world everything appeared the same except for me, I felt so high. But nobody knew why; I had kept the whole thing a secret, from decision to action.

But one Sunday I went to dinner at Jewel's mum's. It was another beautiful day, and as I rode the train to semi suburbia Harrow, I beamed with the peace within.

By the time I arrived my pride in myself was gushing. I practically skipped from the station to her house. The house looked the same, cream and white semi-detached, but I was different from my last visit two years ago.

Now I'm all grown up, a respectable mum, college student and part-time semi-professional.

I sprang through the open door with a fleeting greeting between Karen and me. I rested against the kitchen doorway, engulfed in the aroma of Sunday's best as I watched my aunts cooking dinner.

"Man, you looking real hard, you don't eat?"

Four eyes X-rayed me from head to foot."

I laughed as I spoke.

"Of course, I eat, I'm just slim, I have to keep my body right and tight! I've made sure I'll keep my sexy figure for life, no more babies for me."

"How have you done that, you celibate?" Auntie Kay laughed and shot Auntie Jeanette a snide look.

"Ummmm, I'm too young to be celibate. It's better than that, I got sterilised."

Both aunts stopped what they were doing and just glared at me for a split second.

"Wait… no, you wouldn't do that."

"No man, you too young… they wouldn't do that."

"They will, and I did!"

"You silly girl, why would you do such a thing, you're too young to make such a decision."

I looked for understanding but found nothing helpful in their stance.

"Silly, there is nothing silly about my decision to control my fertility and my life. Silly would be to have children I don't want and can't manage."

"But you're young, what if you meet a man who doesn't have children, what are you going to do then?"

Auntie Kay peered at me as she spoke, while Auntie Jeanette appeared engrossed in cooking.

"Well… if he wants kids, he'll need to find himself another woman because kids are not for me!"

I sulked out of the kitchen feeling dejected. Jewel was away at university and so was my backup.

I cut my visit short but as I journeyed home, I pondered my aunts' response. I just couldn't shake the feeling that they were irritated because I had avoided being a scandal.

The silent air of low expectations seemed to appear whenever I connected with an adult from my childhood. Over time I used this fact to empower me.

❧

With my emancipation I felt free to have fun and date often. Antoinette was my life but dating became my secret hobby. While Antoinette spent every other weekend with her dad, I became a free spirit.

Calvin had taught me to be guarded, like Inspector Gadget. I had to know everything about the guy, where he lived, worked and his inside leg measurement before I could consider dating them.

I loved being young, free and single, I couldn't move without a man whistling at me or tooting his car horn or approaching me. All the attention made me feel like Miss Attractive!

As I enjoyed meeting new men, I sifted through the shit looking for gold. It was hard going because there was so much fool's gold.

One night while raving with Nina at All Nations club, I met Ricardo! He was with his sidekick Linton. They were regular harbour sharks.

Nina and I were doing the most in the basement; Salvador's were playing the best in lovers rock. The place was pulsing with so many people, sweat was running down the walls. As usual Nina was working her way around the room while I danced behind a group of tables.

Ricardo couldn't take a hint. He pestered me for a dance until he wore me down. We became one as we whined seductively while I sang along to the music.

Ricardo insisted on taking me and Nina home. As he drove his BMW we chatted like old friends until I was home.

I liked Ricardo but there was something about him which didn't quite gel.

Apparently, he was a painter and decorator and lived in Wandsworth with his sister, or so he said, but for our brief interlude I saw no evidence of work of any kind and he was always broke.

But before our first date I carried out all my MI5 checks and I got Ricardo to take me to his sister's house. Everything appeared to check out, so we started casually dating.

Ricardo introduced me to 'parté'; the first time he went down on me I thought I was orbiting as I melted into the most exhilarating orgasm. Ricardo was ten out of ten for that.

But after a few months he became Mr Elusive! He was hard to find and unreliable. His sister would always have a story for him. And like a bad odour he would turn up out of the blue with a second-hand gift, some woman's belongings, which definitely wasn't box fresh!

That was it for me, I was done dating men who were beneath me and had nothing to offer except games.

But my abstinence was a fleeting notion which was interrupted by a handsome intelligent Mr Right. Charles looked so kriss! He was dark chocolate with clear skin, like an Asian, he had beautiful hazel eyes and silky pitch-black hair!

Charles and I were introduced by Roxanne, which was crazy because I hadn't seen Roxanne for a few years; the rape mess had tainted our relationship.

But during a rare visit Roxanne took me over to the adventure centre, as she had to collect some money.

Seeing Charles for the first time made my heart flutter. He was so cute. He had a juicy smile and he spoke so politely in a Barry White tone. Our eyes locked after he had caressed me with his twinkle. Oooooh, he made my body hot, upstairs and down!

"Well… hello. Roxanne, who is this lovely young lady?"

"Ummmm, hands off, Charles, this is my sister-in-law, Dominiquè."

"Well helllllooooooo, Dominiquè, I am pleased to make your acquaintance."

I shook Charles's outstretched hand. He cupped my hand in between both his hands, as he leaned in to kiss me on both cheeks.

"Where has she been hiding you?" He kept hold of my hand as he enjoyed watching me.

I giggled, as I was captivated by his beauty.

"I think she's kept you a secret, maybe she wants you for herself."

Roxane pinched my thigh as she faked a laugh.

"We're just friends, aren't we, Charles?"

"Yeah, we go way back."

Roxanne was suddenly eager to leave.

"Is Wendy in?"

"No, but she left this envelope for you."

Charles let go of my hand long enough to retrieve and hand the envelope to Roxanne.

"Thanks Charles, come Dominiquè, let's chip."

Charles caught my breath as he suddenly gently kissed me on the lips and whispered, "Bye… I hope to see you soon."

I was so shocked words failed me, but I could feel his kiss. Roxanne couldn't hide her irritation as we walked back to her place. Her mood was compounded as she begrudgingly gave me his work phone number.

Roxanne also gave me his statistics. Charles was St Lucian and had a daughter but the relationship with her mum had recently ended and he was living back home with his mum. He was dominoes mad and he played professionally.

Within weeks of meeting Charles and I began dating. He loved to take me raving so we could rub up all night, it was wicked. We used to kiss for hours. There was something about his lips and his beautiful face, I just melted away with every touch.

The first time we made love I nearly passed out, his dick was huge. I really had to take my time, or he would have done me serious damage! But slow and easy and he felt so orgasmic.

The only problem was he refused to go down on me or let me go down on him. It was against his Christian values, he told me. As annoying as this refusal was, I loved his love for God. Strangely enough I always seemed to fall for men of God. Probably because of my own Christian roots.

Charles and I were great together, he stimulated my mind and body. Charles worked at the community centre, he taught the community how to use a computer.

He was a great conversationalist, we would debate life's morals for hours, laughing and kissing throughout.

But he was as stubborn as an earthquake. It was impossible to convince him of an opposing opinion. And his other flaw was his lack of domestic skills, which were rooted in his belief that housework belongs to the women.

Luckily, I didn't want him for housework. We dated for about a year, until he started getting serious; he wanted me to have his baby.

That was my cue to run for the hills, relationship's done. I didn't want to be with a man who wanted kids, it was never going to happen.

Charles was crushed, he kept calling me and coming around, but I was done, it was clear we wanted different things from life. He was one of those guys who showed his love by keeping you pregnant and shackled barefoot in the kitchen.

Nope. that was definitely not how I planned to live my life. To me his plan felt like an insult, but he failed to comprehend why I wasn't flattered by his offer of a baby. The more we talked the clearer the end became.

Charles just didn't understand me or know what I wanted or needed. The clarity of our different goals magnified the gaps in all my previous love affairs.

❧

I'm not sure if any of the men I had loved had ever really understood me, so I decided to learn how to love myself.

One thing my life had taught me was that I couldn't rely on any man to fulfil my needs, so I needed to learn to do it for myself. I was sure the inner love would build resilience, which would protect me from becoming dependent on anyone.

My journey of self-discovery began with reading self-development books and I used to say positive affirmations to myself every morning while looking at myself in the mirror.

At first the process felt weird because I hadn't looked at myself for years. I focused on the benefits and fought through the uncomfortable feelings.

Day by day the process helped me to see myself properly, without the public act. At first, looking at me made me cry. I felt sorry for myself. Instead of looking away or closing my eyes or dismissing my feelings, I allowed myself to feel, and by embracing and acknowledging my sadness, which filled me deep within, I began to heal. My personal affirmations strengthened my core.

I spoke my truth, reminded myself of how far I had travelled and how strong I was. I would tell myself how much I loved being me.

By facing myself, I consciously worked to make myself feel better and stronger. I became self-soothing and self-compassionate.

I worked on myself for about one year. During that time I dated no one. I took a vow of chastity, which would only end when I felt complete.

I was determined to meet my own needs, with or without a man. I realised that a man should complement you and a relationship should add to your life, not be your life.

And if by chance I met someone new, I had developed the shortlist of characteristics and qualities he needed to possess for me to date him.

I felt so self-assured; I wasn't fazed about the possibility of a future without a man. I knew I would be fine.

14

A Different Type of Love

It's so funny how things happen in your life when you least expect it. I had never looked into my future and seen myself being married; when I looked into the future I couldn't see anything, and I didn't dare to dream.

After about a year of working on myself, I started raving with Nina again, but it was different this time; my confidence had changed my energy. I was looking fabulous, my body was tight, and I was a perfect Coca-Cola bottle shape (original bottle)! My hair was luscious and long.

Guys were on me like white on rice. But I wasn't playing with time wasters; if they failed the test, it was next, and I moved on.

This particular Saturday night I was desperate to go out, I needed to rave. Charles was back 'sniffing' around me, so I needed to keep moving. I really liked him, but he was looking for something I couldn't offer, a team of kids. And I never really trusted him. He just looked too damn good and he was as smooth as silk!

Thankfully Nina's sister was having a birthday party, so the rave was really local, in the block opposite mine. Nina and I arrived at 12am and the party was dead, just a few of the local 'harbour sharks'.

Nina and I were well vexed; we hadn't put so much effort into looking so fine to spend the night raving with the locals.

But we tried to make the most of it, after all it was still early. We decided to give the party a couple of hours to warm up, and after that if it didn't, I was going home. The party was really hard work. Time moved as if it had stopped or was going backwards, and still no people.

And just as I was about to leave at 2am, a group of guys came in, guys I hadn't seen before. Nina looked at me with a grin on her face and with that we were back in the raving mood.

The guys didn't waste any time, they were all trying to chat us up, except this one guy who broke away from the pack and went to stand across the room.

I didn't think much of the other guys, but I liked the individuality of the one who stood by himself; he had an air of confidence and nonchalance. He didn't look bothered about getting a dance and I liked that. I danced watching him.

He was quietly confident and rocked slowly to the music. I decided to approach him. I didn't know what I was going to say but I went over to him anyway.

I stood in front of him and eyed him up and down. He was attractive and was dressed nicely. He had a low high top and he wore square glasses. I approached him. I smelled his neck and squeezed his bum as he peered at me.

"Can I help you with something?" he asked, seductively.

Just then the DJ played a lovers rock tune.

"Yes, can I have a dance?"

He looked me in my eyes and laughed as he put his arm around my waist. We danced for ages, record after record, without speaking. After working up a real sweat, we went to the bar to get some drinks and then we stood on the staircase, talking.

His name was Mathew. He was living in Harlesden but was

originally from Birmingham. He had been living in London for a few years.

He was a builder and he was on a scheme to build his own home. He was twenty-five and his parents were from Grenada.

While we were talking some facesty guys kept asking me for a dance. They could see I was with a guy but that didn't stop them. I was intrigued by Mathew's attitude. He was so calm and chilled, he didn't react or say a word.

He left me to bat them away. I was intrigued by his posture, he seemed so peaceful and easy-going.

Mathew and I danced a little more and then he walked me home. I invited him in for a coffee and we ended up fooling around. He said it was my fault because I had put on my dressing gown, which was crazy. I thought my dress was too enticing, so I put my dressing gown over it to deter him.

We ended up talking until about 6am. He told me all about himself and his family. He said he was well-educated, had a degree, was a builder and he wanted to have his own business.

He had been brought up in the church, which reflected in his morals and principles. He was the second youngest of five but he had been raised by his dad from the age of six because his mum had died.

His dad had also died a few years ago, and his relationship with his dad hadn't been that great. But he was close to all of his siblings, particularly his sisters. I gave him a peek into my childhood, but I talked mainly about my career path, that I was in university and worked part-time. I told him about my daughter Antoinette.

I told him I didn't do children and if that was something he wanted I wasn't going to be the girl for him.

He was impressed about my career path and said he wasn't bothered about having kids because he had a son.

After talking until the early morning, I escorted him to the door. He said he wanted to see me again which was great, because I really wanted to see him again too. He had passed my test and he ticked all the boxes except he smoked; cigarettes and weed. Eeeeeh, but what could I do; he was on point with everything else.

He didn't have a phone, but he said he would pop by in a few days. I really liked Mathew, he seemed chilled and had prospects, and was just the type of guy I was looking for.

True to his word Mathew turned up two days later. He had borrowed his friend's car. I was so worried about him. I thought he might get lost, not being familiar with Paddington. But he reassured me he always found what he was looking for.

I took Antoinette over to my cousin Jacqui, because I didn't want her to see me with a man who wasn't her father. Child-free, Mathew and I hung out in the house, getting to know each other. I really liked him. He said he was a good guy, but most girls didn't want a 'good guy'.

I assured him a good guy was exactly what I wanted, as I was a good woman. Mathew was really mature, he had clear ideas about the woman he wanted to be with and I seemed to pass his checklist.

We had good chemistry, and we had passion for each other, it was really nice. We spent the next few weeks getting to know each other and then he went missing.

I didn't see or hear from him for about four days. It was so bizarre. I started to wonder if he had gone off me already. Then he finally tipped up. He wanted to know if he could trust me. He was so serious.

"Why... what's happened?"

He looked deadpan serious, as he stared into my eyes.

"I couldn't see you because I was lying low after doing a post office robbery!"

I didn't know what to say. I didn't do prison visits or have criminal friends, it wasn't my thing. When I was in the children's home most of the girls had boyfriends who were in and out of jail. They all got VOs (visiting orders) and visited their boyfriends in jail.

I used to laugh at them. I thought they were stupid or crazy. I told them straight, I had bigger fish to fry and it didn't involve going to visit no man in prison.

But here I was with a criminal staring at me. What was I supposed to say to this mess?

I kept my eyes fixed on Mathew's facial expressions.

"What did you do?"

"I didn't do the robbery, I was just the getaway driver!"

My heart was beating fast. I was thinking, *I hope he wasn't being followed by the police and now they're watching me.*

"Will you come and visit me in jail if I get caught?"

I lied.

"Yes, of course."

I couldn't talk for ages. I just kept thinking, with my new approach to men and my checklist, how did I manage to pick up a criminal?

He seemed so nice. How could my judgement be so off? We sat in silence for ages; I was pretending to watch the telly. After about two hours, he began smiling and then he cracked up laughing.

"Your face, if you could see your face. I'm not a robber and I definitely didn't do a post office robbery!"

He laughed for ages. I was pissed. I hit him with the cushion. He just kept laughing.

"It was a test, I wanted to know if you are loyal."

He killed himself laughing.

"I lied. I was working out how to drop you. I don't do prison visits, so if you have done a robbery you're on your own."

I was so vexed. Even when I knew it was a joke I couldn't laugh. I didn't find it funny, and I didn't like the fact he was so damn convincing. I tried to move down the couch, but Mathew hugged me close and looked deep into my eyes.

"You know you like me, you would visit me."

I didn't bother to answer him. I thought, *let him believe what he wants, I know me, he doesn't.* He also chose that evening to confess that he didn't have a degree and in fact he hadn't finished high school.

"I knew what type of guy you were looking for and I knew you wouldn't give me a chance if you knew the truth."

I was so disappointed. He had lied to me, and yet I was still attracted to someone who didn't pass my checklist.

I decided to focus on the positives, he passed most of the test and he did seem really nice. I opted for the 'give him a chance' option, hoping he would turn out to be more than a liar.

Two weeks later I went to visit him at his place. I was in *Columbo* mode. I needed to make sure he wasn't married with kids or something.

In fact, Mathew was renting a room in a flat in Tottenham. His room was orderly and clean. He had a row of white washing on an airer and his whites were whiter than mine, and mine were Persil white.

The room was sparsely furnished, with a mattress on the floor, but his sheets looked clean.

I was impressed by the clean way he lived; even though he was only renting a room, he lived with pride.

During the visit he told me he had to move out and would be moving to back to Birmingham. I was blown away. I lived in West London. I had no intention of having a long-distance romance, distance makes your heart wander.

A moment of madness took me. I invited him to move in with me. I liked him. And I thought with the right love and care we would be good together. Pure madness.

Mathew jumped at the chance and, after only six weeks of knowing each other, he moved in. I was so caught up in the moment, I hadn't thought about Antoinette, who had never seen me with any man, only her father.

I ploughed ahead, dismissing my misgivings, choosing instead to seize the day. My thought was, we can all learn to live together, and life will be great. I broke the news to Antoinette later that day, and she wasn't impressed at all.

"Why does he have to live with us? We are fine on our own."

I tried to explain it to her, but she was as stubborn as her father, so she wasn't having a bar of it.

Mathew moved in about a week later. Introductions didn't go well. Antoinette refused to speak to Mathew. The silent stand-off went on for about a month. It was such a horrible way to live.

Mathew was trying his best to get to know Antoinette but she refused to engage, choosing instead to hide in her room. Eventually, I had to order her to be polite, and to greet Mathew with either hello, goodbye, good morning or good evening; this was the baseline. Antoinette complied but would speak with total disdain. Mathew even tried to reason with her.

"I'm not trying to replace your dad."

"You can't!" she snapped.

"I know you've got a dad, so we can be just friends."

"I don't need any more friends, I've got enough," she sneered, as she stormed off to her room.

The conversation was done. Antoinette's father even tried to speak to her, but he got nowhere either. So, after three months of sullenness, I just told her, you can either live with us as a family or live with your dad.

She chose to live with us. Over the years Antoinette and Mathew carved out a co-existence. It was strictly business, no real love or affection from either side, but it was amicable. I applied all my efforts to make us a family, but it never really blended.

Despite the issue with Antoinette, Mathew and I were tight. We got on so well together. It was weird; I thought it would be difficult to live with a man, but our similarities made it easy.

We both enjoyed living in an orderly home. My domestic routine remained the same except Mathew loved to cook, clean and do laundry, so we fitted together like a glove. We appreciated our own space and time together.

Raving together was fantastic. I liked his friends and he liked mine. Everything was going great until I discovered he wasn't a carpenter. He was actually unemployed and learning carpentry, so he didn't have a job, unless you count lying. But I was in too deep and it was too late to turn back. The notion of ending it made me feel shallow.

He wanted to work with young people, so six months after we got together, I got him an interview at a youth club, through a contact of mine.

He had a little bit of experience of working with young people and the youth club needed more men in the team. It also helped that the manager was a male chauvinist pig, so he saw Mathew as a 'man's man', and he was happy to give him a chance.

Needless to say, Mathew never became a builder or built his own home, and the scheme folded.

Mathew seemed a bit neglected. His clothes had seen better days and nurturing was long gone. I showered Mathew with love and gifts. I took him shopping and bought him a whole new wardrobe, casual wear and some going out clothes from Cecil Gee's.

He was so grateful. It made me happy to see him happy. And he looked so good in his new clothes. When we went raving we looked like we were meant to be together.

His friends commented on how well I was looking after him. I felt proud. I had a man who I could take care of and who loved to be with me. It felt nice.

I was doing well financially, I was at university and I was also working, so I had money and I wanted Mathew to feel good being with me.

I also introduced Mathew to the world of travel. Mathew didn't even have a passport and he had never been on a plane.

I booked a couples-only package holiday to Grenada. I was really sceptical about going to Grenada. I had heard so many bad things about the people, but I knew it was important for Mathew to go back to his roots.

The package holiday included flights, transfers and a three star hotel in St George's for two weeks. St George's was a tropical picture postcard. The power of the sunshine penetrated our sunglasses as we processed our new surroundings. The smell of Grenada reminded me of Barbados, but the landscape was very different.

Grenada had a mountainous tropical forest terrain, but the heat and palm trees were typical of the Caribbean. The coach drive to the hotel provided a brief tour of St George's and various hotels as fellow travellers were dropped off.

Our hotel was quaint, more like a guest house, so it had a really relaxed atmosphere. By the time we left, we practically worked there. I worked in the office, well really, I was talking to Sonia, who was the receptionist at the front desk, and Mathew was the pool man.

Every day Mathew helped this guy called Fooly to clear leaves out of the pool. After the first week we realised Fooly wasn't his real name.

People called him that because he was so fool, well that's what Fooly told us. He didn't appear to be offended by his pet name.

Mathew and I loved to hang out at the hotel, but we did venture out to cross the major landmarks off our sightseeing list.

During a fun day at Grand Anse beach, we met a local girl called Natalie. While playing in the sea Natalie clung to Mathew. She had a mild asthma attack, she said. Mathew rescued her, and we all became good friends.

Natalie, tall, catwalk model bod, caramel skin, Indian long hair with a pure smile, came with us to the hotel and stayed with us for about four days. She made the most of the facilities and we enjoyed having a local tour guide.

Years later I pondered my acceptance of Mathew's relationship with Natalie. My friends thought I was mad to allow such blatant disrespect. But due to my innocence I took more convincing.

Natalie introduced us to her friend Leon, who was a hotel inspector for the whole of Grenada. Leon was a distinguished older gentleman, probably about forty to Natalie's twenty. It was unclear what he had with Natalie, but he had a nice demeanour.

After hearing Mathew's family lived way across the country in St Patrick, Leon offered to take us to St Patrick.

While Leon drove like a tour guide, we got to see the realness of the island. He stopped along the way to see various friends while we sampled the fruits of the land. Mathew became a native as he climbed a coconut tree to commandeer his own coconut.

Watching him celebrate his victory and salivate over the tasty coconut content filled me with satisfaction. I had successfully connected Mathew to his roots. As he sat amongst the riches of the land he blended in to the tropical postcard.

The mountainous tropical countryside offered wonderful views, smells and tastes.

Each area offered something different. I was sceptical about the cooking conditions, usually a wooden shack with a camper burner or less, just a barrel turned into a barbecue. Mathew embraced the rustic catering and encouraged me to do the same.

As we tried some 'Oil Down' from a street vendor I whispered, "What don't kill will fatten."

Despite the rough servings we enjoyed sampling all the local dishes instead of the tourist fodder.

As we crossed the country we passed through Grenville, where we stopped to enjoy the Claboney Hot Springs for a sulphur mineral bath, which we were told was great for your skin and can heal your ailments. The warm milky water was fantastic. When I came out of the spring my skin felt like butter.

Leon dropped us off in Chantimelle, at the home of Mathew's aunt. The plan was for Mathew to get to see his parents' birthplace and to meet some family. We planned to stay overnight after we had been up Mount Ian, which is where Mathew's father was born.

Unfortunately, when we arrived at his Aunt Madea's house, she told us it was too late to go to Mount Ian because it gets dark up there early.

We were exhausted by the day trip. It was nice to just sit and relax in Madea's gallery. Madea and Mr M's cream double-fronted bungalow looked like it had been plucked from Stanmore, where they had lived for thirty years before returning to Grenada.

As we sat listening to his aunt, we realised we had underestimated the terrain and hadn't allotted enough time. We decided to spend the afternoon with Madea, her husband and Mathew's uncle, who was his dad's last remaining brother. Mathew's genes were really strong because his uncle resembled him and his brothers.

Mathew loved being on 'his' island, but he loved being in the countryside most of all. He fed some local goats and made friends with some of the locals.

Sauteurs was lovely, but it rained like it does in Manchester, England.

"How u say u come from England and bawling you don't like the rain?"

Madea and Mr M were really welcoming, but Madea was shocked that I wasn't Grenadian, like that was impossible because Grenada is the world. I dismissed the small-mindedness, avoiding the small island politics which is entrenched in Caribbean culture.

Mr M put us on a yellow and blue bus and we drove away. The bus was bursting as if it was filled with popping corn. The geriatric bus was designed to hold thirty people, but they packed in at least fifty, plus crocus bags bursting with everything from fruits, veg, to pots and pans, not to mention what was hanging on top of the bus.

❧

As our relationship grew, Mathew and I blended our families and heritage. Contrary to the myth, all black people are not the same. Grenadian and Barbadian cultures have many similarities and vast differences. Our relationship had fused together the best of both, combined with our British nuances.

Travelling became a major artery in our relationship. We prioritised places to visit with family ties. I think Barbados was next on our list. With the freshness of our love everything felt right. We stayed with Auntie Viola.

After many years of life without a trace of Auntie Viola, I bucked up on her as I walked down Third Avenue in Paddington, on my way to collect Antoinette from school.

She had moved from that horrible basement flat and was living in a terraced house in Droop Street, which was just around the corner from us.

The 'happy couple' had broken up, so she was living on her own. She appeared genuinely pleased to see me.

"How you?"

"I'm fine.

"How are you? You're looking well."

"Man, you're as young as you feel.

"How is the little girl?"

She peered at me, looking for failure or bad news.

"Antoinette is doing fine, she's six now."

Her eyes opened wide as she counted the years.

"Six! Man, she get up there quick enough… she learning good?"

"Yes, she's really bright and she loves school."

"Man, bring she, let she see her old aunt, let she know she's got family."

As we parted, her words rang in my ears. After Barbados I had kept my family contact limited to just my siblings and Jewel's family. But I couldn't think of a reason why Antoinette shouldn't get to know her old aunt. My experience of her had been filed away with all the other bygones.

A few weeks after our surprise meeting, I started visiting Auntie Viola with Antoinette. I wanted Antoinette to know her family and after all Auntie Viola was her great-great-aunt.

Auntie Viola loved Antoinette from the first visit. On swinging open the front door I was greeted by the distinctive smell of Jeyes disinfectant, dogs and cats.

As we made our way in, we could hear little dogs yapping behind the closed kitchen door. We sat at the kitchen table. Auntie Viola let the little dogs into kitchen. They steamed in, determined to sniff us. Auntie Viola peered at Antoinette.

"Man, she too sweet, even though you gave her the name of my horse."

She would laugh hard, repeating the same sentence every time she saw her. Antoinette really loved Auntie Viola. She started staying with her at weekends and they would go to church together.

I didn't worry that Auntie Viola would mistreat Antoinette because I had taught her to tell me if anyone hurt her. Antoinette used to love playing with Auntie Viola's dog; she had a new one called Toby, a little Jack Russell.

Auntie Viola and Antoinette were getting on great until one day I went to pick up Antoinette. As soon as I arrived Auntie Viola began quarrelling. Antoinette appeared fine.

"Dat little girl, man she is something else… how she gonna do that to de dawg?"

"What did she do? Antoinette, what happened to the dog?"

Antoinette sat stroking the dogs intently, smiling, with a shrug. I was mystified.

"That little bitch bite my dawg. Why she do that? I hear de dawg holler out and run."

"Bite the dog, no she must have hurt him playing too rough, she couldn't bite a dog. You didn't bite the dog, did you Antoinette?"

I peered at Antoinette, while Auntie Viola mumbled and cursed. But Antoinette was undeterred, she spoke with conviction.

"Yes. I did bite the dog because he bit me first."

"No Antoinette, you can't bite a dog. Why did he bite you?"

"I was playing with him and his toy, it was like tug of war, but as he tugged, he hit himself on the chair and then he bit me, so I bit him back!"

It sounded so crazy I had to fight the urge to roll on the floor laughing.

"Where did you bite him?"

"On his nose."

"How she gonna bite de dawg on he nose? She is wicked, de dawg cried, poor ting."

"Oh well, the silly dog shouldn't have bit her. She was defending herself. Well done baby girl. Don't let nobody hurt you."

Somehow the image of the event overpowered the fact she had actually bitten a dog, so by the time we left we had descended into fits of laughter.

Auntie Viola was getting old. She decided to spend her retirement and die in the country of her birth, Barbados. She applied for a grant from Westminster Council to build a house in Barbados. I helped her with the application and eventually with her move. About a year after she left England, we went to see her in Barbados, all three of us.

Auntie Viola had warmed to Mathew, but her initial prejudice was harsh, to say the least.

"What are you doing with a Grenadian? Dem people are nothing but ignorant thieves!"

Initially I thought she was joking but she didn't change position or turn it into a joke.

"You ain't got no business being with no Grenadian. What's wrong with a nice Bajan (Barbadian) man?"

Shame is all I felt, but all I could do was try to smooth it over.

"Mathew is not a thief, Auntie Viola. You don't have anything to worry about. He is completely trustworthy."

"We will see."

Strangely enough the exchange evoked my disdain for Grenadians as I remembered my own rule set as a child, never be with a Grenadian man. My so-called mother's husband was Grenadian, and I hated him with a passion.

So, at an early age, I had banned myself from dating Grenadian men. But somehow, I had forgotten to add that to my dating checklist. Unfortunately, my memory had omitted this glitch, or my rose-coloured life had glossed over it.

During the holiday Auntie Viola was cordial to Mathew but I could tell she had her eye on him and the jury was still out.

Auntie Viola had built a small two-bedroom bungalow, on the inherited land she was born on, in St James.

Entering my aunt's home was weird. The tropical air I loved to smell had a new scent; the odour of Jeyes disinfectant permeated the air. The place was four thousand two hundred and fourteen miles from the sordid Shirland Road basement flat, yet they could have been the same place.

It was probably the fact that all the furniture and knick-knacks from Shirland Road were all present. The walls and cabinets were filled with the old animal pictures and ornaments that I dusted as a child.

I consciously tried to remain in the present. I didn't want to remember the details of the hellhole I had survived, but the place was one big trigger.

Antoinette was excited to be back in Barbados but staying with her aunt made her sing. She had run into her aunt's arms as soon as the car wheels had stopped turning.

Watching the two reunite was a lovely sight, but I was struck by the size of my aunt, who looked like she was shrinking. No longer the formidable burly size twenty ogre, now a little old white-haired, red-skinned woman.

My mind couldn't get over it as we looked around the place. Antoinette had stated her claim to her aunt's bed.

"I'm sleeping with you!"

"No man, you is too big to sleep with your old aunt. I don't want you rooting around when I'm trying to sleep, no man, not me."

Antoinette laughed as she put her backpack on the bed and ran outside to look around.

The holiday started well. Mathew got to meet most of my family and developed friendships with some of my cousins, which meant he could go off with the boys bunning weed, and drinking, while I hung out with my sister and some of my cousins.

The downside to staying with Auntie Viola was that she was way in the country and the bus ride to town or to the beach was a mundane day trip, unless we went on the yellow buses.

We loved the yellow buses, they made the bus ride fun. They all played music, Grenadian dancehall music or soca, or whatever the bus driver liked. The vibe was pure Caribbean life on the yellow buses.

The yellow buses didn't need a timetable; you could hear them coming from miles away. One bus in particular used to have so much bass, my bum used to vibrate for ages after we got off the bus.

All was going well during our holiday. I had made myself useful, cleaning the house and washing up the 'wares' after every meal. Mathew offered to wash up once and Auntie Viola had shooed him away, so he stayed clear of the kitchen.

Everything was fine. Every day my cousin Rudy used to pass by for dinner. He carried fun and a big character, weighing in at about 300lbs, 6ft and deep black ebony skin.

Apparently, he didn't like his woman's cooking, so Auntie Viola cooked for him every evening. I'm not sure why he didn't eat at his mother's; she was nearer. Every evening we ate together, then Rudy fell asleep, snoring loudly, before leaving about 10pm.

From everything being fine, without warning silence became the norm for Auntie Viola. She wasn't talking to Mathew or me, only Antoinette. If I asked her anything, she replied with either a curt yes or no. She started spending time in her room and not socialising with us.

Then one evening Rudy turned up after work and I overheard him tell Auntie Viola that her phone bill was 300 dollars. She came out of her bedroom cursing.

"Wunna come over here to bankrupt me. Wunna want to put me in de poorhouse. I don't owe a saint one thing an' u'all come here five minutes and want to get me lock up!"

I tried to calm her down as she paced around the house aimlessly.

"Auntie Viola, what are you talking about? We gave you some money for our keep, so what are you talking about?"

"Now she gonna play dumb. She thinks I'm idiot. She got all de sense and I ain't got none. De damn phone bill. Nobody ain't use dat phone but you, so don't try to deny it. I only put the phone in just before you get here!"

"Auntie, I told you I would pay for the call."

"You made more than one call. One call is not going to cost 300 dollars. You must think I am an idiot. I have walked this earth for more years than you could count, and you are not going to take me for a fool or get me locked up. Tomorrow morning, we are going to the phone company and you are going to pay dat bill if it's the last thing you do and after that you can go to hell!"

I was dazed. Speechless. I just couldn't make sense of her outburst. Next thing you know, Rudy's got his mouth in it.

"Man, u'all should know better! You know Auntie Viola is a pensioner. She don't have that sort of money!"

What it had to do with him only God alone knew. I just looked him dead in the face and kissed my teeth.

"My aunt knows I wouldn't take advantage of her, so you don't need to tell me about my aunt, blasted 'hurry-come-lately'."

I just couldn't believe what was happening. There was no way the phone call could amount to 300 dollars, there must be some kind of mistake.

Mathew tried talking to Auntie Viola, but she blanked him like he wasn't there. She walked straight past him, went in her room and blammed the door. She even locked Antoinette out of her room, so she had to sleep with us.

All evening as we sat in the gallery, Mathew and I kept going over and over it. Why was she so angry?

Where was all the venom coming from? We had been model guests. I cooked, washed up, did the washing, hung it on the line, brought it back in. You name it, we did it. Mathew was even sweeping up the yard and throwing away all the rotten fruit off the ground. No matter how hard we debated we just couldn't understand why she was so angry.

The next morning before the cock had crowed, we were in town and at the phone company office. Auntie Viola, Cousin Rudy, Antoinette, Mathew and myself.

We were so early the place hadn't even opened. As soon as they unlocked the doors, we were the first people inside. Auntie Viola requested an up-to-date phone bill from the clerk.

The clerk brought up her records and informed her that she was 300 dollars in credit. Apparently, to get a phone service she had had to give a 300 dollar deposit. The clerk even gave her a copy of the bill, but she still wasn't satisfied.

"I was told I owed 300 dollars," she insisted.

"I apologise, madam. You were misinformed. You do not owe us anything. Your first bill is not due yet but there are no charges on your account to date."

Auntie Viola made the man say it about five times before she would leave the counter. All the way home she had a steely silence. Rudy, who had been muttering things under his breath the whole ride from St James to town, was now also mute.

I realised he was behind the whole conspiracy to cause a rift between me and my aunt. My history with her and presence was threatening his plan to be king of her castle.

Auntie Viola didn't have any children, so I was seen as a possible heir or benefactor if she passed away. I guess he considered me to be a threat to his plan, which he had been working on since she returned to Barbados, hence him eating dinner with her every day.

When he heard we were coming on holiday to stay with Auntie Viola, he must have panicked and started conniving. He could've saved himself the energy because my aunt had told me, when she left England, that she would be leaving her possessions as her mother before her had, everything to be divided between all her remaining family, and she had made a will to that effect.

The silence was killing me. I wanted her to apologise, explain the madness, something. But even when we got home, she said nothing, no apology, nothing.

Well that made my blood boil. After she had cussed me out, accused me of trying to get her locked up, accused me of trying to cheat her, I was boiling mad.

I left her for a few hours, thinking she would eventually come to her senses. But the time never came. Well, I couldn't hold my silence any longer. As she hid behind her bedroom door, I let rip.

"I am to blame for the whole thing because I should have never brought my family to stay with you. After all the abuse you did to me as a child, I must have been mad to think you could change. Don't worry, we will be gone soon but trust and believe as God is my witness, I will never sleep under the same roof as you again!"

Her room remained silent as she refused to respond. She didn't even leave her room again for the rest of the day, except to use the bathroom. That just made my blood boil even more; the disrespect was fuel to the fire.

After she had blabbed the story around the whole family, after she had been cussing me off to everybody, she couldn't even be big enough to apologise. I was disgusted with her.

Unfortunately, we had ten days of our holiday left, and I hated having to stay at her house every day. Despite my best efforts in keeping us busy and out for most of the day, the time dragged by.

The family holiday clarified the fact that my aunt remained a poisoned chalice. With vessels running deep in the family, this treatment reminded me of the wickedness she did to me as a child. I don't know what had convinced me she had changed.

As the days dripped by, I had time to face the harsh reality. I had once again got caught looking for something which wasn't there.

But never again, me and staying with family are done.

ᕬ

Family life back in England was working out great. Despite the initial hiccup with Antoinette, Mathew had settled into the family, with even Keres and Jamie warming to him.

Keres was initially very sceptical of the relationship, and she did her best to put it down and throw shade, but as time passed, her respect grew.

Her favourite dig was my cooking; she used to make snide jokes about it if things came out of the oven a bit crispy or overcooked. I didn't care. I had a man and I was trying my best to impress him.

After the first year together, he introduced me to his family. He was closest to his sister Ria. She had a smile that melted your heart and she had time for everyone. She had everyone over for Christmas and Easter, or birthdays.

All of Mathew's sisters had remained true to their Christian roots. His eldest sister, Hazel, had her own church, but she lived in Atlanta, so we didn't really see her. But Ria, we saw her regularly, she used to cook Mathew's favourite food at least twice a week and all he had to do was pick it up.

She became my kitchen mentor. I wanted to learn to cook just like her. But she didn't just cook, she baked cakes too. Her fruit cake was legendary.

I liked Mathew's family. They were welcoming. I made a concerted effort to get on with them all. I knew how much they meant to Mathew and I respected it. We started spending a lot of time with Ria.

Ria was thirty-six, never been married. She had two children, Kyle, nine, and Andrea, fifteen; they were really nice kids.

We all got on really well. Antoinette fitted right in with them. She loved going to church and after a while she started to go to church with them.

Every Friday we used to go over to their house and order takeout. I'd do Ria's hair, which was no mean feat. She had hair as coarse and thick as a yak's mane.

Her hair took the whole night to wash, blow dry and then cornrow. I didn't mind; I knew how much Mathew loved his sister and I came to love her too. She was meek and mild yet as stubborn as Mathew.

Mathew's routine meant he ate and ran out on the road, to begin his weekend of gambling, raving and smoking weed. He wouldn't come back until early to mid-morning.

When we first got together, Mathew had explained his love of the night. He had been exposed to it from an early age because his dad often locked him out. His dad had favoured his little brother, who was born two years before his mother had died.

Mathew was only six when his mum died. He was really close to his mum. She left a huge hole in his life, and his father never attempted to fill it. Instead, he chastised him relentlessly and offered him no love or affection. Ria tried to fill the void.

As Mathew got older, he started to run away from the harshness. And so his love of the nightlife was born. I trusted Mathew and he never gave me cause to doubt him. I gave him a long rope. I couldn't bear the idea of having a man stuck to my hip, it would have suffocated me. I liked to have my life with my friends too.

Mathew and I regularly had dinner parties with friends and family. I started to feel like I had a real family. Life continued to show us blessings. Mathew enjoyed his job. He loved working in the youth club.

He had great empathy with the young people and he gave them the guidance they needed. The only downside was the report writing and daily logs.

Mathew struggled with spelling and grammar, so every evening I had to spend hours on the phone helping him to do the write-ups for each child. Initially I didn't mind, but years later the full extent of this support proved to be a burden.

There had been no limit to the support I gave Mathew when he got the job. I thought my input would start big and then dwindle down to nothing as he grew into his role. Twenty-five years later, however, I realised his goal was different. He wanted me to prop him up forever.

My career was also going well. I completed my social work training at university and I worked part-time until I finished. I was thrilled when I qualified but I was so career-focused the qualification was only a means to an end.

I had established sound pre-qualifying work experience. When I qualified, I was determined to get a job that paid for my personal and professional experience and my qualifications.

I had been offered a few positions, but they all wanted to start me on the bottom of the pay scale. I refused to work for an organisation which was not going to reward me financially for all my experience.

The job offer I finally accepted was as a senior outreach worker in a new specialist therapeutic project for girls and young women. I negotiated my starting salary; £25,000.

Everyone else in my tutorial group were all on less than £20,000. For the first time in my life I felt financially independent. I didn't have to claim benefits anymore. So with Mathew's and my salary we were living comfortably.

Mathew's son Tremaine started to spend time with us. The integration was a bit bumpy at first. Mathew hadn't seen much of Tremaine because he lived in Birmingham and Tremaine's mum was reluctant to let them spend time together without her supervision.

But Mathew was firm with her, and as soon as she realised that it was this way or no way she got on board. On the first visit, Tremaine's mum dropped him off for a few hours. When I first saw him, I just focused on trying to make him feel relaxed and at home.

Every visit I was struck by his features; his cuteness was unmistakable. He looked like a little coco man, with a striking masculine face, but there was just something. My inner voice said *umm, he doesn't look like Mathew and he doesn't really look like his mum, so who does he look like?*

My attempt to ignore it was futile. The more I looked at him the more I couldn't shake the notion. Mathew's family had very strong genes; they all looked like each other and even the extended family all looked like kin.

I asked Mathew about the relationship he had had with Tremaine's mum. He was clear, the relationship was nothing more than a hook-up.

They hadn't dated or been out together but every now and then they had sex. And out of the blue she was pregnant. As a young man he was pleased at the prospect of being a father.

He had supported her throughout the pregnancy, but just as friends, and he had gone to the hospital after Tremaine was born. But when he left Birmingham, contact had been infrequent.

He was remorseful about not being an involved father and wanted to do better. I respected his honesty and wanted to help him to build a better relationship with his son, who was five. We began to have Tremaine during school holidays.

Antoinette and Tremaine got on brilliantly. They were similar in age and played well together. Antoinette liked the company. Everything was going fine until Mathew had a car crash while Tremaine was in the car.

It was a stupid and senseless accident. Mathew was turning right off a main road. His view was partially blocked by a bus, so he pulled out to turn into the road. He saw the car coming and he saw the driver looking at him but instead of stopping the driver just drove into the side of Mathew's car.

The cost of the accident was higher than we originally thought.

Mathew phoned Tremaine's mum to tell her about the accident. She was belligerent. Within two hours of the call she had driven from Birmingham and was at our front door demanding her son.

Tremaine and Antoinette were playing in her room. Tremaine had been a bit shaken by the crash, but he hadn't been hurt.

Mathew attempted to quell Tremaine's mother's anger, as she batted off offers to sit down and have a drink. It was futile. She didn't move from the doorway.

"I just want my son. Where is he?"

"Hold on. I'll get him in a minute. Calm down. He's fine."

"Fine, how can he be fine when you could have killed him? Nah man, you're too irresponsible. I sent him here in one piece and I'm gonna make sure he stays that way."

"But it's not my fault. The man didn't stop. I can't control other drivers."

Their voices were rising. On hearing his mother's voice Tremaine came running down the stairs. As mother and son hugged, I handed her his bag. Mathew stood powerless as they left, with Tremaine's mother throwing a passing shot.

"He won't be coming back, so don't ask me again."

We heard nothing from her for a few months then, one evening, we were lying on the couch watching a movie when she called demanding money. They got into a big argument.

When Mathew came off the phone he was on fire. He paced. As anger chased him from room to room, I watched from the couch.

"Why is she being so spiteful? I can't see my son, but she wants my money. Everything she has asked for I have given her. It hasn't been easy, but I did it and then one wrong move and she takes my son away from me… she's cold, man."

I tried to hug Mathew, but he stepped back in anger.

"Maybe this is for the best?"

Mathew cut me off.

"How's that? Them people are going to bleed me dry."

"Look, I didn't want to vocalise my doubt, but I've been struck by the absence of your family genes in Tremaine's features, the fact he doesn't even look like his mum… makes me think there's someone else involved."

My eyes searched Mathew's face with a veil of fear.

Strangely enough Mathew didn't try to dispel my suspicions. Silence was his initial response. He finally spoke.

"I'm not silly. I did wonder about him from the day he was born. I searched for a sign, a trait, something, but I just couldn't see it. Nothing, not the 'Simpson' ears, or nose, complexion, nothing. I decided to trust her. I kept thinking it will come when he's a bit older, but he's six now and still I can't see a trace of me."

His silent anger tremored into a pulse. I watched as his temples throbbed.

I wrapped his arms around me as I cornered him in front of the fridge. He was boxed in so he succumbed to my warm hug.

As I held him, I could feel his emotions raging. We hugged in silence for what felt like ages. When I looked up into his eyes, I could see his pain. I stood on tiptoes as I gently pulled his chin down towards my face. I gently kissed his eyes, nose and lips.

"Don't worry, everything will work out. Maybe we're wrong but if she wants more money, she'll do the DNA test, simple."

"Sounds like a plan. I just need to know if he's mine."

When the Child Support Agency got in touch he told them he wouldn't pay any more money until Tremaine had a DNA test. We presumed she didn't agree because we didn't hear anything from her or the CSA again.

Mathew was broken-hearted. He loved Tremaine and during the six months' contact, he had grown quite attached to him. He tried to hide his hurt, but I knew it had cut him deep.

Consoling him was difficult, compounded by the unknown; if Tremaine wasn't his child, he didn't have any children. He had been content with having one child but having none wasn't something he was prepared for.

Over the coming months I used a combination of sex, nurturing and weed to soothe him. And soon his attention was back on me and the love we shared for each other.

Our love grew as we weathered the storm but despite that love I felt a little fear. I hoped our love would survive even if he couldn't have children, but I wasn't sure.

I had been upfront about my aversion to kids, it was the third thing I told him. He knew the score, but that was when he thought he had a child.

As the years passed by, this issue would permeate our love, leading me to question my original decision to voice my suspicion.

I pushed my fear and the whole sordid mess out of my mind and focused on our big plan to buy a house.

15

MARRIED LIFE!

Living on the estate was bittersweet. I loved the community spirit, but I hated living on an estate. The estate's reputation was so bad we couldn't even get a pizza delivered.

I was desperate to get off the estate. I applied for the same grant my Auntie Viola got. The council gave tenants homebuyer grants in return for your council property, a type of repatriation. The grant could be used as a deposit to buy a house.

The day we got the acceptance letter I felt like Charlie from *Charlie and the Chocolate Factory*. We had the golden ticket to get off the estate. It felt unreal. I had never dared to dream but I prayed, and the power of prayer was a miracle.

I was so scared something would go wrong I didn't tell anyone about the application or our house-hunting. I didn't want anyone to jinx us or send out any negative energy.

We agreed on Harrow as our search area of choice based on three key things; being near Mathew's family, Jewel's family and great schools.

The first house we loved was in Northwood Hills. It was a lovely bright semi-detached three-bedroom house with a hundred-foot garden. The house was immaculate. It had a new kitchen and bathroom with a jacuzzi.

We loved the house. We made an offer after one visit. The couple who owned the house were getting a divorce, so they wanted a quick sale. Our offer was accepted, but just weeks before we were due to exchange contracts they took the house off the market.

The estate agent told us the couple had decided to give their marriage another go. We were really disappointed, but we didn't let it keep us down. We started house-hunting in earnest. It took a few months before we found another house, but when we did, it was perfect in every way.

The detached Stanmore house was everything. Walking into the house for the first time felt strangely familiar, just like home, I think partly because it had a similar decor and furniture to our place. The fairy dust was the fact the house was completely detached, with no party walls or noisy neighbours.

The house had three bedrooms with separate toilet and bathroom, two reception rooms and a fireplace. The house was in a lovely cul-de-sac, so no through traffic, which made the street seem peaceful.

On the first viewing day while looking around we had crazy weather. We looked outside; one minute the sun was shining, the next there were hailstones, then snow and this was April. We ended up staying at the house for a few hours waiting for the weather to improve.

We were so comfortable, the house just felt like home. I could imagine where everything would go and see us having dinner parties in the dining room.

We called the estate agent on the way home and made an offer. It was accepted. The couple wanted a quick sale because they had made an offer on their new home. We were in a chain, but the couple said they would sell to us even if the chain broke.

So said, so done, viewed and bought the house within six weeks. Everything went so smoothly. Even moving in was slick. The neighbours were lovely, they kept offering tea and coffee.

I had labelled everything by room so when the removal guys unpacked, we made them put each box and furniture in the right room.

It made moving in simple. With the help of some family and friends we were all moved in and unpacked by nightfall, it was fantastic.

Every room felt like home. Antoinette loved her new room. She could see her new school from her bedroom window. She could roll out of bed straight into her school. Antoinette felt divided about the move, she loved the familiarity of her old life, but was curious about living in a house on a quiet road.

Luckily, she had a six-week transition period as she couldn't start her new school until the start of the new school year. She stayed with Trisha, my cousin, for about six weeks, which enabled her to have a long goodbye and time to adjust to her new area during the summer holidays.

The local kids also helped with Antoinette's induction; they were really friendly. One day a group of kids came to welcome Antoinette to the road and promptly informed her that we were the only black people living in the road. Despite Antoinette being the only black kid on the road they welcomed her, and she settled in well.

We were all so happy and showing our house off became an occupation. We had house-warming dos for months after we moved in, we just loved showing off our new home.

One Sunday we were having Mathew's sisters over for dinner so I was busy cooking while Mathew watched the footie and Antoinette went out riding her bike around the cul-de-sac. The next thing I knew the doorbell rang and the neighbour stood in the doorway with a trembling Antoinette, who had blood pouring out of her mouth.

Antoinette had flown over her handlebars and knocked out her two front teeth. The neighbour was so caring and compassionate, but I was frightened, there was so much blood and she was minus her two front teeth.

Panic-stricken we attempted to play down the accident. We gave her some pain medication, which was all we could do until the next day. I comforted Antoinette. She was shell-shocked from the fall. This was the first bump in our new beautifully manicured, tree-lined cul-de-sac.

❧

With our main family goal achieved, owning a house of our own, we decided to enjoy living and see a bit of the world. We began holidaying regularly, and it was while on holiday Mathew proposed to me. It came completely out of the blue.

We had just checked into the Sea Breeze Hotel in Barbados. It was a lovely four star hotel on the beach. After dumping our cases in the room, we went to the bar for a few cocktails. We were having such a laugh, chatting to the other guests. All of a sudden Mathew's kissing me. He looked so happy, like he had discovered a genie in the bottle.

"I love you and I want to marry you."

I thought he was joking, so I started laughing.

"Stop messing about. You don't want to marry me. You're just feeling sweet on holiday."

But while I laughed his face looked deadpan serious.

"You're joking, right?"

He took my left hand in his.

"I love you, D, and I want to marry you."

I was so blown away. We had never really discussed marriage or our future plans. I still wasn't convinced; he was always pranking me. My eyes X-rayed his expression for the truth.

"Are you serious? I don't think you are serious because you didn't go down on one knee!"

"Do you want me to do it here on this dirty floor?"

"No, don't mess up your clothes. If you're serious let's go back to our room."

We hurried back to the room. I kept cracking jokes along the way.

"I know your tune's gonna change to making love as soon as we get inside."

"We'll see, D!"

But as I sat down on the bed Mathew went down on one knee.

"Dominiquè, will you marry me?"

"Oh my God you're serious… yes, yes of course I'll marry you."

I helped him up from his knee and we kissed passionately. He looked at me with love in his eyes.

"I love you. You make me so happy. I want to spend the rest of my life with you."

Tears trickled down my face. I had never dared to dream of happily ever after, but Mathew made me feel so loved. I definitely wanted to be his wife.

As we sat on the bed Mathew spoke so endearingly.

"Sorry babe, I'm not even prepared. I don't even have a ring for you. I didn't plan this, but the moment just felt right!"

I didn't care. I was engaged. I was getting married. Just being able to say that was enough for me. The ring could wait.

Our engagement made the holiday really meaningful. We barely left the room, instead we enjoyed each other like people with no technology. Morning, noon and night, at least seven days a week.

As soon as we got back home, we went straight to Hatton Garden, spurning tradition and choosing our rings together. I fell for a lovely diamond ring set, which had a wedding band and engagement ring which fitted together. I bought Mathew a nine-diamond pinkie ring for his engagement present.

Everything just flowed. We decided to get married abroad because we couldn't afford to cater for a wedding in England, as we were paying for the wedding ourselves and didn't have parents to provide any dowries. We decided to have a destination wedding in Grenada and then honeymoon in Barbados in June. We had eight months to plan our big day.

No sooner had we booked our package wedding when I found my dream wedding dress. My plan was to go looking for a wedding dress with Jewel and my sister but one morning on my way to work it found me.

As I made my way through Stratford shopping mall, I passed a boutique bridal shop. Curiosity called me inside. Looking around the shop filled me with giddy excitement. The wonderful wedding gowns sang, you're getting married. Your man loves you. You're going to be a Mrs.

Feeling like a bride-to-be, I looked through the rack of wedding gowns, rows and rows of them, but nothing seemed right. The dresses the lady showed me had way too much ruffles or puffiness.

I knew exactly what I was looking for. I wanted an ivory, elegant, timeless, lightweight, figure-hugging something.

I explained what I wanted and as if by magic the seasoned sales lady pulled out my dream gown. It was ivory, off the shoulder, covered in mother of pearls and mother-of-pearl sequins. It was close-fitting, accentuating my hourglass figure, knee-length with a detachable train which fastened around the waist with sequins and mother of pearl.

Looking at the reflection of the beautiful young bride in the mirror was humbling, tears trickled down my cheeks.

I didn't need to try on another gown. I had found the only one for me. I called Mathew from the bridal shop as I paid for it. He couldn't believe I had found my wedding dress already.

"You just left to go to work. When did you get time to find a wedding dress? It's only 9.30! I better find my suit. I'm not going to get left behind."

And true to his word he found his wedding suit by the end of that week.

Mathew knew this guy who sold designer suits. He found a dark blue Versace suit, and we went into Bond Street and bought his shoes. Pinuet (luxury shoe brand) ostrich-skin shoes, they cost £350 and he loved them. So within a month of getting engaged we had our wedding attire.

I loved being engaged. I was marrying the man I loved and I knew he loved me. We were so compatible. We shared the same family values and morals. We felt like two halves that fitted together. We didn't need each other, but we wanted each other.

We loved the life we had made together, and we wanted to continue it for the rest of our lives. It felt so right. I didn't want to change anything about Mathew.

He cooked, cleaned, washed clothes and even ironed better than me and that's saying something, given I had been ironing since I was eight years old. He shopped, took Antoinette where she needed to go or picked her up.

We complemented each other. We finished each other's sentences or communicated with our eyes. It was fantastic.

I was the happiest I had ever been in my whole life. I actually felt content and loved, in a way which respected my experiences. He loved me for who I was and how I was as a person. He loved me despite my flaws.

And I loved him despite his flaws. He was the most stubborn man I had ever met in my life. Once I flicked him with cold water playfully and he didn't talk to me for two days.

He smoked. I found it totally disgusting, which he couldn't understand because I used to smoke. I had started when I was sixteen experimentally and developed a habit of five a day.

But I gave up smoking after I had Antoinette. She was about one year old. As I stood in the shop counting my coins, I was torn between buying nappies, Andrex toilet paper or cheap toilet paper and cigarettes.

And right then and there, I quit smoking. I wasn't going to start using tracing paper on my ass for anybody.

But Mathew loved to smoke, cigarettes and high-grade weed. He made it clear that he would only give it up if he wanted to and I supported his right to decide. The downside to him smoking was the five-minute tooth brushing and mouth wash ritual he had to go through before we could French kiss.

My mouth just couldn't stomach the taste of tobacco. It made me feel so sick. We couldn't kiss spontaneously unless he and I had been drinking alcohol, that seemed to mask the taste.

Mathew loved the nightlife but that didn't really bother me, but the gambling not so much. But his biggest fault was his addiction to lying. He lied for the sake of it. And he lied with a straight face. I don't know why he felt the need to be deceptive, but to love him was to love the best of him and the worst of him.

Deep down I felt this undercurrent of fear. It wasn't anything big, but it was there. Fear that something bad would happen to spoil our happiness. My past had taught me pain was waiting to pounce.

And I still didn't know who my father was. I needed to know before I got married. Could you imagine the heartache of finding out we were siblings or cousins after we were married?

Mathew knew the details of my childhood and was sure we weren't related, but I couldn't leave it to chance.

So I wrote to my so-called mother. It was a very simple letter. *Dear Mrs Grenadian, I am getting married and I need to know who my father is.*

Please fill in the blanks below and return in the stamped addressed envelope provided, signed Dominiquè Moore.

I posted it and hoped for the best. The suspense was ridiculous. At the age of twenty-seven I still didn't know my father's name. For so many years I had learnt to live without knowing, but it had always caused me pain. I felt ashamed when people asked me about my father because I knew nothing about him.

To avoid embarrassment, when people asked me about my parents, I'd say they were dead. I had learnt early on it was easier than dredging up my past. People never understood my journey or my pain, so what was the point, my past was too painful for people to truly understand or appreciate.

It was easier to be an orphan. People never dared to ask any questions about dead parents, so it was a great cover. But deep down I wanted to know the backdrop to my conception.

Well, weeks passed and the self-addressed envelope never came back. After three months of waiting anxiously I was livid. My wedding was getting closer and I couldn't bear the suspense.

That fucking woman was fucking with me again. Why didn't she want me to be happy? Why couldn't she just answer a simple question? Did she hate me so much? I was furious, so I called her. She answered after one ring. She sounded so sweet, like candy floss.

"Hello, this is Dominiquè. I sent you a letter. Did you get it?"

"Yes, I did," spoken coldly.

"Well, why didn't you return it?"

"Why are you asking me about my business? Why do you have to know my business?"

Hearing her coldness ignited my fire. I thought I was going to combust.

"Your business? It's not just your business. It's my business too. I have a right to know who my father is. Why won't you just tell me his name?"

"I don't have to tell you anything. You are a big woman. You don't need to know, so stop asking me!"

Blam. She dropped the phone down in my ear. I was incredulous. I couldn't believe it. The conversation was over so soon. I was upset and furious all at the same time.

How dare she put down the phone on me. I thought, *she must want me to go down there.*

I was pacing up and down in the front room. I called her back, but she didn't answer.

After about an hour of repeatedly calling, Keres answered the phone. I told her what had happened. She tried to console me, but I was out of my mind with rage. I wanted to kill her mother with my bare hands. She had nothing but hate for me and I felt the same for her.

Keres offered to get it out of her mother, but neither of us was hopeful. I needed love and tenderness. I called Mathew and he came home to console me.

⌒

Our wedding was scheduled to be the wedding of the century in Grenada. We invited all our friends and family formally and ended up with a very select number.

My sister and brother both made excuses as to why they couldn't come. But I didn't care, I had Antoinette and Jewel and I was marrying my man.

A destination wedding was a great way to get married. We spent the first week just enjoying being in St George's, Grenada. We stayed at the Secret Harbour hotel.

Our wedding party moved en masse to enjoy the island. We made a pit stop at a small guest house near the famous Claboney Hot Springs. Mathew's cousin Simone took Mathew inside to see something but when he came back out, he had his cousin Donavon and family friend Scully with him. They had flown in to surprise Mathew.

The guys added the missing male aspect of the wedding party which, thankfully, stopped Mathew acting like a sheik with a harem of women. Everywhere we went guys would ask him if all the women were his and he would say yes.

The guys were staying about one hour away from us. They didn't have any transport, so from the day they came to our hotel they never went back to theirs. They didn't formally check into our hotel either, but they took up residence anyway.

On the night before our wedding, I had arranged to stay in Jewel's room, but Mathew and I were so close, he refused to let me go. He told me it would be too strange. We had been living together for nearly five years and he wouldn't be able to sleep without me.

We broke with tradition and spent the night before our wedding together. But the next morning I woke up feeling sick. My stomach was having kittens. I knew it was nerves, but I just couldn't shake the queasiness.

Jewel was wonderful, the perfect maid of honour. She claimed the room and shipped Mathew off to the boys. She refused to let me give in to my stomach. She organised breakfast in bed and we sipped champagne. She laid out my wedding gown and tiara, and she had even bought me sexy lingerie to wear.

Jewel organised everything.

We went off to the hair salon in town for them to do everyone's hair. We arrived at 9.30am and left at 4pm. My wedding was at five o'clock. Eventually they got around to styling my hair, which was a pointless exercise because by the time we got back to the hotel every carefully tonged ringlet I had on my head had gone, along with Antoinette.

And to make matters worse, I was running so late I didn't have any time to do anything about it. I had no time to shower. I had to do a cat wash. Slap some soap and water under my arms and between my legs; throw on my gown, shoes, tiara and veil and run downstairs. I was in such a daze as we walked to the ceremony, it was only when I saw people's faces that I remembered I was the bride.

People were oohing and aahing. All the hotel front desk staff came out from behind the counter to wish me good luck. And then I saw Mathew through the floor to ceiling window, he was standing beside Donavon.

As I took my first step down the spiral staircase, I could see the big smile on his face. He looked so happy talking to the guests, looking fine in his Versace navy blue suit.

He had been so involved in the planning of our wedding; I knew he really wanted to marry me. Seeing his radiant smile made me feel so happy I began to cry. Jewel was in a flap, I don't know why; I wasn't wearing any make-up, so nothing was going to smudge.

She said she didn't want to see any bogeys in my wedding pictures. Luckily, she had a hanky and she mopped up my tears and gave me a pep talk. I couldn't hear what she was saying, I was too busy watching Mathew; he looked so happy.

We didn't have time to succumb to the romantic beach setting. We were running so late the pastor galloped through the service but not before he told us about the extra pressure we would have in our marriage. As he spoke Mathew and I peered intently at him, wondering what extra pressure he was talking about.

"You will have cross-culture problems in your marriage because your wife is from a different country and they do things differently. You must face the cross-culture dynamics together, and remember you love each other and that is all that matters."

On hearing his insight, we laughed with relief. We had no idea what he was talking about, but soon his words would ring in our ears and come to pass.

The hotel provided us with a beautiful white heart-shaped wedding cake. We linked arms to serve it to each other. Sadly, the cake didn't taste as good as it looked. It tasted so bad, I couldn't keep my face straight for the pictures. It was disgusting.

We served the cake to our guests with some champagne, but the reception was as brief as the wedding because the wind had whipped up and dusk was nearly on us.

Our wedding supper was booked at the nearby five star Half Moon Resort in St George's. After a brief intermission, where Mathew and I went back to our room for a quick kiss and cuddle, we went to our reception.

The white modern two-storey thatched roof, palm tree-lined resort looked special under the evening sky. In the courtyard, management had arranged a little entertainment, three old men, playing on instruments; one playing the tambourine and the other two playing spoons. This was our wedding music.

I think they were supposed to be a folklore band but instead they sang about what was happening at our table and they had a lot to sing about!

Unfortunately, the food was a disaster, to put it mildly. It was either too hot or too cold, no flavour, too salty; nothing was right. The band sang about it, "Dem don't like da food, me say dey don't like da food. She push up she face, she push up she face. Me say dem don't like the food, dey don't like da food!"

They were so funny. They commented about everything that was happening at our table in song until we left. They made us laugh and take our mind off the bad-tasting expensive food.

I was so glad to leave the dinner. I was so tired from the day. Back at the hotel, Mathew and I retreated to our room. Antoinette was sleeping in Jewel's room, so we had the night to make Mr and Mrs official.

I put on my beautiful wedding lingerie and lay in the bed. The new Mr and Mrs were just getting happy when the phone rang. Despite me begging Mathew to ignore it, he answered the phone. After a brief exchange Mathew hung up the phone and hugged me as he whispered, "Babe, Donavon and Scully don't have anywhere to sleep. Can they sleep in here?"

He watched my expression closely to see my reaction. I masked my irritation.

"Why can't they sleep in his sister's room?"

"They're not answering the phone."

Bearing in mind they had come all this way to surprise us, I had no choice but to agree. I put Mathew's bathrobe on over my sexy lingerie and wrapped myself up in the bed. Within minutes the pair were in the next bed to ours on our wedding night.

I tried to laugh it off, but deep down I couldn't understand how we ended up being their only option.

I focused on replaying flashes of our wedding and being Mrs S. I just kept looking at my diamond wedding set on my married finger. Before long I had drifted off to sleep wrapped in Mathew's arms.

❧

When we got back to England, we found out that we had inadvertently become part of a family tradition. Apparently, Mathew's parents had shared the wedding bed with Donavon's parents on their wedding night some thirty-five years before.

Mathew's family loved the fact we hadn't turned Donavon and Scully away, and had followed family tradition; they said it would bring us good luck in our marriage.

We had flown back to England for five days of intense activity as we were having a wedding party on Saturday before flying to Barbados for our honeymoon.

Mathew didn't really want to have the party, but I wanted my girlfriends to see me in my wedding dress and to see me have my first dance with my husband, surrounded by our loved ones.

Up until our return our wedding plans had sailed by without any problems. We had had two glorious weeks in Grenada. We returned to wedding party chaos.

Before we left for Grenada we had met with the caterer and had bought a goat and untold chickens from a cousin-in-law who had a farm.

We had organised the drinks, booked a DJ; Young Bushman, a popular north-west London radio and event DJ. Everything was organised before we left, so what could go wrong?

As soon as we reached home, I got a call from the caterer.

"Why you don't want me to cook the curried mutton? Don't the Grenadians think we can cook curried mutton?"

My lady was well vexed.

And that's how the cross-cultural problems reared their ugly head. I spent about an hour pacifying the caterer, who was also the mother of my childhood friend.

The next day I got a call from Mathew's auntie/cousin. Can I ask the caterer if she can borrow a pot to cook the curried mutton? How the hell was I supposed to ask the caterer if the Grenadian family could borrow a pot after she was already feeling slighted?

Ewww, it wasn't easy. I had to do a merry dance, but somehow, after about an hour of cajoling and telling her that I really wanted her to cook the curried mutton, but I had to go with what my new husband wanted, she finally agreed to lend the pot, but not before insisting that Mathew had to pick it up and she would be leaving with it at the end of the party. She had lost too many pots that way and she wasn't taking any chances!

So in addition to all the other running up and down we had to do, Mathew now had another journey added to his plate. By Saturday, the day of the wedding party, we were 'mash up and buy back!'

On top of that, we had family staying with us from Birmingham who had come down for the party, so the house was in chaos. On the morning of the wedding party the phone started ringing from 7am.

First the caterer rang. She wanted to know what facilities the kitchen had and what time Mathew was going to pick her up to take the food to the hall. As I put the phone down from her, his auntie/cousin called. She wanted to know what time Mathew was going to pick up the curried mutton and the wedding cake.

And that's how the phone carried on all day until it was time to go and decorate the hall. Unfortunately, we had underestimated how long decorating the hall would take. We needed the whole day, but we only allowed three hours. Even with all the balloons and banners the hall still looked like a school gymnasium.

✑

Mathew set up the bar with his friends and then ran off to collect the food and caterer. He had underestimated how much food was coming so he had to make two trips because he couldn't find anyone to delegate the job to.

I had to run home from the hall to get dressed just as people were arriving. When I got back to the hall the chaos had intensified, because all our guests had arrived, but the bride and groom were missing.

As soon as I arrived our guests were greeting me and wanting to hear about the wedding, but I couldn't stop to chat with them because Mathew was missing, and I had to sort out a crisis in the kitchen.

I say kitchen but actually it was just a room with a hatch. There was no oven or warmer or anything needed to prepare food. We had inspected the hall but somehow failed to notice that there wasn't an actual kitchen, and we definitely had not been advised of this fact.

So here I am at my wedding party with no kitchen. Luckily the caterer used to serve food at Notting Hill Carnival, so she had portable cooker rings, but it meant that Mathew had to collect her from the hall and take her back home to get them.

I tried to make the most of the party, but it was hard because I was on my own and my husband was missing in action, still unable to find anyone to delegate to.

I'm not even sure when he managed to get home to get dressed but he finally turned up and we began enjoying the party together. We cut the cake, thanked everyone for coming and invited guests to watch the wedding video in another room.

We had asked the DJ, Young Bushman, to play our wedding song, 'Here and Now' by Luther Vandross, and as we began to dance all I could hear was 'Endless Love'. I tried to ignore the error, but it spoilt the moment for me.

Mathew looked into my eyes, trying to reclaim the moment.

"Don't worry, babe. We are married and tomorrow we are off on our honeymoon!"

The words melted my disappointment. I tried to enjoy the dance, which was spoiled by the fact that Mathew could only hold me with one arm because he was dancing with a bottle of champagne in the other.

We invited our guests to come and dance with us and I really began to enjoy myself. I started raving with my friends and cracking jokes. One of my friends, Alison, who I met in the mother and baby home, bit me on the cheek as she whispered in my ear, "Bitch... you're married. You bitch!"

I broke free to twirl around in my gown. She needed to get the full effect.

She was so happy for me, and jealousy was killing her. I laughed so hard I nearly choked. I was so smug seeing my friends' faces as they watched me.

I took off my train to reveal a cute wedding cocktail dress. It was the fairy dust I needed. But as I re-entered the room, I sensed the vibe in the hall had changed.

People began running up to me saying, "He's dead, he's dead." I looked around the room as I spoke.

"Who's dead?"

My heart was racing. What had happened? I felt sickly. I hated dead people and I definitely didn't want one at my wedding party.

I began looking for Mathew before I went to see what the commotion was about, but I couldn't find him. Then somebody told me not to worry because he's not dead. I felt relieved and apprehensive at the same time. I went to see what was going on. To my shock and horror, it was my boss Yvonne's new husband. They had only been married three months.

And he was passed out on the floor at my wedding party, all 6ft 5 of him. Luckily, we had at least three nurses at the party, so they took care of him until the ambulance arrived.

Unfortunately, the ambulance had difficulty getting through to the hall because Mathew had parked his car blocking the path of the ambulance. Nobody could find him to move it. No sooner had the ambulance left, than people began to leave.

The place felt as if it was cursed. Lorraine, Mathew's sister's sister-in-law, whispered in my ear, "Nooooooo, something is going on in here. Me gone!" and with that she was through the door. Mathew still hadn't appeared.

And then a woman got a bone stuck in her throat. I don't even know who she was, but she too had to be rushed to hospital. It was a nightmare.

Debate amongst the few remaining guests gathered momentum; was it a Bajan fish bone or a Grenadian curried mutton bone that got stuck in her throat? I was at my wits' end when Mathew turned up with his brother Roy.

The party was done. I was so vexed. I couldn't hold it in.

"Where have you been? How can you disappear from your own wedding party and not even tell your wife you're going?"

I stared at him, waiting for a response to satisfy me.

"I had to collect my brother from St Pancras Station and then he didn't have anything to wear so I took him home so I could give him something to wear."

I think my brain exploded. All I could think was, *you left your own wedding party to drive a thirty-mile round trip, when you've got a hall full of people, how could he be your priority today?*

I stared at him incredulously. Luckily, his cousin Sandy pulled me away.

"Leave it. You're going on your honeymoon tomorrow. Forget it!"

I had had enough. I left the venue cradling my champagne cocktail. I was blind with rage, so I have no idea who took me home. I went straight into my bedroom with all the gift bags.

The only thing that stopped me from getting a divorce at that moment was the fact we were going on our honeymoon in a few hours.

Over the years Mathew developed his pattern, prioritising those less important or maybe, to him, pleasing the caterers or the guest was his priority, but it definitely wasn't putting me or my needs first.

16

What Is the Point of Big Eyes That Can't See?

So much happened in our first year of wedded bliss. People kept asking us what marriage was like and when I said the same, they seemed disappointed. I explained I got married because I loved the life we had together and wanted it to stay the same. We had everything working in a natural rhythm.

Antoinette had the best of both worlds, both of her parents were married just to other people. She enjoyed spending time with her father, but it wasn't as often as it used to be because he had moved to south London.

That really pissed me off. What father moves to the other side of London when he knows his daughter lives in north-west London? But he now had a new daughter, Rochelle. She was the image of her mother, which sweeted me because Antoinette was the stump of her father.

I initially tried to talk to Anthony about moving closer to his first daughter, but he was definitely marching to a different drum. So

Anthony's visits went from every other weekend to every few months until there wasn't any pattern or frequency.

Mathew and I were working hard at our careers and things were going really well for both of us. After working as an agency youth worker for two years he finally got his permanent contract. He was really happy.

My social work career was going really well too. The young women's specialist project, of which I was senior outreach worker, had received national recognition for a therapeutic service.

While working with disillusioned young women I stumbled on the idea to write a book. My aim was to give young black girls positive role models, which would motivate them to achieve their own dreams. I wanted other girls to have what Antoinette had, which was a family full of positive role models.

Her godmother Jewel was a solicitor; her sister Karen was a barrister. My sister Keres was a teacher, my so-called mother was a chief officer in charge and I was a qualified social worker in a senior role. My daughter had so many role models who could inspire her.

I wanted all girls to have the same inspiration. So I wrote a series of role model books which portrayed successful black British people from a wide range of cultural backgrounds and careers.

I found a publisher quite easily, after contacting about ten publishing companies.

My publisher was a small publishing company, so I had to do my own PR. I went on local and national radio; I had interviews in the local and national press.

I attended lots of cultural events, which gave the book good exposure. I was also invited to the House of Lords by Shareela Flather. Shareela was the first Asian woman to become a Member of Parliament and become a baroness in the House of Lords.

Shareela was wonderful; she introduced me to very influential women and often invited me to events. My life was so busy. I was juggling so many different balls.

But while promoting my book at the Notting Hill Carnival, my sight suddenly went in my right eye. I couldn't see a thing out of it. I knew something terrible had happened, so I took myself off to Marylebone Eye Hospital.

The treatment at the hospital was awful. They took my contact lens out of my only seeing eye and abandoned me in a room. I was terrified out of my mind. I couldn't see anything. I felt terrified.

When I arrived at the hospital, I called Mathew, but he was on a day trip to Chessington Zoo with the children from the youth centre.

So, alone and terrified, I waited and waited. The nurses kept sending me down corridors to different rooms and no matter how many times I told them I couldn't see without my contact lens they still wouldn't guide me.

I was left to feel and fumble my way along unfamiliar white corridors. For the first time in my life I felt disabled. I felt so sad and sorry for myself.

After a few hours of tests and peering at my eyes, a doctor told me that I had a detached retina and I needed an operation. As I sat there all alone, I thought back to the beginning of my eye problems.

I started wearing glasses as a little girl. My eyes were so bad I had to go to the children's hospital. My NHS milk-bottle-thick glasses were so heavy they hurt my ears. And children taunted me, calling me 'four eyes' and 'froggy'.

I tried my hardest to choose nice frames, so the children wouldn't make fun of me, but it didn't work as my choice was limited to thick ugly NHS frames.

Oh, how I wished I didn't have to wear glasses, but when I took them off, I couldn't see anything, not even my face in the mirror. The funny thing was I had really big eyes. Looking at them perplexed me. No matter how hard I squinted I still couldn't see a thing, near or far.

My glasses were such a hindrance. I loved swimming, but my glasses didn't.

They would fog up and get wet, so I couldn't see a thing. I had to hold my glasses to my face with one hand while I attempted to swim or somersault with the other.

When I was about ten my Auntie Viola got me contact lenses. £1,000, she told me they cost. She threatened to kill me if I lost them.

The contact lenses were minute and were made out of glass. The optician showed me how to put the contact lenses in my eyes and gave me detailed instructions. The only problem was that my eye didn't like the thought of a piece of glass being put on it.

Every time I tried to put the lens in my eye, my lid would close, and I'd drop the lens, and then I would have to start the process all over again.

The process took me ages to get one lens in my eye, never mind two. To compound matters those lenses used to make my eyes itch so bad, so much so my eyes cried.

Those lenses were unbearable. My eyes eventually rejected them. Every time I put them in my eyes popped them out, at which point my optician told us my eyes were allergic to the contact lenses. I was so relieved. I preferred having the kids call me names rather than suffer with those things in my eyes; that was pure torture.

My Auntie Viola was stinking mad but there was nothing she could do; the optician had spoken. I was back wearing glasses.

When I went to live with Auntie Jeannette (my foster parent) she took me to the Royal Free Hospital where I met my new consultant, David. He also had his own optician's in Hampstead.

He informed us that because my eyes were so bad, I was entitled to get free contact lenses on the NHS. Luckily by then, contact lenses had changed to soft plastic, but it still wasn't easy to find a type of contact lens that my eyes could tolerate.

It took about a year of trial and error to find a pair of contact lenses which my eyes didn't reject. I loved wearing contact lenses once I got the hang of them.

Over the years the solutions changed, and the cleaning process got easier. But my eyes didn't keep up with science, choosing instead to deteriorate. My eyes were bad to begin with, but now I had a detached retina.

It was crazy how it had happened. The night before Mathew's family had had a family gathering for some family from America. We had all been having a laugh, drinking and chatting.

I had been laughing with one of his cousins when I threw my head back and banged my head hard against a wall display cabinet. I hadn't thought anything of it until later, when I saw a dark liquid covering my eye, as if blackout curtains were blocking my vision.

I didn't realise it was serious until the morning, when I couldn't see anything out of my right eye. I should have gone straight to the hospital, but I had promotional work to do at the Notting Hill Carnival, which included being interviewed for a live television programme.

So I went to the Carnival. I did the interview and then went straight to the hospital, but my delay had caused unimaginable damage to my eye.

The enormity of my situation began to sink in as I waited for Mathew, sobbing. I felt so frightened and alone. The waiting just made things all the more unbearable.

When Mathew arrived, I told him about my horrible ordeal and he was furious. He wanted to make a complaint, but I just wanted to get out of there.

The next day I went to my optician, hoping he had better news. I had remained with the same optician since I was eleven or twelve. But David just confirmed what the hospital had said. He informed me that I would not get my sight back in that eye.

Shocked and devastated, I couldn't stop crying. Why hadn't someone told me what could happen if I had a blow to my head or advise me what to do if I did? None of my opticians had given me that advice.

David told me to go to Moorfields Eye Hospital in London. So that's what I did. Mathew drove me, as I sobbed all the way there, which was about an hour's drive.

When we arrived at the hospital, from the moment I registered in A&E, there was an air of excitement. I instantly became a teaching case because I had a 360-degree retinal tear which is extremely rare. Only two people in every million will have one.

Doctors and nurses from all over the hospital kept coming to have a look at the back of my eye. The crowd was a great distraction. It kinda helped take my mind off the fact that I would never see out of that eye again.

I was taken under the care of Mr Levy, who was a world-renowned consultant retinal specialist. He assured me he would be operating on me personally.

Mr Levy was very gentle and kind. He made me feel special for giving him the opportunity to operate on such a big retinal tear. He talked me through the surgical procedure, which involved putting my eye in a plastic brace which would hold it in position. I would have to keep my head down for six weeks, which included sleeping on my face.

He also confirmed that I would never see out of the eye again.

The shocking facts gave me a rollercoaster of emotions, but the main one was fear. I was terrified about everything, the operation itself and the thought of living with only one eye.

As I lay in the hospital holding on to Mathew's hands, I felt a bit of his strength and love until visiting hours finished.

After begging him not to go, the light left the ward with him. Alone I felt like a lost child, very sorry for myself and scared. With no other escape, I hid under the sheets in my bed.

The next day I met Charmaine. She was the same age as me and she had high myopia like me. She was really short-sighted. Her glasses were as thick as mine.

Charmaine had had a retinal tear, too. I saw her curled up on her bed looking how I felt. From the moment I introduced myself and what I was in for, we became instant support for each other. Charmaine was my first angel and then came the second.

As the porter parked me in a waiting bay outside the operating theatre, the clinical sanitised area told the time. I felt overpowered as I inhaled. But just as I was taking off my glasses, I saw a familiar big smile. I refocused as I pushed back my glasses to see my cousin Mags.

Mags stood in surgical scrubs. Cute, petite. Her 5ft structure masked the British Barbadian bulldog within. Seeing Mags took away all my fears. She hugged me and kissed me and told me she would be with me during the surgery and until I came around from the anaesthetic.

And so said, so done. But as I lay on the gurney after surgery and before I could exhale, I had a bad reaction to the anaesthetic. It made me feel like I was freezing cold. My temperature dropped as my body went into shock. Mags sprang into action, covering me with foil blankets which helped me to warm up.

I thanked God for Mags. She was my angel. I hadn't seen her for about a year. We used to be close, for about a minute, but we lost touch after I got married.

The way she looked after me was like we had never lost touch. She accompanied me up to the ward with the porter and Mathew. She told the nurses to take extra special care of me. I felt so grateful but most of all I felt safe.

After I was discharged from hospital, I didn't see or hear from Mags, but I will always be thankful for her care and compassion.

My hospital discharge presented new challenges. I had to keep my head face down for six weeks, including sleeping on my face. I couldn't risk moving the eye brace or I would have to have the surgery again and that wasn't an option.

Unfortunately, time passed at an inordinately slow pace. I thought the six weeks would never end. When it did I had to learn how to hold my head up. But my biggest issue was learning to live with only one limited eye. With every blink I felt the fear of blindness.

At the age of twenty-eight, I felt bereaved without a body. My loss was life-changing. I had to adapt to a limited life. The biggest challenge was to give up driving.

I loved driving, it was part of my 'Miss Independent' life. I had learnt to drive with BSM, even though they were more expensive than other driving schools, but I had decided to invest in getting the best lessons money could buy.

I took twenty-one driving lessons and bought myself a car. I passed my test on my second attempt, which sickened me, because Mathew passed on his first attempt, without a single lesson.

I loved driving. I loved having a car. I was free to come and go as I pleased. I hated not now being able to drive, but I hated the idea of killing someone more, so I learnt to accept the cards which fate had dealt me.

Learning to live with sight in one eye only was so hard, but I tried not to let it get me down. After having a few months off sick, I went back to work.

Apart from a few minor adjustments to my computer and changing my hours so I could get home before it got dark in the winter I tried to carry on as normal.

But there was a part of me which felt, why do these horrible things have to happen to me. Haven't I suffered enough? Isn't it bad enough that I didn't have parents but now I can barely see too? How much more am I supposed to endure? With no answers forthcoming, I tried to be positive and just carry on one day at a time.

I decided to keep busy and motivated, so I started promoting my book again. I managed to get my book national exposure and stocked in bookshops, schools and libraries nationwide.

With the success of my first book, I wondered what next. As I continued building my career by day I added another ball. I became the agony aunt for a major African-Caribbean magazine, which specialised in everything beauty and lifestyle.

Helping people with their problems was my aim. I thought I could do a much better job of answering people's worries than the culture-less drivel I often read in magazines.

I felt so excited. I was actually getting paid to write an agony aunt column. It was just the distraction I needed. I tried to focus on my new job. In amongst all my idiosyncrasies I felt the warmth of success. Happiness swelled as I continued to juggle my roles and responsibilities.

Eight months after I lost the sight in my right eye, Mathew and I celebrated our first wedding anniversary at the Dorchester Hotel, London.

Mathew surprised me with an eternity ring, and I surprised him with a gold pinkie ring, which had two hands clasped together with a heart inside. Our one-year celebration was wonderful. Our first year of marriage had been so eventful the months had flown by. We both hoped that such an eventful start would mean a smooth happily ever after.

17

WHY CAN'T THINGS STAY THE SAME?

Smooth lasted three years, during which I never drew breath. I loved to see Mathew smile. I spent so much time thinking of ways to make him happy.

I threw Mathew a surprise party for his thirtieth birthday. I had managed to organise everything including hiding all the drinks in the garage. I had our favourite DJ, Young Bushman, playing, and I had invited all his friends and family.

The ruse was taking him for a meal at the Taste of China, our favourite restaurant. As we ate each course I had my eye on the time. To speed up the meal I told him I wasn't wearing any panties. Mathew practically dragged me out of the restaurant. As we drove down our road he noticed all the parked cars. I distracted him by rubbing his penis. He barely drew brakes, he just threw the car in our drive and ran into the house.

He was so shocked when everyone shouted, "Surprise!" He had a wicked party. We raved all night until the last stragglers left at about 6am. Mathew's joy was infectious. He made love to me all morning.

❧

Things were going great for both of us. Mathew still loved working at the youth club and I had started a new job as a lead children's inspector at Hammersmith and Fulham council. I used to inspect children's services, including children's homes, nurseries, childminders, secure units and a children's hotel.

I loved my new job. I was working in a different part of London. Being nearer to home and closer to Mathew allowed us to meet for lunch and occasionally he picked me up after work and we drove home together. It was nice. I went from four hours a day travel time to about an hour and a half, which improved my work/life balance dramatically.

Antoinette was growing up nicely. She blossomed into a beautiful young lady, at twelve years old. She was so well behaved, and we had a lovely close relationship. Mathew and Antoinette had maintained their distance, despite the fact that Antoinette was seeing less and less of her father. I tried to build a better relationship between them, but they remained distant, but cordial.

Mathew yearned to see his son. He attempted to contact Tremaine's mum, but she refused to return his calls. His pain was palpable. I wanted to ease Mathew's pain.

So I contacted one of Mathew's brothers, who still lived in Birmingham. He got me a work number for Tremaine's mum. I decided to call her to find out once and for all if Tremaine was Mathew's. As the phone rang I was unsure how to broach the issue and she answered before I could think.

"Hello, this is Mathew's wife."

"Yes, how can I help you?"

"I'm calling because Mathew's really missing Tremaine…"

"Well, Tremaine's fine."

"Fine. How can he be? He must be missing his dad."

Her chilly response gave way to silence.

"Look, I don't want to offend you, but I think you know why you're not bothered if Tremaine sees Mathew or not."

"What... what do you mean?"

"Look. I know you're a good mother and you wanted the best for your baby. You knew Mathew was a good guy and would be a great father. You did what you thought was best for your baby... but they deserve to know the truth. I'm not trying to judge you or trying to put you down."

After another long pause, she spoke in nearly a whisper.

"Tremaine doesn't need him. He has enough positive male role models, uncles, grandfather, he's fine."

"Yes, but he, they, deserve the truth. Woman to woman, is Mathew Tremaine's father?"

The silence was sooo long I thought she had hung up.

"No. He's not his."

"Thank you for telling me. It takes courage to own your truth. Take care. Bye."

As the words sank in, I felt the weight of her lie. How was I supposed to tell Mathew that the boy he called son and had loved for nine years wasn't his son? It was one thing to suspect it but to know it for a fact was a whole other thing.

As the words sank in, I felt the impact of her deception. I didn't know how I was going to tell Mathew, but I knew I had to; I just had to pick the right time.

❧

We were still travelling around the world as a family and as a couple. And we also had a few family holidays with Mathew's sister Ria and her son Kyle.

On one trip we went to Los Angeles, to go to Disneyland and to meet Mathew and Ria's cousins, who lived in Venice Beach. The holiday wasn't without its challenges. Right from the planning stage I should have taken the hint, that Ria and I had different ideas about where to stay. Mathew and I liked to stay in four star hotels, but Ria was happy to stay in a two or three star.

I tried to compromise as she was a single parent, so I knew her money was less than ours. I booked us into a three and a half star hotel in Anaheim, which was across the road from Disneyland.

The day we arrived at the hotel I nearly passed out, it was so basic, and I knew when I saw the game arcade the place was more like a three star than a four star. The hotel was clean, but I missed the opulence I was used to. Antoinette and Kyle had a ball. They were either in the pool or in the games arcade.

We spent our days either exploring the local area, eating at different restaurants or at the theme parks, including Disneyland and Universal Studios. We really should have hired a car, because it was difficult to get around without one. We were a distance from most tourist spots.

Not long after we arrived in Anaheim, we phoned Mathew and Ria's cousin Pauline. She was so glad to hear we were in town she arranged to meet us the next day.

On sight Pauline wouldn't stop hugging us all. It was ridiculous how alike the family all looked. They all had the same face structure and features; small Chinese-looking eyes, straight noses, really small ears and the same red caramel complexion.

Pauline's mum and Mathew and Ria's mum were sisters, so they were first cousins. After the hour-long introductions Pauline refused to leave us at the hotel, so she kidnapped us. No joke. She bundled us all into her car. She was driving what looked like a Honda or something. It only had five seats but somehow she managed to get all five of us plus her and the luggage into the car.

Pauline took us to her apartment in Crenshaw. She opened her home to us, which was amazing, particularly as she only had two bedrooms and two bathrooms. And her two sons lived with her.

As we looked around, I felt perplexed. I appreciated her generosity, but I couldn't see how eight people could be divided between two medium-sized bedrooms. But somehow Pauline did magic, and we all had somewhere to sleep. Pauline went above and beyond to make us comfortable; she even gave Mathew and me her bedroom.

We were embraced by the whole Cali family. They took us sightseeing and they all had dinner parties for us. While staying at one of the cousins', Mathew became quite forlorn. It was strange because we were having such a great time. He wished Tremaine had come with us. Hearing this erased my silence. I wanted to end his pining. He needed to know the truth.

As we lay looking up into the darkness in the guest room of his cousin, who had a beautiful home in Beverly Hills, I broke the news. Initially Mathew seemed reluctant to hear the truth. He made me tell him verbatim what Tremaine's mum had said. As the words sank in Mathew sobbed like his heart was breaking. I tried to comfort him, but he was inconsolable. Telling him I love you didn't touch the sides.

He was hurting, and nothing I said or did helped him. Luckily being on holiday was a good distraction during the day, but at night he was sad. He made me repeat the conversation over and over again. I stopped when I realised it was doing him no good. I used my body to distract him but not even that worked.

I felt like I was dodging land mines. I knew what was coming next, I could tell Mathew was looking for a solution I didn't have.

Right from the start, he knew I didn't do children. I had my daughter and the shop was shut.

But now Mathew wanted to talk about nothing else. I couldn't get him to understand that I only had capacity to love one child, him and me; anything else would send me mad. He just couldn't or wouldn't understand. We became irritated with each other. Exasperated, we agreed to park the issue and focus on enjoying the remainder of our holiday.

Getting home from LA turned into a lifetime memory. We had travelled on United Airways staff tickets, which Mathew's brother-in-law had booked for us. We had standby tickets and could only get on flights which had empty seats.

Getting on our flight to LA had been a breeze but as we approached the heaving United check-in desk at Los Angeles airport, the reality of standby travel dawned on us.

All the flights to Heathrow were full or oversold and the picture was the same for the next two weeks. We were stuck in LA. The only way out was to go to Chicago, which had more daily flights to London. We took a gamble.

We all needed to get back to England to go to work, so really, we didn't have a choice. But when we got to Chicago all the flights were full. We had to check into a hotel.

All five of us had to share a room. We had no choice. We were broke. We had just had a three-week holiday. Every day we called the airline to be told the same thing, "the flight's full". We lived on rationed fast food for a couple of days.

On about the third day, we were all sitting eating takeout while watching BBC World News, when Mathew read out the newsfeed. Princess Diana had been in a car crash. We all sat in disbelief as the horror unfolded, switching from channel to channel hoping it wasn't true.

As the hours passed and ended with the announcement of the death of Princess Diana and Dodi we tried to comprehend the news. The next day we felt the impact of losing such an icon. All empty seats on flights to London had been filled by journalists from the world's press.

United's airline staff advised us it would be at least a month before we could all get on a flight. Faced with limited options we decided to split up. Ria and Kyle went back to LA and we managed to get on a flight to France. With only our prayers we managed to land in France, and our credit cards got us seats on Eurostar. Our lack of French compounded our frustration as we fought more and more barriers obstructing our way home.

The significance of landing in the country which had taken our princess hadn't dawned on us but as we emerged into Waterloo Station, we were struck by a country gripped in mourning. It was eerily quiet.

Back home, we attempted to click into our normal life/work pattern. Everything looked the same but Mathew felt off.

The first day I really noticed it was the day we went to see my cousin Chrystal. She had had a baby boy. I was excited because we hadn't had a baby in the family for years. When we arrived, it was clear that Chrystal needed a hand. I bathed the baby and tidied up a bit. I gave Chrystal some things for the baby, nappies and wipes and some chocolates for her.

But the whole time we were there Mathew hid his face in his coat. He barely spoke to Chrystal and he refused to hold the baby. During the drive home I attempted to get to the root of his silence.

"Are you okay?"

"Why? I'm fine."

"You didn't look fine. You hid under your coat and barely said two words."

I looked into his face as he stared at the road.

"It's hard for me to watch you with a baby when you don't want mine!"

Boom. The nuclear bomb went off. I was totally unprepared. I glared at Mathew, speechless.

"I don't understand why you are so good with other people's babies, but you won't have a baby for me. I just don't get it."

"But I've told you what it means to me. When I have a child, I give so much of myself I don't have anything left for me. I knew when I had Antoinette I could only do it once. I don't have anything left to give to another child. And I just don't like the responsibility of having a child, they aren't just for Christmas, they're for life. It's just not for me. I'm sorry."

Silence replaced words, and when we got home Mathew went straight to our bedroom and he threw himself on the bed without saying another word.

A few months later my brother Jamie had his first son. We took champagne to the hospital to toast the new addition to the family. Mathew faked his way through the festivities but on the long drive from Holloway, he opened the sore again.

"Look how good you are with the babies. Why can't you be good with our baby? Our baby will be so cute. I know you will be a good mother. We love each other so much it will be perfect."

My level of irritation had hit a new high. He just didn't get me. I just ignored him. My silence for the rest of the journey was palpable.

When we got home, Mathew begged me to go to see a fertility doctor to see if they could reverse my sterilisation. I was so annoyed with him. Why couldn't he hear me? Why didn't he understand what he was asking of me? I had told him in no uncertain terms, I didn't want to have a baby. Period!

The more I refused, the more he begged and pleaded. Eventually he wore me down, but I only agreed to go to the appointment and listen to what the doctor had to say.

I was so upset. He was basically asking me to kill myself, but he didn't care, he wanted a baby.

In the weeks leading up to the appointment with the fertility consultant I tried my best to get Mathew to understand what he was asking of me.

But he just wasn't listening. We went to see the consultant. He informed us that the sterilisation could be reversed, but the success rate was very low. The procedure required me to have an operation (under general anaesthetic) but the likelihood of us conceiving a baby was only about 5%.

The consultant asked me directly if I wanted to reverse my surgery. My answer, "No," was definitive, so the meeting was over.

As we walked out of the hospital, Mathew couldn't hide his fury.

"Why did you tell the doctor that you don't want to reverse the sterilisation? You said you would listen to the doctor."

I looked at him incredulously.

"I did listen, and I heard what he had to say, but nothing he said changed my mind. My reasons for getting sterilised haven't changed; I still do not want to have any more children. I'm sorry if that's not what you want to hear but I just can't do it."

I attempted to hug him, but he shrugged me off him. He said he was so hurt. But so was I. He was putting me in an impossible position.

At that moment, I regretted unearthing the truth about his son. I should have kept my mouth shut, better yet, never opened the hornets' nest. I should have kept my suspicions about the paternity of Tremaine to myself. The truth had brought nothing but misery.

Mathew was no longer content with what he had. I didn't know what to do. Should I just let him go, so he could have a family with someone who wanted to give him the child he yearned for, or should I carry on trying to make a life with a man who wanted some things I couldn't give him?

The whole thing was maddening. I loved my husband and would do anything to make him happy, but I drew the line at having a child; that was a step too far.

It was an awful time. I felt so unsupported. Nobody understood my position. Mathew had everyone on his side, particularly his family. I was the wicked bitch who wouldn't give her husband a baby.

It's not that the women in my circle didn't understand my position; nope, they begrudged me living a life they couldn't. Jewel was the only person who knew me well enough to understand how I felt.

About a year after the appointment with the fertility consultant, Mathew was still sulking, and I was busy living life. But for some crazy reason my period was five days late.

Despite being sterilised for about ten years, I still used to panic if my period was late. It had been late before but only a couple of days or so, never five days late.

The strangest thing was I could feel my period coming. Twice at work I had run to the toilet to put a sanitary towel on but when I got there, still no blood. On day five, I called Jewel, frantic.

"Where is my period? Why is it five days late? What the hell is going on?"

"Stop fretting. You are probably worrying it away, just relax and it will come. It always does."

She was right, it usually did come after I stopped worrying, but something told me this was different.

"To put your mind at ease, do a pregnancy test. It's a waste of money, but what have you got to lose? At least it will put your mind at rest."

I sent Mathew to get a Clearblue pregnancy test. When he came back, he handed me the packet.

"The woman in the shop said I should buy a double pack because nobody ever believes the first test and it's cheaper than buying two single pregnancy tests. But I'm not wasting my money on a double pack when we both know you're not pregnant!"

I ripped open the package and peed on the stick. Before I could finish reading the instructions the thing went blue. I nearly passed out. I couldn't speak; I just gave Mathew the stick as I sat on the toilet, dazed.

I didn't have to speak. He knew what my face meant. He was elated. He couldn't contain his happiness. He kissed me on the cheek and said he was off to celebrate with his friends. He grabbed a bottle of champagne and a Cohiba cigar and he was gone.

I phoned Jewel. She was working on a big case in Brighton. She answered the phone sarcastically.

"I told you, you were worrying for nothing."

"It says I'm pregnant."

I couldn't say another word. I was shocked by what I had just said. She couldn't believe it either. I sat on the toilet, holding the phone for about three hours. I couldn't hang up, I didn't want to be left alone in this mess.

You have a choice, she said. But I knew I didn't. What kind of choice is it when one road leads to no husband and the other road leads to no sanity, what kind of choice was that?

I felt sick from the moment I peed on the pregnancy stick and that feeling didn't leave me, it just got worse. I went to my doctor, hoping she would say it was all a terrible mistake; instead she told me the tests were extremely accurate, so she didn't have to test me herself.

Then she took delight in telling me when the baby was due. I nearly threw up in her office. My head was spinning, and my stomach felt so sickly it was unbearable.

And nothing improved my perspective. I was trapped between the devil and the deep blue sea. I had no way out. I was powerless. If I had a termination, what would the people say about the woman who killed her husband's only child? I couldn't bear the thought of it or the thought of losing my husband. It was mind-blowing.

But I couldn't face the alternative either. I just didn't have the capacity to grow another child and what's more I didn't want to. What could I do? What was the solution?

The pregnancy was a nightmare. I felt sick for the full nine months. I couldn't eat the things I liked, which added to the madness I felt. I had been a chocoholic since I was a teenager but now I couldn't eat chocolate, I mean not even one bar or square.

I loved eggs, but now I couldn't eat eggs. If it wasn't bad enough that I had morning/all-day sickness, when I could manage to eat, I couldn't eat what I wanted.

I was so unhappy and people's happiness for Mathew compounded this feeling. As the news spread that I was pregnant, we had family and friends from around the world ringing to congratulate us and it was only then that I realised that Mathew had had a prayer circle going. His cousins in America and Grenada and even my family in Barbados said they had been praying for us to have a baby.

How did I stand a chance when so many people were praying for what I didn't want? The pressure was immense. My pregnancy was considered high risk because I had a history of late miscarriages. I had to go to the hospital every two weeks, it was an absolute nightmare.

From three months I had dropsy. Every afternoon at 1pm, it didn't matter if I was in a meeting, on the toilet or standing at a bus stop,

I just fell asleep. I mean, out cold, for about half an hour. At first, I thought I could fight it, but after I fell asleep in a few meetings I had to surrender to it.

I had to schedule my meetings around the dropsy time. Luckily, as a team manager I had a lot of autonomy.

At six months I suffered with a softened pelvis, which felt like I was going to drop the baby, so I had to go on early maternity leave. I couldn't lift or carry anything heavier than a glass of water. It was a nightmare. I couldn't do the housework or go anywhere or do anything, it was horrible.

But amongst it all, my biggest disappointment was Mathew. He wasn't at all supportive and at times he looked as miserable as I felt. I kept saying this is your dream, so why aren't you happy? He said he was, but he didn't look it or show it. Worse still, he wasn't loving or nurturing towards me, which I couldn't understand, given we were living his dream and his prayer.

Instead he carried on living his usual street life while I was trapped at home. I was already living my fear, which was he only wanted me to have his child so he could control me, so he could feel secure in the knowledge I would never leave him.

The months just dragged on like time was going backwards. In the midst of my nightmare, we were having a new kitchen and wardrobes fitted and we were also having the family for Christmas dinner.

Despite choosing a well-known local kitchen company, we ended up with a demolition site and an unqualified kitchen fitter, who brought his wife with him each day and used her as a labourer.

I started to believe Mathew was on the fitter's payroll because he made so many excuses for his shoddy work. But after the guy cut short the worktop and put a plug directly under the sink, I was done and so was he.

After firing 'Bob a job' we were left without a kitchen for two months, which included Christmas. The horror only ended when the company owners returned from their cruise at the start of January. Thankfully, our new kitchen fitter was a perfectionist and a complete contrast to the 'Bob a job' guy. Our new kitchen was superb and looked like it came from the pages of *House Beautiful* or *Ideal Home* magazine.

With our home back to normal, I went back to counting down the months. Irritation and discontent was the title of my life.

At seven months I had a strange dream. We had the baby, but we didn't have anything for it, so we had to put the baby to sleep in a drawer. The dream brought me to reality. I realised that the baby was coming, ready or not, so I had to prepare. I didn't want to, but I had no choice.

Unfortunately, Mathew's energy added nothing but gunpowder to my emotional dynamite. He couldn't even make shopping for the baby positive. He sulked around the shops as if he was irritated and disinterested.

As we walked around John Lewis nursery department, I felt like a water crab without water. I kept holding up baby clothes or pointing at cots, trying to get a reaction, but he offered nothing, just worried lines and the smell of smoke.

I couldn't make sense of him. I knew I wasn't happy because I was living my nightmare, but it was his dream although he didn't act like it. And he did nothing to make it enjoyable for me or to keep my spirits up. It was awful.

Unfortunately, forty weeks wasn't enough for the baby. He or she was overdue by two weeks, during which I had blood-curdling contractions for the whole time.

The contractions indicated I was in labour twice, but the midwives said not. After doing some 90s swing beat dancing to VH1 90s music my waters finally broke and I was finally in labour. My labour could be used as a form of contraceptive for women. But for me it just magnified the horror I was living.

When I arrived at WG Maternity Hospital, I was two centimetres dilated. I felt hopeful that the labour would be smoother than the pregnancy, but my hopes were soon dashed as the contractions intensified and my body refused to let the baby out.

The baby went into foetal distress and even did a poo but the midwife was not concerned, despite me repeatedly telling her that my body was not going to open up on its own.

The pains were making me feel like the girl from *The Exorcist*. After about five hours I had an epidural, but to my dismay it didn't do anything to ease the pain.

At first the midwife couldn't understand why the epidural wasn't working, but after she examined me she told me that the baby was facing down instead of up, so with every contraction the baby was coming back in instead of coming out.

Hearing her explanation sent my head reeling. It was a miracle I didn't get sectioned, the pain was driving me so mad. I had never heard of an epidural not working, it was held up as the pinnacle of pain relief in childbirth so why wasn't it working for me?

What made the situation worse was Mathew. From the time he brought me to the hospital all he did was sleep under his coat in a chair on the other side of the room.

He was so embarrassing. Every time the midwife came in she looked at me and then at him and then back at me. She even attempted to wake him up, but realised it was pointless after he grunted, "What do you want me to do? There's nothing I can do for her, she just has to get through it."

The midwife was stunned by his response. She shot him a stinking look as she left me.

Despite my being married and my husband being in the room with me, I felt more alone than when I had Antoinette. But what could I do? I had no choice but to endure.

After being in labour for about ten hours the baby was in distress again and did another poo. This time my new midwife was concerned. The baby's heart rate had dropped drastically so I had to have an emergency C-section.

The C-section was another horror. Unfortunately, none of the mother and baby books or magazines had prepared me for it. I had exceeded the maximum dose of epidural, so pain relief was limited to morphine. Unfortunately, morphine did not numb the body. Nobody bothered to inform me I would be able to feel the surgeon's hands in my stomach. I felt him moving my organs and wrenching the baby out.

It was horrific. And to make matters worse I had asked my obstetrician to give me another sterilisation, but he had not recorded it in my notes, so the doctor refused to carry out the procedure. This meant I was going to have to have another operation. I was beyond distraught. Mathew was supportive when I had the C-section but once he got his son in his hands, he was done with me.

For me, seeing the baby for the first time was weird, it felt surreal. I had a newborn baby boy, but he looked white.

He didn't look anything like me; he looked like Mathew, but most of all he looked like Mathew's sister, Ria. The baby looked like her twin or her baby.

During the pregnancy, I held on to one small nugget of hope. It was the only thing that brought me comfort. Somebody was going to have to pay me for a bodged sterilisation. I had paid the Mary Stopes Clinic for a sterilisation. And not just a run of the mill sterilisation like on the NHS, which was just clips on the fallopian tubes. No.

I had paid for a private clinic's triple sterilisation procedure, which included cutting away two inches of each fallopian tube, four clips and heat sealing the tubes. But despite all of the fail-safe cutting-edge procedure I had gone through, I still managed to get pregnant and have a baby.

Somebody had to pay me. During the nine months, I, we, had spent the money a million times over. The compensation for medical negligence was the only thing which gave me hope.

My consultant had assured me he would get all the evidence I needed to sue the clinic, so after the baby was delivered, I waited eagerly to see him. He arrived the next day looking rather chipper. I didn't wait for him to stand still, I just launched straight in.

"Hello, have you got all the evidence and pictures I need to sue?"

He paused as if he was unsure how to answer.

"I have good news and bad news, what would you like first?"

I studied my consultant's face for a clue, but there was none, just a furrowed brow.

"I would like the bad first, let's get that out of the way."

As he spoke my eyes were locked with his.

"You were still sterilised… the clips were still in place, and the fallopian tubes were still one inch apart and sealed."

I felt deflated by his words as I sank into my pillow. I held my breath, still hoping for pound signs.

"What's the good news?"

"You have what is termed by the British Medical Association journal as a miracle."

He looked at me with such delight.

"How much does a miracle pay?"

He laughed, but I was serious.

"Unfortunately, you cannot sue for a miracle."

I was dumbstruck. I had no case, just a miracle. But how was I, were we, going to afford a baby? Who was going to pay for this baby?

My consultant must have left when he realised I was not happy with his news; I didn't even see him go. My head was trying to make sense of his words. From what I could gather, the only person who was going to pay for this baby was me.

During my stay in hospital, I forced myself to bond with the baby; we called him Monet after Mathew's father. He was a really cute baby, but he was hard work, right from the word go.

He was constantly hungry despite me breastfeeding him on demand. My nipples were so sore from all the sucking, the skin around them cracked, and bled. It was awful. I felt abused.

The nice part of having a new baby was all the visitors to the hospital, including Antoinette. Ria brought Antoinette to see her baby brother. She was so funny. She peeked at her baby brother, but she was more worried about me. She said I looked grey, like I was sick. I tried to reassure her that I was fine, but she looked worried. Antoinette had taken the full nine months to believe she was going to have a sibling from me.

She had long since given up on the idea of having a brother or sister, particularly when she found out I had been sterilised. So when we told her I was pregnant she didn't believe me. She didn't even believe the scan pictures.

Antoinette had held nothing back when she vocalised her opinion; she was sixteen, so she was over the idea of having a brother or sister. I wasn't surprised by her lack of interest in the baby once he was born. But by the end of her first visit she did ask to hold her baby brother; thankfully the bond had begun to grow.

I was discharged from hospital when the baby was five days old. Arriving home with a new baby felt so surreal. I felt sick to my stomach and it wasn't morning sickness, it was the stark reality of being a mother to a newborn baby.

I'd sit looking at the Moses basket in the corner of the room with this little white bundle gently sleeping. He didn't feel like mine, but the hospital assured me he was.

18

A Stork Can Bring More Than a Baby!

The first morning back home after I had been discharged from the hospital I got up and readied myself for the midwife's visit. I sat downstairs looking at the Moses basket, trying to come to terms with the reality, when I heard letters dropping from the letterbox.

I went and picked them up and flicked through them, seeing who they were for. Amongst a few greeting cards was a letter marked National Statistics Society, which was addressed to me.

I wondered what the National Statistics Society was and why they were writing to me. Just as I was about to open the letter the doorbell rang. I opened the door to the midwife.

The midwife was happy to see I was up and prepared for her visit. She only looked at the baby in the Moses basket but asked me if he was feeding well and if I had any concerns.

I kept feeling a bit light-headed and kept getting palpitations in my chest. She told me I was probably anaemic and gave me a prescription for some iron tablets. The midwife stayed all of about twenty minutes, but I was eager for her to leave so I could open my mail.

I don't think the door had even shut good before I opened the letter from the National Statistics Society. My heart nearly stopped as I read at the bottom of the page 'from your sister Melissa'.

Melissa had contacted the National Statistics Society and had asked for their help in trying to find me. They used my national insurance number to locate me.

Inside the covering letter was a letter from my sister. She explained that she was my sister from my father. She didn't know if I knew about her, but she wanted me to know that she loved me, and she wasn't angry with my mother if she hadn't told me about her, but she wanted me to know that I had a sister and a brother from my father.

She said her name was Melissa and her brother was called Johnny. Our father, Tyrone Brown, died in 1989 and she didn't know if I knew he had passed.

She just wanted to know if I was okay. She enclosed her contact information. I sat there looking at the letter and reading it and re-reading it, over and over again. Could it be possible that I had a new baby and new siblings all at the same time?

But my dad was dead. Tears rolled down my cheeks as the reality touched my heart. My father was dead. I would never know him. I would never know what he was like. I would never know how he would hug or kiss me.

He would never know how I had turned out. He'd never know my children or my husband. He wouldn't know me. My heart was broken. I had missed out on knowing my dad before he died. I just couldn't stop crying. Oh, how my heart ached.

The baby must have sensed my distress. He began crying. I picked him up and hugged him to me. He tried to suck my face, hungry again. I kissed him for my father, who he would never know. It was like my son had come to connect me to my father.

I felt the timing just had to be linked or why else would these things be happening at the same time? I sat feeding the baby while looking at the words on the letter; tears ran down my cheeks again as I read the words over and over.

I just couldn't believe it. My sister was looking for me. She wanted to know if I was okay. I couldn't wait to tell Mathew, who was upstairs sleeping. As soon as the baby was finished feeding, I changed his nappy and put him down.

I wanted to run up the stairs, but my stitches gripped me, so I just hobbled upstairs to tell Mathew. I gave him the letter to read. He was as shocked as I was. As he handed me back the letter, he looked concerned.

"What are you going to do? Are you going to contact her?"

"I don't know. I'm not sure. I can't really think straight, I can't believe it. I have a sister from my dad and she is looking for me. And my dad is dead. I have a dad!"

The excitement of each word burst out, as I began shouting, "I have a dad and I know his name. My dad's name is Tyrone Brown."

What a lovely name, I thought, as I shouted it over and over again.

"Sssh babes, you're gonna wake the baby."

I didn't care really. I knew my dad's name. I had a dad and his name was Tyrone Brown. I felt so proud. I knew who I was; I was the daughter of Tyrone Brown.

I felt weird. My joy was mixed with so many different emotions. It was bittersweet but at least I knew his name. I decided to let everything just marinate for a while, it was such a shock; I needed time to process the information.

After three days, I had absorbed the information and with great excitement I decided to speak to my sister. Curiosity bubbled as I wondered what she was like; I wanted her to tell me what my dad was like.

But Mathew was sceptical. He said he didn't want me to get hurt. He was sick of seeing my siblings hurt me, so he wanted me to prepare myself in case the union didn't go well.

I agreed with him. I wasn't expecting a relationship with my sister. I just wanted to get some answers to my questions. Questions I had had since I was a little girl. I had waited such a long time to find out about my dad and I refused to waste the opportunity even if it meant getting hurt again.

Anyway, I didn't intend to get that close to her. I called the number on the letter and listened as the phone rang. Then I heard this chirpy husky sultry voice.

"Hello."

As I heard the voice my heart began to race.

"This is Dominiquè King, your sister—"

Before I could finish the word, she began screaming down the phone.

"It's my sissssssstttttttter! Auntie, it's her. How wonderful. It's really you. I'm talking to my sister."

She let out a squeal of glee.

"I'm in the car with my auntie, I mean our auntie."

She squealed again.

"Our auntie. Auntie C is our dad's sister."

Melissa sounded so exhilarated she made me feel giddy too. I wanted to meet her, even if it was only once.

"Where do you live?" I asked.

"I live in Brentfield Road, it's near Harlesden, do you know it?"

"Yes, I do. My cousin lives on Brentfield Road."

"Who's your cousin?"

"Trisha, do you know her?"

"Oh my God! Trisha's your cousin? It's a small world, we must have met at her wedding, were you there?"

"Yes, I was, I was serving in the kitchen."

Melissa's tone saddened briefly.

"Wow, you probably served me a drink and we didn't know we were sisters. Wow, so near but so far apart."

The thought that we had been in the same room about three years before felt odd.

"Shall we meet up? It may be easier to talk." I couldn't bear the suspense any longer.

"Yes, yes, I can't wait. I've waited so long to meet my baby sister. When?"

"I've just had a baby so…"

"Oh my God, I'm an auntie. Auntie, I'm an auntie. What did you have?"

"A boy called Monet and I have a daughter, Antoinette, she's sixteen."

"Oh my God, a boy and a girl, how lovely. I have a daughter too, her name is Porshia, and she's fourteen."

"Awwww, I can't wait to meet her and you."

We arranged to meet on the Sunday, because she was busy moving.

After all the anticipation of a first date, when the moment arrived, it was like we were old friends. There was nothing strained or awkward. We hugged for ages, she nearly squeezed the life out of me with the bear hug of a lifetime.

I told her I had had a C-section, but she didn't seem able to let go. I looked at her face and into her eyes, trying to see a resemblance or evidence to prove she was my sister.

We shared some facial features, but I think she could sense what I was doing because she said she looked like her mum and our Auntie C. She said I looked like her Auntie C too.

I found it strange because I knew I looked like my maternal grandmother Baa, but I never imagined I looked like my father's family too.

I hugged her daughter Porshia and introduced her to Antoinette and Mathew and showed them the baby. Antoinette took Porshia to her room and Mathew went to our bedroom with the baby, so Melissa and I could talk.

We talked for ages. Melissa started. She told me what she knew about our father and my so-called mother. She said she couldn't remember how old she was when she overheard a conversation about me. She asked her mum who I was, but her mum refused to answer her.

While Melissa talked, we held hands and when things got hard, we both gently caressed each other's hands.

Her mother remained tight-lipped but eventually she asked Auntie C, who told her the backdrop to us being sisters. Apparently, my father was living with Melissa's mum.

They lived on the same road as my so-called mother. My father started to have an affair with my so-called mother and they were not very discreet.

My father took my so-called mother in their home to show her his new baby girl, Melissa. Melissa's mum came home and found my so-called mother in her home, bacchanal broke out and my father had to break up the fight. The next thing my father told Auntie C that my so-called mother had had a baby, me.

My father wanted to be with my so-called mother, so he took her to live with his cousin A in Bedfordshire and then he kidnapped Melissa, so we could all live together.

But Melissa's mum stormed Bedfordshire to reclaim her daughter.

Then my so-called mother ended the relationship, leaving me and my dad in Bedfordshire. My father went back to Melissa's mum, leaving me in Bedfordshire with his cousin A's family.

Unfortunately, Melissa's memory of our father was limited. She was sent to Barbados to live with her maternal grandmother. She spent many years living there, so she only saw her parents when they came over on holiday. By the time she returned to live in England her parents had broken up and our father went to live in Barbados.

Melissa's biggest regret was he never got to meet his granddaughter. He died a year after Porshia was born.

Tears ran down Melissa's cheeks as she spoke. I gave her a hug. Listening to the detail sounded foreign. Hearing about my father and so-called mother's story was so weird. I felt awestruck. I actually had a beginning to my story.

Then Melissa told me about her life. She didn't really get on with her mum, but Auntie was like a mother to her. She loved Auntie so much, she had always been there for her and she didn't know what she would have done without her.

When she was pregnant with Porshia, she lived in a mother and baby home in Harlesden, which was crazy, as she was just one Number 18 bus ride away, so near yet so far.

I guess that's why people kept saying they had seen me places and I knew it wasn't me. They must've seen my sister. Hearing our paths had crossed throughout the years felt crazy and cruel, yet it made sense.

Melissa had had a difficult time when she had Porshia. She practically had to raise her on her own after the break-up of her relationship when Porshia was only one. Her mum offered no help, so she relied on her friends.

It was crazy to think we were both alone raising our daughters when we could have been doing it together.

Melissa finally got her flat on Brentfield Road. She had lived there until she bought a flat in Heathrow. She had considered buying in Stanmore but decided to get a flat closer to her work. She worked for United Airways at Heathrow Airport.

As she talked about her job she glowed. She loved her job because she loved people and loved to travel.

I laughed.

"I love travelling too."

Melissa giggled as she spoke.

"Wow spooky, I'm gonna add you to my concessions. You will love staff travel. We travel First Class."

"Yes, it's interesting. We use my brother-in-law's, Virgin staff travel."

"Well, you're going to love United, we go all over the world. As soon as I go back to work, I'm going to add my sister."

Melissa beamed with pride.

Melissa talked about her dating life. She had dated a lot but hadn't found anyone serious until she met Philip, who happened to be my cousin Trisha's good friend.

I knew Philip. I couldn't understand what she saw in him, but she said he was a freak like her, as she winked at me.

"I'm a Scorpion, you know what that means."

I laughed so loud it made my stitches pull.

"Yes, I do, because I'm a Scorpion too!"

"No way, you can't be!"

Melissa peered into my face as I laughed

"I am, my birthday is on the 26th October."

"Mine is the 5th November."

"What year were you born?"

"1967!"

"Oh my God. We are only eleven months apart. I was born in 1966."

Melissa started laughing hard.

"Our dad wasn't messing around, man."

We chatted for hours. We had a lot in common.

It was funny to think that she didn't get on with her mum and I didn't get on with my so-called mother. And she didn't grow with her father and I didn't either.

Melissa was about to make excuses to explain why my so-called mother hadn't told me about her. I cut her off by telling her about my childhood.

Melissa couldn't believe what a horrible time I had had but she was still reluctant to blame my so-called mother. Then I told her that I didn't know who my dad was until Monday when I got her letter.

And that's when she realised who she was dealing with. She switched emotions quickly. She resented my so-called mother for denying me the chance to know my father.

Melissa and I talked for hours. I was exhausted after she left. She had given me so much new information which I needed time to digest, but I felt a sense of relief. I knew my beginning and that provided me with a peace of mind I had never felt before. I went to bed with a new feeling of contentment.

After our first meeting we began to see a lot of each other and spent time together as a family. Melissa admired the fact I was married. She said I was like the big sister.

The more time we spent together the more I began to agree with her. Melissa seemed naïve, like she was living her life wearing rose-coloured glasses. She was cute.

Unfortunately, my experience of the world had forced me to take my rose-coloured glasses off when I was seven; after that life was too real.

After a few months Melissa took me to meet our father's family in Bedfordshire. I left Monet and Antoinette with Mathew, so I could take the time to focus on meeting my family I hadn't seen since I was a baby.

My father's cousin A had a big family, six children, but after a long marriage he had separated from his wife and had a new partner, so we had to go to so many houses.

We started off with Auntie A. As we pulled outside the house there was something familiar about it. I don't know what it was, but I could feel it. The front door of the terraced house blended into the neighbouring old red brick houses, there was nothing distinctive about my aunt's home.

From the moment the door opened Auntie was so glad to see me. I studied the face of my sweet-smiling, walnut-skinned, 5ft 4, hat-wearing old aunt.

She wouldn't stop hugging me. Then she started to cry. I thought she was just glad to see me, but she was in pain. Auntie explained how for years she had longed to see me, since my so-called mother had kidnapped me from her home over thirty years ago.

Auntie had looked after me from when I was about six months old until I was eighteen months old. My so-called mother had come to visit me. She asked Auntie if she could take me out to the park. Auntie had agreed reluctantly, and that was the last time she saw me.

As my Aunt relived my kidnapping, the pain overwhelmed her. I hugged her tight.

"Your mother was such a liar. You could never believe a word she said. I shouldn't have let her take you to the park. You were my baby. I had you from when you were six months old. You used to sleep in the cot with Imani."

I felt strange hearing the details of my early life. My aunt looked so heartbroken, but I felt so wanted. As she spoke, it was the first time I had ever heard that someone in my family had actually wanted me.

She stroked my hair as we sat on the sofa.

"You always had lovely hair. I used to brush it, it was so thick and long."

Auntie looked at me with such fondness, I hugged her tight. She showed me a picture of me as a baby. I had a pretty white dress on and my hair was in little bunches. I looked so cute. I had never seen me as a baby before. I finally knew what I looked like as a baby.

Looking at baby me made me feel wounded, I pitied myself. Looking at my picture made me feel deep sadness. I looked so content. I had no idea what horror I was yet to face. I felt such sadness for the little me in the picture.

Melissa could see it was getting overwhelming. She led our retreat. Auntie didn't want me to leave so she came with us to her daughter Imani's house, which was just around the corner, less than five minutes in the car.

As I stood in the doorway my cousin Imani hugged me close. She said she remembered me because everything she had she had to share with me. It was nice to hear someone else's fond memory of me as a baby. It was so new and surreal.

We chatted with Imani for a while and then we had to go to see her sister Maureen, who lived around another corner, with her husband and three sons. She remembered me too, but all I could remember was the way her dad called her name.

Next, we went to her dad's. As we entered the cramped maisonette, which was heaving with oversized furniture and cabinets full of china and glassware, he asked where we had been, and the way he said 'Maariaaan' resonated in me. It was just the way I remembered hearing it as a baby.

His Bajan British accent had a Barry White masculine tone which sounded familiar but that was my only connection. Looking at his bulging muscular bourbon frame, with youthful perfect teeth, triggered no memory.

Uncle A hugged me with love, like he knew me. Before we could sit down, he offered me a drink of rum and I couldn't say yes quick enough. I really needed a drink to help me, calm my racing emotions.

"You're your father's child. He loved a good drink. She's like him too."

Uncle pointed the rum bottle at Melissa and laughed as he poured us a round of rum.

While we sipped on our rum, straight, because he didn't have any Coke, he recounted the time when my dad had kidnapped Melissa and brought her to live at his house with my so-called mother and me.

"Your father loved your mother, and he really wanted to be with her. But it only lasted about six months and then Melissa's mum came and got her, and your mother left too. So your father went back to Melissa's mum and tried to work on the relationship. But you need to know, your father loved you so much, he wanted to be with you, but he couldn't cope when your mother left him."

As I watched my father's cousin, I couldn't deny his genuine loyalty and love for my father.

"He left you with us and though we had five kids already we loved you like the rest. But one day your nightdress caught fire, you was sitting too close to the gas fire."

As uncle recounted the incident, I could see my pink nightdress and I remembered how the fabric had melted like plastic at the bottom of my nightdress. Up until that moment this memory had no significance. Uncle continued, "The following Sunday your mother came to visit. She asked to take you to the park and never brought you back."

"Your mother was so wicked. She could have let us say goodbye, not run off with you like that... I was so mad with her. She nearly broke your aunt's heart. We didn't know where she had put you."

As he spoke, I could see the pain in his eyes and quizzical expression on his face. The event still didn't make sense to him or me. Why would she take me from my loving family to put me with white strangers?

Why did she take me away from the place my father had left me and where he could visit me to put me in a place where my father didn't visit me?

Hearing the backdrop of my life just confirmed what I knew already, my so-called mother hated me and wanted to get rid of me. Out of sight, out of mind.

My head was wrecked. I wanted to go home and sleep, but we had to go back to cousin Imani's because her sisters and brother were there waiting to see me and Melissa. Only one of Uncle A's children was missing, Ian; he lived in Australia with his wife.

As I drank more rum, which my uncle had given me, I got reacquainted with my cousins. They were all lovely and welcoming except for my cousin Vexelle. She was miffed. She blamed me for the fact her mother didn't love her like she loved me.

"My mum was so preoccupied with you she didn't really bond with me. Things were so bad I practically grew myself."

As I looked in her face I couldn't work out if she was joking or serious.

"Oh no, but you had such a big family, I'm sure you had lots of love."

She dismissed me with a fake laugh. I felt bad for her but what could I do? It wasn't my fault or my intention. I wasn't even aware that I had a family who loved and missed me.

My sister and I had a lovely summer's day with the family in beautiful Bedfordshire countryside; however a huge cloud hovered overhead, confirming my so-called mother's hate for me had held no bounds. Right from the start she has systematically sought to cause me optimum misery.

Back home, I attempted to process my early life. I had a father who loved me and wanted me.

Knowing this warmed my heart but my joy was tainted by the knowledge that my mother had ripped me from my family and my father to put me with white strangers. How do you reconcile being loved and hated for your sheer existence?

My emotions were in turmoil. I masked them by portraying the image of a doting mum, but on the inside I was a kaleidoscope of emotions. My feelings were jumbled and my sense of reality was askew.

And in the back of my mind I couldn't quite shift the question, is the arrival of my sister a good or bad omen?

19

KILLER DREAMS!

Having a miracle baby opens the floodgates. We had lots of visitors. Friends and family all came to see the miracle baby.

Mathew was a proud doting father. He felt so proud, he was like a lion with super sperm. He beamed as he was congratulated.

Mathew was good with the baby. He did the night shift while I slept, and I had the baby all day. Which did help because I was a slave to a good night's sleep.

I tried to bury my feelings deep inside me, so I could be the best mother I could be. I didn't want my son to feel unwanted or unloved, like I did when I was a child, so I put all my efforts into giving him the best care I could.

Monet was a really clever baby. He reached all his milestones early. He sat up at three months; crawled at five months and took his first steps at seven months. His speech was also advanced, so he could speak in sentences by eleven months.

At six months old, I put him in nursery part-time. I had to get back to work. Staying home staring at a baby was driving me out of my mind. Luckily, I got an agency team manager's post at Jewish Care in Stanmore and the nursery was in Stanmore, so everything was local.

Mathew was good with the baby, to a point; nappy changing, feeding him and singing to him, but the baby was very attached to me. Probably because I played with him all the time. I did activities with him on the days he was at home with me, and in the evenings, I read to him.

So despite my best attempts to help Mathew bond with the baby, Monet was a mummy's boy. A fact that drove me mad. The more I tried to escape from Monet, the tighter he clung to me. Mathew was pleased really, it meant he didn't really have to do much with him.

But I refused to let Mathew off the hook so easily. I endeavoured to share tasks with Mathew regardless of his protests. His main role was to bath Monet and put him to bed, but even that we took in turns.

But in the main Mathew continued with his old lifestyle. He was still out Thursday, Friday, and Saturday night to early morning or midday. It began to grate on me. I didn't mind it when I was out and about living my life but being stuck in with a baby wasn't my plan.

I attempted to bring the focus back to us. I proposed date nights. I wanted him to show interest in me and my needs. But it was pointless.

He didn't do anything to stimulate our marriage or me. My lifeline was regular moan calls to Jewel or a moany me camped out at her house. Auntie Kay's response was militant.

"You picked him, so make it work!"

So at the end of a few hours' solitude I'd return home determined to improve things, but change eluded me.

Mathew proved to be a huge disappointment. He had had his prayers answered, while all mine were unanswered. My life would've been bearable with a supportive husband. Instead Mathew became more and more self-serving.

Our relationship hit a brick wall for the first time in ten years. Our arguments included the possibility of breaking up.

I often considered running away and in my darkest despair, I contemplated jumping in front of a train. But the thought of my children's heartbreak blocked my plans.

Shackled to my life I focused my energy on Monet. His beautiful pale caramel, dimpled-filled smile and loving eyes insisted I give him the best of life.

Years later I realised how much I had blanked out periods of time. Looking at pictures of Monet aged eight or nine years old, I was struck by his chubby cheeks. How come I didn't know he had cheeks like a chipmunk? I had clearly detached my consciousness without knowing.

The christening provided a brief distraction. I organised the royal event of the year. We had an ivory and gold theme. Monet was a miracle, so he deserved a grand theme.

Despite it being a 9.30am service the church was packed. At the service I wore a lovely gold dress and gold shoes, I had my hair up with barrel rolls on the top and straight down my back with big curls.

Mathew wore a blue suit with a gold tie and a wicked pair of Patrick Cox shoes. Monet had a beautiful linen ivory and gold suit with a little hat to match and ivory shoes.

He looked gorgeous. Monet had six godparents. We knew this was a once in a lifetime thing as we would not be having any more children, so we wanted Monet to be spoiled by a big support network.

I really wanted Jewel to be a godparent, but she refused, saying she didn't want Antoinette to have to share her godmother.

Monet was great during the service. He didn't cry when they put the water on his head, but he wouldn't go to a soul, not even his father, which was deeply irritating to me. I wanted Mathew to carry his bundle of joy; instead Monet was stuck to me like glue.

Because the service was so early there was a big gap until the reception. Luckily Alan's girlfriend Maricka was a great help. She cooked breakfast for everyone, which was about twenty people, and Mathew cleaned up.

Before I knew it, it was time to go and set the hall up. We decorated the hall with gold and ivory decorations and balloons. Monet had three christening cakes, which included a two-tier cake. We had lovely speeches, except for the ones where people said they knew we would have a baby. I don't know where they got their information from but clearly they had the inside track. A shame they didn't use their gift of foresight to make us rich.

Apart from the irritating speeches we had a lovely reception, with great music, and an abundance of food and drink. We partied until 11pm.

What I liked the most about the christening was the fact I didn't have to do anything except carry the bundle of joy. Our family and friends, including Melissa, served the food and drinks and even cleaned up at the end. It was wicked.

Once the christening was out the way we settled down to normal life. Mathew and I were both enjoying our careers but now we had to balance a new ball, a baby. However, I was the only one balancing the balls.

Distraction was my key to ignoring the inequality of the division of labour, but it was hard. I struggled to understand how a man can pray for a child but refuse to alter his life for the child once he gets it. I just didn't expect Mathew to be that guy.

Jewel and her family were a great support to me for about the first two years and then Jewel decided she wanted to go travelling around the Caribbean and then settle in Barbados.

Her decision rocked my world. I was so used to having her around to keep me on track and to keep my spirits up, I just couldn't imagine my life without her nearby for support.

Jewel was more than just a friend, she was my mother and my father, she was my confidante. Jewel had been my constant, reliable friend since I was eleven years old.

Jewel knew my pain, she knew where I had come from, how far I had come, she loved me and kept me moving forward on my track. I had no backup plan, no alternative support, no one who I could trust like I trusted Jewel. I begged her not to go but somehow I assisted in making the dream come true.

Jewel wanted a travelling companion and by some crazy coincidence a member of staff in my team had mentioned to me that she wanted to go travelling too.

Despite my internal objections and resistance, I linked them up and the next thing I knew I was waving them off at Jewel's leaving party. They travelled around the Caribbean for about six months and then Jewel went to live in Barbados.

I talked to her two or three times a week and visited her often, about three times a year. Those trips saved my life. They gave me space to recuperate from juggling all the balls and gave me a break from being Monet's mummy.

Luckily my sister Melissa kept her word. She put me on her concessions and so it was really cheap for me to travel to Barbados.

One time I went to visit Jewel while she was staying with Uncle Granham who lived in St George.

Jewel and her mum were building their home in St James. It was a huge three-apartment block with shared garden and garage. While it was being built Jewel stayed with Uncle Granham.

Uncle Granham was a big man, about our parents' age, but despite his age, he was really great fun. He used to live in England before retiring to the island of his birth.

Unfortunately, his wife didn't share his dream, so she stayed in England and visited regularly.

Uncle Granham knew everybody on the island, so his house was always buzzing with visitors. He loved to entertain and he loved to cook for his guests. We always had such fun with him.

One night Jewel and I decided to go out into town. Uncle Granham gave us a front door key. Unfortunately, we had not planned our night out well because once in town we found out that on a Monday night the whole island is dead. Not a thing was going on.

Somehow we ended up in After Dark, which was usually a nightclub, but on a Monday night it was just a bar with a few drunk karaoke singers.

Reluctantly, we stayed for a few drinks. I think the barman spiked my drink because the next thing I knew I was pissed. Lightweight Jewel was killing herself laughing.

We took a taxi home and attempted to get into the house. But for some reason our key wouldn't work. We both tried to get the key to work, but no luck. Locked out, we knocked and banged on the door and the living room window, but we just couldn't wake up Uncle Granham.

I was so pissed I found the whole thing hilarious until I needed to go to the toilet. I held it for as long as I could before I had to surrender to nature and pee in a bucket in the garage.

Jewel found it hilarious because I was stumbling all over the place. She wasn't sure if I could get the pee in the bucket.

We ended up sleeping in the gallery with towels from the washing line around our shoulders to keep the chill of the night off us and the mosquitoes at bay. About 5am Uncle Granham found us sleeping in the gallery.

He found it so funny. He couldn't understand how he had managed to give us the wrong key but the whole thing 'sweet him' none the less. Jewel and I kept that joke alive for time. It had been such a funny night.

About three years after Jewel left to go and live in Barbados, her mum decided to go too. And then about one year after her mum went Chrystal went too. I was devastated. It was bad enough not having Jewel nearby but at least I had the rest of the family. I understood why they went; Auntie Kay had retired, and her sister Auntie Jeannette had already retired in Barbados and they were inseparable, so I knew it was only a matter of time before Auntie Kay would go too.

But Chrystal shocked me. She had struggled to cope without the support of her mum and then when her dad died suddenly in Barbados, she just decided to pack up and go for good. It was the final blow to my infrastructure. I found life really hard without my support network.

Luckily Melissa and I had been getting on great, we had so much in common. She loved to rave and so did I. She loved to drink rum and brandy and so did I.

Neither one of us could get drunk. No matter how much we drank we still couldn't. Apparently neither could our dad or his brothers, so the inability to get drunk was definitely in our genes.

Melissa loved lovers rock and so did I, and what was scary we both used to say, 'tune' when one of our favourite songs came on.

The first time it happened we said tune in unison. It was scary. We both looked at each other and laughed. It was like we were twins.

I had introduced Melissa and her daughter Porshia to my family. They blended in really well.

Before Jewel left to go off on her travels, she kept saying you'll be all right, you have your sister now. You don't need me. I was not as optimistic because I knew the relationship I had with Jewel was beyond comparison.

My experience of blood relations to date ensured I had no intention of putting all my faith in my relationship with Melissa.

Luckily, I had other good friends, like my friend Rose. She and I worked together for about five years. We established the specialised project for young women together.

Rose and I had a fantastic relationship. It was so good it used to bother Mathew. Rose and I used to work together all day and speak on the phone all night; it used to drive Mathew crazy.

At one point Mathew was convinced Rose was in love with me. But what Mathew didn't understand was that Rose and I were counsellors for each other and we provided support to each other which was free but professional.

We also used to provide good caring, compassionate support to each other because we both came from traumatic childhoods and our families were challenging. When Rose went into counselling our supportive relationship changed but we remained great friends.

My other sistren is Annemarie. Annemarie's childhood had been so traumatic we had bonded because we were child soldiers, and we had battled against all odds to make a life for ourselves.

Another lifelong friend is Pat. We met through her sister, in the early 90s. We bonded over day-to-day life as we raised our families. After a twenty-five-year relationship, I shared the details of my childhood. Pat couldn't believe how close we had become without her really knowing my past.

252

All my friends were a great support and motivators, but Jewel was gone. I missed her terribly. When the family departed, they left a great big hole in the family.

Festive occasions were different. We had to go to Barbados to get a taste of the good old family times, but that's life, it moves forwards not backwards, and nothing ever stays the same.

As is my way, I attempted to stay focused and motivated. I tried to make the most of the changes, but it was hard.

Melissa and I began to have difficulties. The first big one was one Christmas. We had started to spend Boxing Day with our cousins in Bedfordshire. It was great fun. There was something for everyone. We played games, played music, and it was great.

But this particular year, I couldn't find my sister Melissa. I had called all her numbers. I had called her mum. I had called our Auntie C, but I just couldn't track her down.

By the time I got to Bedfordshire, I was fraught. I started to panic that something awful had happened to her. I pretended to enjoy myself at Imani's, but I just couldn't stop worrying.

Then just when I was contemplating calling the police, I got a text from her to say, 'Happy Christmas. I'm having a great Christmas in Barbados. I didn't tell you because I didn't want you to be jealous!'

I was livid. Who does that? Who just goes on holiday and doesn't tell their family? I was so pissed off, I couldn't even speak. Pure madness. Her behaviour felt cruel and thoughtless. I put my irritation aside and moved forward.

The next issue of concern for me happened after a night at our cousins in Bedfordshire. We had been having a great time and we had been drinking.

We all left together at about 2 or 3am. Melissa drove with Porshia and Antoinette, while Mathew and I drove together with Monet. Melissa drove ahead as we followed her.

After several miles of driving behind her Mathew became concerned about her driving. She was driving really fast, which was usual, but she seemed to be swerving in and out of her lane.

Mathew and I observed Melissa's erratic driving through the morning dew, for several miles, getting increasingly anxious. At the end of our deliberation, Mathew decided to flash his fog lights to get her to pull over. Confused about what to do, I approached the car.

As Melissa looked back, bewildered, I opened the back passenger door and I took Antoinette out of the car.

"What's wrong, did something happen?"

"We don't like the way you're driving. Antoinette can come with us."

I didn't wait for her response. Before we reached our car, Melissa had sped off. Once home, I texted her to check she got home safely. She responded saying she was home, but it was about a week before we spoke again.

When she eventually took my call, she told me she was really upset with me because I took Antoinette out of the car and I left Porshia. I said my priority was to my daughter but as Porshia was her daughter, she was her responsibility and I didn't feel it was right to take her daughter.

Talking it through didn't result in a shared understanding, so we just agreed to disagree. I thought we were fine for a while until our Barbados trip.

Melissa and I had planned the holiday together. She wanted to take me to meet our grandmother and the rest of our father's family.

We couldn't all stay together so I had arranged to stay at my friend Gloria's apartment in St James and Melissa was going to stay with our cousin Colin, who lived behind our grandmother's house.

Mathew, Antoinette, Porshia, Monet and I were all set to stay at the apartment but when we arrived in the late afternoon it was clear that we would not be able to stay there.

Standing outside the front door we could pass a screwdriver through the door frame. The apartment needed major repairs including secure front and back doors. Against my better judgement we ended up staying at my Auntie Viola's.

I had sworn I would never stay at her house again after the last incident over the phone bill, but we were in a desperate situation and it was the only plan B I could think of which wasn't going to cost us money we didn't have.

Amazingly, Auntie Viola was delighted to have us all; she rolled out the red carpet despite us turning up without prior notice. It was clear that she was prepared to eat humble pie, so I tried to put the awful memory of our last visit out of my mind.

The first meeting with my father's mother was strange. I felt devoid of any emotion. I felt quite matter of fact, definitely detached, like I was just checking people off my list.

My experience of family had taught me blood didn't mean a thing, especially when that blood was acquired in such shady circumstances.

I knew meeting my grandmother wasn't going to change my life. It just meant I would know who my people were, so we could avoid breeding monkeys.

My grandmother did hug me but she kind of read me, like she was looking for proof that I was her kin. I guess she found something in my appearance because she did kind of mellow.

Gran showed me pictures of my father and other family members. We also took some pictures with her and our families together, three generations together. Just our father and his siblings were missing.

Our gran had four children, including our father, three boys and a girl, but all three of her sons had died and she only had her daughter C left. Auntie C was in England, so it was a picture with just us.

Connecting with Gran highlighted how easily I had bonded well with Auntie C, she was so gentle and kind. She was easy to love.

But this introduction felt cold. I knew I wasn't going to bond with my gran. She seemed so distant and I couldn't be arsed. Maybe all we had in common was blood and mutual respect and that's all we needed.

After the family bubble had burst after meeting my cold new grandmother, my need to meet all the family dispelled too. I felt emotionally drained. I didn't need any more family, just knowing who my father was and how much he loved me was more than enough.

A few days later Melissa and I had planned to go raving, so Mathew and I drove over to Gran's house.

Despite our relentless searching we just couldn't find the small gap in the road which led to the house. We drove up and down the main road, but we just couldn't find the turning. We asked people, we went into the gas station and asked for directions, but we just couldn't find the road. (This was in the days before mobile phones). After nearly two hours of driving around, frustrated and jarred, we just went off into town on our own.

The next day cousin Colin cussed me off, on the phone, telling me how wicked I was for leaving Melissa dressed waiting for us to pick her up. My man wouldn't even listen to reason, he just hung up.

Melissa and I ended up having separate holidays. I gave up trying to explain. She was too pissed off to listen. Two weeks later we met up at the airport to fly back home.

⁓

Back home my life was overwhelming, but I just kept running, hoping things would get easier. When Monet was about seven years old, I realised for the first time I was depressed. I felt so unhappy with the life I was living.

Looking at Mathew confirmed to me some dreams should remain just that, a dream. Mathew didn't appear to be living his dream. He was just living like nothing had changed.

While I was trying to live his dream, he did absolutely nothing to nurture me, to make me feel it was all worthwhile, or I was appreciated.

I was working as a senior manager in social care and I loved my job. I had developed into a successful strategic manager.

My fostering and adoption services received national recognition for innovation and trailblazing standards.

As a result of my rewarding salary and bonuses we could live the high life. Mathew's work with young people was also making waves as he continued to work as a youth worker.

Luckily our finances increased sufficiently to pay for a local nursery place, the price of which astounded us. For sixteen hours per week, we paid £950 per month, plus a supply of nappies and soya milk.

Our options were none; the borough of Harrow had only two full-time nurseries. Acorn Nursery provided an exceptional standard of care and early learning.

Monet developed socially and academically, which helped us to accept the high cost of his childcare. It also prepared our pockets for private school.

I thought as long as we could afford the school fees, putting Monet in a private school would be a breeze. I wasn't prepared for the assessment/selection process and neither was Monet.

His response was the same at every school. He'd look around the school, clinging to my leg, then he'd refuse to go with the other children into the assessment room.

Regardless of my attempts to prepare him or coax him, he could not be moved. Needless to say, he didn't get a place at any of our preferred schools.

After weeks of trying to successfully get him through the process, he finally got a place at Quainton Hall Boys School. Reluctantly we accepted the place, mindful that an all-boys school wasn't going to be a natural fit for Monet, who enjoyed playing with boys and girls.

Monet's transition from nursery school was smooth until he moved up a year. The new teacher brought with her a disdain for boys, which was crazy, given she worked in an all-boys school.

Monet went from being a happily confident, creative, six-year-old to an unsure, weepy silent child.

We had several meetings with the teacher and the head of the school, in an attempt to identify what was going wrong and what support Monet needed.

The horrible teacher deflected her issues onto Monet, saying he had special learning needs and she thought he had a learning difficulty, but she wasn't sure what it was. Pure madness.

As I attempted to tread water in the shackles of my idiosyncrasies, this was just something else I had to address.

I was aware that Monet was struggling with reading and maths, but I didn't think he had a learning disability. I was convinced he just had an awful teacher.

My commitment to support Monet's learning was relentless. Every evening after a full day's work, making, serving and eating dinner together as a family, I'd spend at least an hour helping Monet with his homework and reading.

I found it really jarring after a hard day managing people and resources, particularly as Monet struggled with the basics.

I couldn't figure out the block to his learning. He was so bright. From the age of one I started teaching him colours, the alphabet and numbers, to spell and a little bit of reading.

I duplicated the same early learning method which worked with Antoinette. But my approach had hit a blockage. As I battled to help I realised my method was making things worse. Monet became more and more stressed and anxious as he fought to read a word or work out a sum.

I just didn't have the patience Monet needed. I tried to get Mathew to help him, but he couldn't be bothered. To appease me he'd pretend to listen to Monet read. Every time I spied on him, I'd observe him watching the TV, just letting Monet read without correcting his punctuation or missed words or anything.

I might as well have got Monet to read to himself. And it was pointless asking Mathew to help Monet with his spellings because he said he struggled with spelling himself, so he couldn't teach him.

It was just an excuse and a way to get out of doing what he was supposed to.

So I had to do it all. I decided to get Monet tested to see if he really did have a learning disability, because if he did, I needed to know what it was, so I could get him the help he needed.

I paid for an educational psychologist assessment. The assessment confirmed that Monet did not have a learning difficulty, but he had not learnt what he needed to during the year he was with the awful teacher and instead his confidence had been knocked.

The process also identified Monet's high level of IQ and understanding, which was assessed as being the age of thirteen or fourteen, fantastic for a seven-year-old.

Monet's learning block was cured by an exceptional black male tutor, Ian. He provided Monet with a great male role model while teaching him the basics in English and Maths, starting from word building and one plus one.

Ian rebuilt Monet's confidence and knowledge. He was great. So on top of paying for a private prep school we also had to pay for a tutor for two hours per week.

Unfortunately, when Monet started private school we couldn't find any one to collect him from school, so Mathew had to go part-time for about two years.

Life just wouldn't give me air… outside of school, things weren't much better for Monet. None of our friends or family had children his age, all his cousins were much older than him, which caused problems for Monet and me. We were both lonely.

At his first birthday party he was the only child. His cousins came to celebrate with him, but they were all between nineteen and twenty-five years old. He only had children to play with at school. And as a result, he was really mature, like a little man.

Antoinette used to play with him every now and then, but she was sixteen years older than him. Mathew didn't really bother with him; he said he was too much of a mummy's boy.

His main complaint was that Monet didn't like anything he liked, and he didn't like watching children's TV. As if I enjoyed watching *Teletubbies* or *Tweenies*.

But when you have a young child that is what you have to do, unless you are Mathew, in which case you don't have to, you can leave it to somebody else.

Mathew failed to be wowed by Monet's gifts. From about three his artistic buds began to bloom. As he succumbed to his creative energy, he'd make so many things out of paper and Sellotape, including shoes, skirts and wigs.

Monet's talent was amazing. On his fifth birthday he made me a pleated skirt to wear to his party.

The design detail was fantastic. Each pleat was exact, like a real skirt, and he finished the design with some ribbon which he used to tie it around my waist. It fit perfectly.

I was so proud of Monet's genius. Unfortunately his father wasn't; he'd rather he focused on playing football.

"Too much gal business. He doesn't play with boys' things."

I attempted to get him to understand that toys aren't gender specific, but he refused to accept it. Mathew nearly lost his mind when I bought Monet a *Girl's World*.

"Why do you keep buying him girls' things? Can't you buy him something for boys?"

His ignorance pricked me.

"I buy him what he likes. He likes to do hair, so I bought him a head, so he can practise doing hair. What is your problem? Is it the toys or are you frightened he is going to be gay?"

He was so angry.

"I don't think he's going to be gay but if you keep treating him like a girl he soon will be."

I looked him straight in the face.

"If he's going to be gay, he's going to be gay. What he plays with is not going to affect his sexuality. Let the boy play and be happy."

This was the first of many ignorant arguments, but I didn't care. I wanted my son to be a happy child, free to play with any toy he wanted to.

As Monet's artistic flair developed so did his medium of choice. When he was seven, Melissa bought him his first sewing machine. And so Monet was left to me to raise, with a father who focused on his street life more than his home life.

As I began to drown, I ran faster. I think this is how I started travelling on my own. Usually I visited Jewel and occasionally I went on holiday with Melissa.

It was on the way back from a trip to Dubai with Melissa, as I sat enjoying the flight, that my feelings overwhelmed me. I don't know what the trigger was but all of a sudden, I was sobbing, uncontrollably. I just couldn't stop my tears from falling. Luckily, I was in a First-Class pod, away from the rest of Melissa and her friends.

I fought to regain my composure but inside I had this overpowering feeling of impending doom. My tears just kept coming. I sobbed for about an hour and every time I thought the sadness had passed the tears started up again.

I felt so deeply broken inside, but I just couldn't understand why. After a few hours of trying to make sense of my feelings with no luck, I had to just accept my heart was in pieces. Acknowledging my pain gradually stopped my tears from flowing. Thankfully, my breakdown went unnoticed. Neither Melissa nor her friends had seen me. I was able to disembark with a fake smile.

Returning home from a five-day holiday robbed me of the opportunity to decompress as my escape was only temporary; I had to go back to my life. And Mathew hadn't bothered to take Monet to school for at least two days, which was all he would admit to.

He was full of excuses. He hadn't heard the alarm and when he eventually woke up it was too late to take Monet to school or for him to go to work.

His ridiculousness lit a fuse paper in my head with questions fuelling the flames. How could a grown man fail to take his child to school? What message did it send to Monet? Was Monet going to grow up to be irresponsible too?

I just couldn't do it anymore. I wanted a partner in life, not another child. But I ended up with two for one. I felt so exhausted. I was tired of having to do everything. I was tired of having to arrange everything.

All Mathew had to do was show up, and he would, but late. I guess it's a side effect from smoking too much weed, which remained his passion. High-grade weed first, then nightlife and gambling.

Upon reflection my initial decision to compromise and date a man who smoked set a pattern in motion which led me to overlook the impact of living with a man addicted to drugs and vices which compromised my own standards of living.

Culturally, weed is ranked with smoking, but if he was an alcoholic, starting his day with a drink, I would've left his ass long ago.

Mathew's lifestyle was incompatible with normal family life. Regardless of our plans he always showed up tired and sleep-deprived. His contribution would usually be to serve drinks and do the washing-up. And then he would fall asleep, even if we had guests.

Going out together became a distant memory, and so too was Mathew's interest in having fun with me. He never took me anywhere. If we went out for a meal it was always to our local steak house or Chinese restaurant.

Like a spoilt teenager he refused to try some new cuisine. Determined to get my needs met, I took him to a local French restaurant in Harrow on the Hill, near Harrow School.

He ensured the night was a bust by sulking and complaining about everything and nothing. My attempts to enjoy the ambiance and lovely food was futile with a brat at my table.

As we drove away from the restaurant, I felt irritated and at the end of my frayed rope. I voiced my thoughts.

"Why is it you seem to have so much fun with everyone except me?"

"What did you expect, D? You know I don't like that type of food. You know what I like, we should have gone to Leaf Robinson."

"Why couldn't you just make the most of a romantic evening with your wife? No, that was too much to ask, instead you had to snarl all night."

"It wasn't that bad, but I just don't like the French or their food. If you want romance, you should have taken me somewhere else."

I peered at him in the dark car. He looked reticent. His arrogance grated on me.

"Why is it always on me to do everything? You can book a table somewhere, but you can't be bothered. You'd rather get high with the man dem or go gambling. You never think about me and what I enjoy."

"What do you want from me? We just went out together. Nothing's ever enough for you, I just can't win."

My pressure began to boil as his words hit my last nerve. I laughed instead of punching the dashboard.

"You don't even try to please me. How could you, doing you is a full-time job!"

"You have changed since you had Monet. You're never happy anymore. You need to stop letting your childhood affect your life, start enjoying the life you have."

As he parked the car in our drive, I studied his face to see if he was serious. My inner voice screamed, what do you do to make me happy while I'm living a nightmare? But he got out of the car without answering me.

It was clear he couldn't hear my inner voice or frankly-spoken words.

I heard though, loud and clear; the problem was me. So I continued running and balancing every demand without dwelling on the void in me. I focused on the family and my work. But deep inside I was screaming, what about me? I am so unhappy. What about me? Why won't you just comfort me? I had to be a good mother to my son but all I really wanted to do was run for the hills and do me.

A few months later, Monet woke me out of my sleep asking, "Why did the lady put the willy in her mouth?" I was so disorientated. I was still half-asleep and didn't know what he was talking about.

"Who's putting what in their mouth?"

I tried to surface but sleep was killing me.

"On the telly the woman put the willy in her mouth."

I jumped up and went downstairs where I saw Mathew asleep on the sofa. On the television was a porn movie. And true enough the woman did have a man's cock in her mouth.

I switched the TV off while shouting at Mathew. Monet beat a speedy retreat upstairs.

"What is wrong with you? Can't you take this thing out when you're done? Why do you have to leave it playing for your son to see it? What are you doing? What is wrong with you? You say you want a child and when you get him this is the stupidness you do."

"D, I didn't do it on purpose, I fell asleep."

His response floored me. I was incredulous. I couldn't bear to look at him and I definitely didn't want to hear another word of foolishness. I just went back into my room and shut the door.

Mathew's reckless lifestyle had hit a new low. Now he was corrupting and abusing our son while putting our careers on the line, with the possibility of a child protection investigation if Monet told his teacher what he saw.

My fury hit seven on the Richter Scale. I was ready to erupt. I sought out the support of my friends, but I didn't get any, just women making excuses for the inexcusable.

All my hope had diminished in time for my big 40th birthday. He confirmed my disillusion by saying, "You know I can't buy for you… I'm not a great organiser like you." Code for, I can't be arsed to do anything unless it's for myself.

Lazy doesn't go far enough to define Mathew. Regardless of how many clues I gave him. I love gold, diamonds. I could never have too much jewellery.

My perfumes have stayed the same since we met and are on display on our dressing table. I love Chinese or French cuisine, so how hard could it be to buy me a nice gift or arrange something for me?

To rub salt in my wounds, over the years I had gone above and beyond for his birthdays. I had surprised him with a Formula 1 driving experience which included arranging for his friends to be there to see him do his circuit.

I surprised him with an all-expenses paid trip to Las Vegas, which included limousine transfers, a suite at the world-famous Bellagio Hotel, plus gambling money.

I had thrown him three surprise birthday parties, the last one being his 40th birthday party. Melissa's husband had a link to use a private members club in Westbourne Park.

I hired our usual DJs, bought £1,000 of drinks. His sister had made his cake and I had some family do some nibbles. I even hired a limo to take us to the club.

On the night of the party I told Mathew I had VIP tickets to see Morgan Heritage, so he put on his tailored cream silk linen suit. He must have heard the limo pull up outside, so he peered out of the bedroom window.

"That limo won't be able to turn around down here, I wonder who's got a limo booked?"

When he looked in my face, he saw my grin.

"Babe, you got us a limo, wow you are really going to town! I'm only 40! Awww, you're too much!"

He pulled me close and kissed me so passionately. I laughed inside, thinking *wow, if he's that happy with a limo, what's he gonna do for a surprise party?*

My sister Melissa was lookout and greeter at the club. The limo took us on a 45-minute tour of London before arriving at the club. Melissa called to check where we were, so I made out that she wanted us to pop in for a drink before we went to the concert.

When the limo pulled up outside the members only club, Mathew got excited.

"Wow, how did Melissa get in this club? It's members only. Me and T have been trying to get in here for years!"

I acted a bit shocked.

"I think she knows a member or something."

Mathew led the way up the stairs to the first floor.

As we entered the lounge area everyone shouted, "Surprise!" Mathew was so shocked to see all his friends and family.

I gave him a bottle of Chrystal champagne. As I gave him a kiss on the lips, "Happy birthday, darling," I whispered.

He hugged me so close.

"D, you shouldn't have done all this, how did you do it?"

I just laughed and walked away, leaving him to celebrate with his friends.

I guess he never did work out how I planned a surprise birthday party because he never planned any parties for me.

Two years later, when it was my 40th birthday, I organised my own champagne party with performances from two of my favourite lovers rock singers: Caroll Thompson and Paul Dawkins.

All I asked him to do was to find me a small intimate venue, which would allow late night parties; definitely no school halls.

About a month before my birthday he told me he had found a great venue in Harrow, which we could have until 2am, but usually he just gave the keys and asked the people to lock up the venue and return the keys the next day.

I spent the build-up to my party losing weight, so I would fit into the most perfect figure-hugging gown. I paid for professional decorators to decorate the hall with a champagne theme. I had paid Scandals to do the catering and I booked my favourite DJs, Bushman and Young Bushman.

On the day of my party I turned up at the venue to discover that it was exactly what I didn't want, a school hall.

There was no possible way of having an intimate party, so having a wicked rave went out the window! I was so pissed off; my face was like thunder.

Mathew attempted to appease me.

"The hall can be divided." When he showed me some cricket curtain, I was too angry to respond. I just left to get ready.

I had planned to make a dramatic entrance at 9.30pm. Mathew was due to pick me up at 9.15. My prep went to plan, bath, dress, make-up and ready to go.

I waited and waited for Mathew. I should have got a cab but I just kept expecting him to turn up and every time I called him, he kept saying I'll be there in five minutes.

He eventually arrived at 10.45. I was so furious. I thought I was going to explode. Instead I seethed in silence. Years later, when I recounted how I felt arriving 'tardy for my party', Annemarie said she didn't realise I was upset. It was at that moment I realised that since Nanny had died when I was seven, I had learnt how to mask my pain.

As I walked towards the hall, oblivious to my special guests, Caroll Thompson and Paul Dawkins, the property manager stopped me as I approached the door and whispered, "The party will be finishing at 1am on the dot." I didn't reply.

I entered my party with a red-carpet catwalk as they played 'She's Royal' by Taurus Riley. It was 11pm.

Vexed and disappointed, I attempted to enjoy my party but as I greeted my guests all I could think about was the fact it would be finished in a flash.

The performances by Caroll Thompson and Paul Dawkins were exceptional, they really made the night for me.

The lack of time really bothered me. Luckily my cousin Toni talked the property owner into allowing the party to go on until 2am, so my party lasted three hours.

At the end of the party I began my speech, but my words were distorted by my tears as I had a meltdown. Suddenly my stacked-up frustration and the harsh reality of my marriage leaked out of me uncontrollably.

My tears wouldn't stop. At that moment I knew my marriage was over. I was sick and tired of being last on my husband's list. The party had amplified the problems in my life in a way which unmasked my feelings. All my emotions ran free as I ended the chapter in my speech.

A few days later a dear friend chastised me for having a meltdown in front of people. She was more concerned about what my guests would think than about me.

Thankfully the spill-over party back at the house delayed Mathew and me from talking. But the moment came as we lay in bed the next day.

I listened to Mathew's attempt to blow off my emotional outburst by giving me the details of what had gone wrong, but even in his narrative he failed to see the error of his judgement in putting other people before me.

What irritated me the most was the simple fact that I did everything I could to make him feel like my king, but what I got back in return was less than nothing. And worse, leading by example had been less than useless because he just didn't get it.

For months after, I attempted to put my emotional jack back in the box, by hiding my feelings. I motivated myself by trying harder to improve my relationship, with the mantra, if I gave 100%, eventually things would click into place and my marriage would again be a happy one.

His stockpiled response was to blame our problems on my childhood. What did that have to do with the fact he wasn't present in our marriage or capable of living his own dream?

Exhausted, I kept running.

20

CREATIVITY IS A GREAT DISTRACTION!

To take my mind off my problem(s), six months after my party I started a travel journalism course at Harrow College.

The course was a step out of my comfort zone but I relished the opportunity to expand my mind. The first class had gone well. Feeling chuffed with my accomplishment, I beat a hasty retreat down the stairs, when some guy bumped into me while another guy laughed.

Slightly miffed I attempted to ignore the fool but the guys were laughing at me. I opened my mouth to cuss them when I clocked my ex, Charles. He peered at me with his Adonis smile.

"Why didn't you cuss the man for bumping into you?"

Looking at him made me smile.

"I'm a peaceful person. It's not that serious."

"You lie, you lie. You know you wanted to cuss him!"

I just laughed. Charles didn't take his eyes off me as we chatted.

"What are you doing here?"

"I'm doing a travel journalism course. What are you doing here?"

"I work here, teaching computer classes."

We talked until we got to the bottom of the stairs and, as we took the last step, Charles swept me up off the step into a tight hug.

He kissed me on the cheek and told me he had missed me. As he looked into my eyes, I felt a sudden chill. Charles looked so good, he hadn't aged a bit. His hair was still jet black, his eyes were still hazel brown and his lips still looked as juicy as ever.

"You better put me down before your wife gets one of her spies to kill me."

He laughed through his smile.

"You mean your husband will kill me!"

I could feel a rush of sensations. I had to get away from him. I made a feeble excuse and ran off out of the building. But all the way home all I could think about was how beautiful Charles looked and how gentle his kiss had been.

I decided I had to do whatever it took to avoid seeing him again. It should've been easy; my course was one day a week.

My strategy was to arrive promptly and go straight to class and leave immediately after. And if I bumped into Charles, I would not let him kiss me again.

Unfortunately, the plan was not foolproof. The very next week I attended the class I bumped into Charles in the canteen during a ten-minute break.

Charles crept up behind me and hugged me. I wanted to reprimand him or even shake him off, but I just couldn't do it.

He made me sit down to have my snack. I should have just left. I didn't even want the snack anymore, I suddenly felt sick. All I could manage to do was drink my Ribena, as he talked and flirted with me.

We did a quick catch-up, talking about our children and siblings. And out of nowhere he changed the topic.

"My marriage is in trouble. We haven't been getting on for years, but we have stayed together for the children!"

I didn't know what to say, so I said nothing.

"How are you and Mathew? Are you still happily married?"

I lied, "Yes. We have been married for twelve years and together for seventeen."

"Wow. Congratulations. What is your secret?"

I gave him some garbled response and then we started to reminisce about our relationship.

"Why didn't you want to have my baby? We would make a beautiful baby."

I laughed uncontrollably. Charles sounded exactly the same as he did seventeen years earlier. I couldn't believe he hadn't got over it. All of a sudden, and I don't know why, he put his hand on my knee.

His touch created a rush of sensations, which ran through my body. It took every fibre in my body to take his hand off my knee.

"What are you frightened of? We are both married. You are perfectly safe with me!"

He spoke with a grin on his face. I knew at that moment he could feel what I was feeling, and I was not safe with him. I jumped up and ran to class. I didn't even say goodbye.

But he did. I could hear his words echoing behind me.

"I hope to see you soon!"

As I sat in the classroom, I felt panic as I battled to think straight. I don't know what the tutor was teaching, I couldn't concentrate.

I felt warm tingles as my mind replayed seeing Charles. I knew the feelings were wrong, but I just couldn't fight them. I tried to think about Mathew's handsome face but just as I could see it Charles's face would replace it.

It was so strange. I had never ever thought about another man since I was with Mathew, well, except Denzel Washington, and he doesn't count. I refused to fight my imaginary crush. But Charles was real and the warm sensation I felt wasn't my imagination.

Despite my avoidance strategy, Charles had another plan called 'find her'. No matter where I'd go he'd seek me out. He distracted me to the point I couldn't study. All I could think about was him.

We started having our breaks together off-campus. And it was during a lunch break he kissed me for the first time. I knew it was wrong to kiss him back but I just couldn't stop myself. His kiss caressed my whole body and I felt the sensations to my core.

As the warm feeling touched my vulva I pushed him away.

"I'm married. And I love my husband. Don't you dare ever kiss me again!"

I ran out of the restaurant. He tried to run after me but he had to pay the bill.

From then on, I attempted to put distance between us by skipping a couple of classes, and I refused to take his phone calls. I didn't want another man. I just wanted my man to be the man I needed him to be. I refused to be compromised. I had never been a cheater and I wasn't about to start now.

Charles refused to give me up without a struggle. He kept blowing up my phone. One morning Mathew was dropping me to the train station, when my phone started blowing up. I kept rejecting the calls, but Charles just called back.

Mathew asked, "Who is that blowing up your phone? Why don't you answer it?"

So, like a fool, I did.

"Good morning."

Mathew heard Charles' deep Barry White tone.

"So, it's like that. You're talking to another man? Oooookkkkkkk!"

I didn't know what to say. Words failed me. Mathew pulled up at the station. I got out of the car and looked back at him, pleading with my eyes, but my mouth said nothing.

I'd never been a cheater or a liar, so I just didn't know what to say. I called Mathew from the train. Before I could utter a word, he laid it out.

"You don't need to say anything. Your face said everything!"

"Matt, it's not what you think. He's just a friend from college."

Mathew wasn't listening. I knew it was pointless trying to talk to him over the phone, especially when I really didn't know what to say. We agreed to talk later.

All day I was in a mess. I felt like I was in the hot seat and I had to confess everything but at the same time I didn't really think there was much to confess.

Charles provided the catalyst, but he was not my solution. My desire for another man confirmed I really had come to a full stop with Mathew.

Rather than confronting the issues, Mathew chose avoidance mode. He stayed out until early morning. I think that went on for about a week. That avoidance tactic just played into how I was feeling. If he wasn't going to fight for our relationship then neither was I.

I just needed to tell him so. But timing was the issue. We had two big family events coming up. My sister Melissa was getting married at the age of forty-one and my friend Annemarie had a 'belly wash' baby, at the age of forty-three.

I had popped to see Annemarie one afternoon. Before I could get comfortable in the sofa Annemarie dropped her news. I would have thrown myself on the floor to express my shock, but I was still recovering from having a hysterectomy. Annemarie stood in the doorway, showing me her four-month bump, as she explained, "Didn't you think it was funny that you haven't seen me? You know I'm always there for you, but I've been in a mess. Look at me!"

My eyes were locked on her bump as I fought the urge to fake-faint.

"I'm looking but I can't believe it. I did wonder why you hadn't come to visit me. It feels like I haven't seen you for months."

"But you know that's not me. If I wasn't in a mess I would've been there for you but look at me. I don't know what is happening."

She didn't have to tell me. My eyes hadn't moved away from her bump.

"I expected to see you after I told you about my private hospital nightmare. But when I didn't see you, I put you on the top of my visit list for when I could move about, hence my unannounced knock at your door."

Annemarie laughed, but we both knew she was not the girl for drive-bys. All visits to Annemarie's house had to be scheduled.

For the whole visit Annemarie detailed her surprise pregnancy. The family were all still in shock, but happy. Annemarie and Tony had been together for about twenty-eight years. They already had two grown-up children together when they were blessed again.

Annemarie's news trumped my need to talk about the details of my hysterectomy or problems in my marriage. I parked both issues.

But by the time the 'Save the Date' christening card hit the mailbox my marriage had hit the buffer. The problem was Mathew and I were both godparents to the baby so it didn't seem the right time to break up. My strategy was simple, we just needed to hold it together for about three weeks and then we could make a clean break.

I didn't know what Mathew's strategy was because he deflected all my direct questions. But under his smoked-out exterior he looked lost. For the six months after my party, I had been asking him how he felt, and he just kept saying, "If you're happy, I'm happy."

I hated how he just linked our emotions without trying to understand how I felt. Why couldn't he express how he felt, or what was going on in his head?

In the early days of our relationship our hearts were conjoined, we could feel each other's pain, but that feeling had gone a long time ago.

Now it just felt like he was codependent, like he had lost the ability to feel or think for himself and, more importantly, the willingness to communicate his own feelings to me.

The waiting game proved too difficult for me. Despite my best efforts, I just couldn't keep the cat in the bag. Being around him was driving me mad, the awkward silence was too much.

Looking at Mathew's dejected face was a step too far. Not to mention the new level of tension which was consuming the house. The situation was untenable.

I just couldn't breathe. The fact he couldn't or wouldn't do anything to save our marriage was driving me crazy.

Having made the decision, I felt like a pressure cooker bursting to call time. A few days before the christening I couldn't take it anymore. My truth overpowered me, as Mathew and I lay in bed in silence.

"Look Mathew, we, I, can't go on like this... we need to accept it, we are done."

His body stiffened as he spoke.

"Do what you want, you always do!"

My relief at his marginal acceptance was short-lived as his rigid body lay beside me. I worried about the slightest touch. The awkwardness of the situation kept us awake. Eventually Mathew went downstairs to sleep in the front room. I was so relieved. I could finally get some sleep.

Things remained awkward between us for months, as silence remained our only form of communication. Even when we attended social events, we kept our distance.

At Melissa and Basil's wedding I used my role as matron of honour to avoid Mathew, so much so that it was days later that I realised the 'happy couple' gave me a hug instead of the engraved keepsake that they gave to the rest of the wedding party. It felt deliberate, but the moment had passed.

The christening was hard going, too. The church service went fine but at the reception, I lost my mind. I was flirting with other guys. I even ended up taking a walk with one of them and just as we were about to kiss, Antoinette appeared. Shame is all I felt.

I know I was wrong, but part of me wanted to see if my husband would fight for me, not physically, but at least make a scene, profess his true and undying love for me.

But I got none of that, just a red face as I looked into my daughter's bewildered eyes. Shame, shame, I was beyond embarrassed. On the drive home, in what felt like a decompression chamber I considered my next steps, while watching Mathew's silent roar.

As the genie's bottle lay in pieces, I had to explain what was going on to the kids. Antoinette's age required the direct approach, while Monet needed sensitive handling.

Antoinette received the news like she had been expecting it. Her maturity always surprised me, but she was twenty-two. She wanted to know if we were sure. She worried about her brother. I assured her life would return to its natural rhythm once the clouds cleared.

Mathew and I agreed we would tell Monet together when we knew what we were going to do.

Despite the public humiliation of seeing me go off with another man, it didn't progress our break-up. Mathew refused to move out. Having him around was driving me mad. I felt stifled, unable to move on while he was still in my face.

But he didn't seem to care about any of that or the atmosphere or the effect it was having on our children.

I felt so overwhelmed by it all that one evening after work, I sat down and begged him to leave. I asked him to go and stay with his sister, who had a spare room, but he refused. I asked him when he would be moving out. He replied, confrontationally, when he was good and ready.

The next thing I knew, I was outside looking for a brick. Brick in hand I smashed the windscreen of his Mercedes, causing a big crack. Feeling like an erupted volcano, I went back inside to discover Mathew had smashed up my new Sony plasma TV.

I guess rage was all the motivation he needed because, as quick as a flash, he filled his car with his clothes and shoes and drove off into the night.

⁓

Calm replaced the tension at home. Antoinette's life carried on with no effect, while Monet plodded along.

Soon after Mathew moved out, he and I sat Monet down to explain our decision to separate. He took the news well; he just wanted reassurance that he could stay with me, which we gave him.

But up until that moment when we gave Monet that reassurance, I hadn't given it much thought. Why should I get left holding the bundle of joy? Surely, he should go with his father, who had begged and prayed for him. I parked the topic until I could think more clearly.

With Mathew gone I could finally exhale. Being on my own gave me time to focus on healing my broken self. But after weeks of enduring turbulent emotions ranging from sadness to jubilation, I felt exhausted. I realised I needed help to stop the cycle and reset my default position.

Within a few months of Mathew leaving, I started attending self-development workshops which helped me to focus on me. I even made a vision board and began to look to the future.

As I grappled with the idiosyncrasies of my new life I failed to consider how our families and friends would deal with the break-up until one of Mathew's sisters had a family dinner.

Initially, I refused to go. I still felt raw after the break-up, but his sister Hazel called, insisting the get-together wouldn't be the same without me. I reluctantly agreed to attend.

Monet and I had only been at Eve's house for about an hour, we were busy socialising, when, my nephew Tristan whispered that Auntie Ria, Mathew's sister, wanted to see me in his mum's room. I made my way up the stairs. As I entered the bedroom, I noted Ria's thunderous scowl.

"Hello Dominiquè, I wanted to have a word with you."

"Hi Ria. Good to see—"

I approached her to give her hug, but she stepped back.

"I've been meaning to talk to you. I want to know who you think you are, dashing out my brother. You're so selfish. All you think about is you. You're never happy. He's too good for you, I'm glad he's not with you. I never did like you. I can't stand you."

I felt dazed as I bounced off the ropes with my 'dukes' up.

"Him. Too good for me. What does he do for me, burn weed from sunup to sundown? Stay out all night? Manufacture parking fines and clamps? Stay out all night gambling? Well, since he's that great a catch and you haven't had a man since Noah was a boy, you have him!"

With that I was gone. As I sat at home, drinking my Martell brandy and coke, I realised I had left Monet at Eve's house. I felt livid as I replayed her words. "I never did like you"; that was a knockout blow.

I just couldn't believe it. I thought we were close. We had spent so much time together over the seventeen years and out of all Mathew's siblings I believed we were the closest.

But she never did like me. Even though I had been there at a moment's notice, I had helped mediate her relationship with her kids. I helped her with application forms for jobs, prepared her for interviews and ensured she got a job in one of my residential units.

Her disingenuous demeanour shook me to my core, but worse, she broke another piece of my heart. Never again would I feel secure in a friendship. I can't trust anyone.

Suddenly, I felt exposed. My every nerve sparked under the criticism from family and friends. Support for me and my decision was little to none.

Mathew's mask had worked so well, everyone thought I was crazy to end our relationship.

Being outnumbered by all the supporters in Mathew's camp forced me to reconsider my decision. If I couldn't convince people of my argument maybe I didn't have one.

Reality was harsh. When we first broke up, I hoped Mathew would run to me. I was prepared to wait and see if he really did love me or was it just the life we had that he loved.

But Mathew hadn't pissed on me since he left, not a phone call or a visit. Months passed and nothing. At first, I had stayed firm, trying to focus on my future. But deep down I missed my life. I wanted my husband and to be a Mrs again.

I loved the status of being married. British society respected marriage. Without it, I was just seen as another black woman with kids without a father. That label didn't fit me. I had worked too hard and invested so much in that married label.

When Christmas came and I still hadn't heard anything from Mathew, I felt so down and low. I missed our big family Christmases. We used to invite family and friends to Christmas dinner at our home or we would go to either Mathew's family or one of my aunts.

But this year, everything seemed grey and lonely. Monet had gone off with Mathew to have Christmas with his family and Antoinette had gone to have Christmas with her father.

All alone, I spent Christmas day in bed, with a brandy and coke, while watching Christmas TV. In between adverts and programmes, I sobbed and shouted.

Why me? Why couldn't I have happily ever after? Hadn't I suffered enough? I bawled so much my head throbbed and my nose was sore. I must have eventually fallen asleep. I awoke to find myself in a sea of soggy tissues and peanuts and Quality Street wrappers.

It was Boxing Day and Melissa had convinced me to go to Bedfordshire to see the family. I didn't want to go but she insisted. She was going to come for me shortly. I was tidying up when I spotted Mathew's phone on the dining room table. I looked at it for ages trying to determine when Mathew had left it there.

I had no memory of him coming in the house, far less him being in the dining room. But there it was, just sitting there. I snatched it up and began reading texts and Whatsapp messages.

My heart was racing. I felt sick in my stomach. I was frightened that I might find something from a woman.

And just as I tried to calm myself down, I found a string of texts from some woman, calling my husband 'babe'.

One text said how much she missed him and was looking forward to seeing him again. I felt so sick and fearful as I continued searching. Looking through his pictures, I found a video of Mathew watching a woman feeling herself up and then Mathew started kissing her. It was all on video.

Tears ran from my eyes. I cried my heart out again. I had seen enough. I closed the phone and put it back on the table. Reality dawned. We really were over, and he was already seeing other women.

Distraught, I had just about finished throwing some clothes on when Melissa and her husband Basil started banging on the door and ringing the bell. I let them in and told Melissa to follow me upstairs, so she could help me with something. As soon as she stepped in my bedroom, I began to cry.

She hugged me and told me not to cry. But I just couldn't stop. My heart was breaking with every flashback of Mathew with that woman.

"Arrrrrgh sis, what's wrong? Has something happened?"

"I, I, I saw Mathew with another woman. He's got another woman."

"No way. He wouldn't do that, he loves you. It must be a friend or something. How do you know?"

"Look."

I showed her the video on his phone.

Melissa looked perplexed as she handed me the phone. She hugged and kissed me.

"Don't worry. It's probably nothing. Just sex. Put him out of your mind. We'll go to Bedfordshire, have fun with our cousins and get pissed."

I reluctantly got in the car and we drove to Bedfordshire. I cried on and off for the whole journey. I just couldn't seem to stop the tears from falling.

When we arrived, I wasn't in a fit state to visit with anyone. I told Melissa I would go to my cousin Imani's first and, if I felt better later, I would pop down to cousin Vexelle's house.

Melissa and Basil went off to Vexelle's and I spent the day with Imani. I told her about the video on Mathew's phone. She tried to comfort me, but I felt awful. I didn't feel up to seeing people, so I waited it out at Imani's house until Melissa and Basil were ready to go.

They drove me back home. I was so happy to be home, so I could cry on my own, in private. But before I went to bed, I phoned Mathew.

"Hey D."

"You left your phone here."

"I couldn't think where I had left it. That's a relief."

"I see you've got a woman. How could you move on so quick, just like that?"

"I'm not going to let no woman drive me mad. Life goes on. You don't want me, so what do you expect me to do?"

I felt so hurt I just hung up the phone. He sounded so cold. He obviously didn't care about me. I went to bed and cried myself to sleep.

The next day Imani phoned me. She wanted to know how I was feeling. I told her I had called Mathew and what he had said.

"Cuz, don't worry about it. It was probably just sex and didn't mean anything. You two need to talk face-to-face and try to sort this mess out before it goes too far and it's too late."

"It looks too late to me already!"

"You won't know for sure unless you talk to him. If you want him back, then you better talk to him and find out if he feels the same."

"You're right. I don't have a choice. I have to get my husband back."

Then Imani fell silent.

"Imani, are you still there?"

"I need to tell you something, but I want you to know I'm only telling you this because I think you have a right to know."

I felt panicked. I thought it was something to do with Mathew. After a pause, she spoke.

"Melissa told Vexelle and Donna about the video."

I was so shocked.

"Dominiquè, Dominiquè, hello!"

I just couldn't believe what she had said. I couldn't believe that my sister had broken my confidence like that.

The information was so fresh and new. I was still coming to terms with it myself and she had gossiped about it within hours of me telling her. She had seen how broken-hearted I was and yet she had the audacity to chat my personal business.

"Imani, I'm stunned. I can't believe that my sister would chat my personal business."

"Well, she was laughing about it with Basil and them, like it was a big joke."

281

"I thought she was my sister and had my back. It's clear she doesn't value our relationship, and she let everyone know except me."

I paused for a moment while my mind processed the betrayal.

"Wow, you have blown me away. I'm shocked and hurt but thank you so much for having my back. If it wasn't for you, I would be going around thinking I have a sister who I can trust but thanks to you, now I know the truth. Wow, did she tell them everything?"

"Oh yes. Vexelle gave me a blow-by-blow account of the video. I really didn't want to tell you, but I had to. What are you going to do?"

"Hmmmmmm... I don't know. I need to sort out my marriage first and then I will deal with Melissa."

By the end of the call my head was spinning. My feelings were mixed up, anger and sadness were at war, but I felt too exhausted and broken to referee. I poured myself a large Courvoisier and coke and retreated to bed.

A few days later Mathew came to pick up his phone. He looked awful. When he hugged me I could smell his locks; they smelt like stale cigarettes and old grease. He was unshaven, so he looked like Father Time with black whiskers and white flecks.

He smelt musty too, without a trace of aftershave or cologne. He looked stressed, with large bags under his eyes. He just didn't look like my man. I felt sorry for him.

"We need to talk—" Before I could finish my sentence Mathew butted in.

"She doesn't mean anything. She's just a girl. You didn't want me, so I was getting on with my life. But I'm not seeing that bitch anymore, who does she think she is, talking about my wife? She doesn't know my wife, the mother of my child. I told her to fuck off and I haven't seen her since. Cheeky bitch!"

His tone unnerved me. I wasn't sure who he was angry with.

"Mathew, we need to stop this before it goes too far. I can't bear the thought of you with another woman. Seeing that video made me feel sick deep down in my stomach. I hated the idea of another woman touching you, touching my man. That's when I realised, I still love you and want to be with you."

I stared at him longingly, hoping he felt the same, but Mathew just looked stressed.

"Dominiquè, you know I love you but it's just too hard. You are not easy."

He stared at me intently and then shook his head.

"You like to war with people and I just like a simple life. You are too loud. You don't have to be loud all the time. You don't have anything to prove. If you could just tone it down a bit. You don't have to be the loudest in the room. People don't need you to speak for them. You can't control people, and you have to let people do what they want."

I knew what he was referring to. I had always partied like the world was going to end and I could never walk past an injustice without getting involved. But if he wanted me to be quieter, then that's what I'd be. My husband was my man and I was prepared to do whatever it took to make my marriage work.

I started to cry. The loss of my marriage made me feel hurt and tortured. I couldn't bear it. I wanted my husband. As my tears ran down my face, Mathew swept me up from the couch into his arms.

"Dominiquè, don't cry. It's going to be all right. We can turn this around. You just need to relax and take it easy. Let your childhood go and we will be fine." He kissed my tears and then my lips. The passion was unmistakable. He looked into my eyes.

"This is going to take time, but we will get there. Let's take things one day at a time."

So that's what we did. On New Year's Eve, I went out with friends while Mathew looked after Monet at our house.

Under normal circumstances the rave would have been a great start to the new year, but I still had carpet burns from my awful Christmas. Not even the splendour of Kensington Roof Garden could distract me.

Raving without Mathew felt strange. All I could think of was him. Me and my girls looked like 'money', but the rave lacked lustre. There was also a shortage of men. Not that I was looking, but I thought if I was pickings were very slim.

The women who came with a man clung to them, clearly aware of the disparity. I enjoyed watching them defending their territory. They didn't have to worry about me. I had a man, my husband.

We partied hard, but I watched the clock. I wanted to go home but my girls wouldn't leave until the last song played, so it was about 5 or 6am when we got back to mine.

Mathew hadn't moved back home yet, but I was hoping he would stay the night. I was yearning to feel his body next to mine. Thankfully he was still awake when we got back.

He made coffee for the girls and he sat chatting to them for a while. I was mashed up and eager to get to bed, so I gave them some bedding and bid them a good sleep.

About ten minutes later, Mathew came in our bedroom and lay on top of the bedding, saying he would just have a little nap and then go home. I eventually convinced him he might as well get in the bed and be comfortable. After he took off his clothes in slow motion he got in the bed.

He lay with his back to me. I wrapped my naked body around him and eventually my warmth penetrated his reluctance. He turned around and kissed me. He bit me, and licked me, starting with my lips, my neck, my breasts, my belly button and my thighs.

I was so desperate to feel him inside me. I couldn't wait. I just pulled him up by his face, kissed him and pulled him down on top of me. My legs were wide open, and I squeezed his bum cheeks as I pulled him into me.

He felt so good, so hard, my body was tingling. I fought to keep my moans within our room because we had guests, but I couldn't. He felt so good, ecstasy couldn't be silenced. We were finally back together.

21

CAN I FIX IT?
YES, YOU CAN!

Over the next three months, Mathew and I worked on our relationship. I started to see a therapist. I wanted to put my childhood demons to bed once and for all. I refused to allow them to ruin my life.

My therapist, Sally, was fantastic. She specialised in childhood trauma, and so she was perfect for the job.

On first sight, I wasn't sure the therapeutic relationship between her and me was going to work because she looked just like Auntie Viola's ex-girlfriend, Toni.

Sally was a short little white woman, who wore glasses. She had grey and white short cut hair and I could detect a subtle accent, either Welsh or Scottish.

But I refused to be deterred. It had taken me so long to get to that point, I was ready to work, so I dismissed my possible transference of unresolved issues relating to Auntie Viola's partner Auntie Toni, who was Scottish. I chose instead to focus on me.

In the first session, I talked nonstop for the full fifty minutes. She said I was so clearly in need of therapeutic space, she had to extend the session.

Sally assessed me as being at risk of having a nervous breakdown. She offered to see me once a week even though I couldn't afford it. She reduced her fee so I could afford to see her as regularly as needed.

Over about two months I told my therapist about my journey. It had been really hard. At times my pain blocked my vocal chords and I couldn't speak or swallow. Sally skilfully comforted me until my tears eased and I felt able to swallow again.

Sally informed me that I had experienced abuse trauma and I needed to learn to be self-compassionate and take the time to heal.

Just hearing her validated the impact of my journey. I found the purging process to be rather cathartic. I began to feel better, but I also felt angry.

The anger I felt for my so-called mother overwhelmed me. She had a lot to answer for and I was tired of carrying emotional baggage which didn't belong to me.

Things became clearer and clearer with each session. My so-called mother's legacy impacted on my sense of self and my ability to love, affecting every relationship I'd ever had and nearly destroying my marriage.

Despite my determination to be nothing like her, by virtue of my goal to be nothing like, she had had a hand in every move I made.

❧

A few days after a therapy session I went to Tottenham, to have my hair done in African twists by my lovely African hairdresser called Grace.

I arrived at her house like normal, and after the usual catch-up, Grace began to do my hair. A few hours in her husband came home from work, so she stopped to make his lunch.

While she took care of him, I sat watching the TV, but I wasn't really watching it. Suddenly I felt compelled to phone my brother Jamie.

"Hey bro, can you pick me up later? I'm in Tottenham."

"No, but Mum's here."

That was such a strange thing for him to say. But for some crazy reason I told him to put her on the phone. Hearing her say hello, I realised I didn't have a plan.

"I wanted Jamie to pick me up when I finish getting my hair done but he said he's going to work. What are you up to?"

I listened as my craziness spread to my so-called mother.

"I'm supposed to be going to work, but I can call in sick. I'll pick you up."

I felt baffled. She was going to change her plans for me. She had never done anything for me which didn't involve me having to cuss or carry on, but here she was wanting to do something for me.

Dumbfounded, I gave her the address and she confirmed that she would pick me up when I was ready.

For the duration of time my hair was being twisted, I replayed the conversation in my head, over and over again. When my hair was finished, I watched through the kitchen window as my so-called mother pulled up in her blue Polo. I laughed.

Not even time had interfered with her passion for VWs. She had had a Beetle for many years and then she moved on to Polos. Some things did stay the same.

I stepped into the car, bewildered. I couldn't make sense of what was happening.

She started talking hurriedly about nothing consequential, as if she had seen me just yesterday. I ignored her topic.

"Don't you want to know why I wanted to see you? Why did you want to pick me up?"

I looked at her face as she answered me. One thing that always sickened me about my so-called mother was how beautiful she always looked. But today she looked old. I had never seen age on her before, it was striking. I hadn't seen her for at least eight years.

"I just wanted to see you. I've never had the urge before. I was fine until I retired, then I had all this time to think.

"Now I can't stop the things going around in my mind. When I was working, I didn't have time to think, so I didn't have to but now all I do is think back."

She looked straight ahead as she spoke. She never once looked at me, but I could sense her torment. Her hair looked a mess, which was unusual. Her hair was always immaculate; she used to go to the hairdressers every week.

What was this? Had my so-called mother developed a conscience? Had her ghosts and demons caught up with her? I refused to believe it. This woman was as hard as nails. She was like Teflon, nothing stuck to her and definitely not her emotions, she didn't have any.

The whole thing was rather baffling.

"Where do you want to go?"

I had no idea. I didn't even know what I was doing with her, so I definitely didn't know where we should go.

"I don't want to go to your house. It holds way too many horrible memories for me and just being there gives me the creeps!"

"That place gives me the creeps too!" she said.

I had to laugh. Who was this woman? What had she done with my so-called mother?

"Are you hungry?"

I had to admit I was.

"Shall we get some fish and chips?"

"Okay."

As I agreed, a memory of her local chip shop flashed through my mind. They had really nice fish and chips. She bought the fish and chips, and despite what we had both said about her house we ended up there.

Oh how I hated that house. As I entered it, the feeling of doom and gloom I experienced as a child engulfed me. I forced myself to shrug it off and instead looked for changes to the house since I had last set foot in there about eighteen years ago.

Everything looked exactly the same. There were pictures of Jamie, Keres and Jamie's two children throughout the house. There was not one trace of me or my family, despite the fact that Antoinette was her first and oldest grandchild.

Just as I was coming to terms with the absence of me and mine, I saw my wedding invitation.

"Where did you get this?"

I picked it up. Just as she was about to answer I said, "Jamie, damn traitor."

"He's not a traitor. He just likes to keep me informed about you."

"Why? You don't show any interest, so why does he bother?"

"That's not true. I am interested."

"You have a funny way of showing it."

"Come and eat this food before it gets cold."

We sat and ate together, without speaking. Then she jumped up in a panic.

"Do you want something to drink?"

"Sit down, I'll get it."

I went into the kitchen and opened every cupboard and the fridge, just looking to see what kind of food and drink my so-called mother had.

I was pleased to see she still had Idris ginger beer, my favourite, but I wasn't in the mood to drink that. I needed something stronger.

She must have read my mind because she directed me to the cupboard where she kept the Bajan rum. I poured myself a glass of rum and coke and gave her a glass of ginger beer.

We continued to eat in silence. It was a nice silence. I used the peace to gather my thoughts. This day had been a long time coming but it felt surreal. She seemed on edge. I had never seen her look so out of sorts.

When we finished eating, I watched as my so-called mother washed up the few wares in the sink.

I sipped on my rum and coke and tried to connect with the reality of me being there. Why was I there? I couldn't bear being with her.

Then the answer hit me. I was sick and tired of carrying all the stuff which caused me pain. I had paid the toll for her choices, but above everything I wanted to know why she hated me so much.

As she sat down in the sitting room and began playing with the TV remote, I stared at her. She now looked very comfortable compared to earlier in the car, while I percolated with a combination of resentment, anger and fear as I remembered how horrible she could be and how easily she had dismissed me for forty years.

Courage overpowered my fear as I focused on the forty-year path littered with misery which had led me to this day. My well was finally dry. I had no more capacity to carry her burden. I needed to be heard.

I peered into her eyes as I spoke sternly to her.

"I want you to know what I have been through because of you, but more importantly I want to give you what I have been carrying. I'm tired and this stuff doesn't belong to me. It's your stuff. It's all yours. I'm sick of it. I can't lug it around anymore."

I didn't stop to draw breath, but I could see she was actually listening. As she was about to speak, I continued, "I had a stroke because the doctors couldn't control my blood pressure. I am forty-two years old and I have the health of an old woman. I have to take three tablets to try to keep my pressure down." She appeared shocked as her eyes widened.

"What tablets are you on?"

"Irbesartan 300mg, Amlodopine 5mg and Bisoprolol 2.5mg. I also suffer from chronic migraines and I'm registered blind. I am tired, in fact exhausted, but I didn't realise how truly broken I was until I had a stroke six month ago. But before the stroke, my marriage broke up after eighteen years.

"At first, I thought it was just one of those things until I realised how much my childhood had affected me, my marriage, and it even prevented me from celebrating the creation and birth of my son."

She was about to interrupt but I shot her a look and she held her peace.

"My husband loved me. He was overjoyed at the prospect of being a father, but I couldn't share his joy. The whole thing was a nightmare for me. Do you know why?"

She shook her head.

"Because I didn't want to be like you. I refused to have a child I didn't want. No child of mine would grow up feeling unwanted and unloved, like I did. This fear consumed me throughout my pregnancy. I knew I didn't have the capacity to give another child what they needed or deserved. I knew I was emotionally tired and exhausted. I had done well with Antoinette but the thought of having to give my all to another child was just too much. I knew I had nothing left."

Tears began rolling down my cheeks. I tried to suppress them, but they just kept rolling down faster. I quickly wiped them away. I didn't want my so-called mother to see them, she didn't deserve to see my pain.

I watched her through my tears. She looked a little grey, but she said nothing.

"Why did you call me when I was pregnant? What did you want?"

"I don't know. I just wanted to speak to you."

"But why, after all that time, and why didn't you just say that? Instead when I asked you, you said, 'Oh your grandmother was asking for you'. Why did you lie?"

"I don't know. I just didn't know what to say."

I watched her as she spoke. She looked different, not like her usual self, from what I could remember.

She looked like an old woman. Although she was only sixty-five she looked more like seventy. Her forehead was full of worry lines. It was weird. I had never seen her look sad or vulnerable before.

She was no longer the carefree self-assured pretty woman I remembered, now she just looked old and troubled. I carried on regardless. This was my opportunity and I wasn't going to let pity derail me.

"The birth was a nightmare and looking after him was challenging. Mathew just didn't know what to do to make me happy. I continually reminded him that he had his dream and prayer, while I was living a nightmare. How was he supposed to enjoy being a father when he had to contend with my negativity? Despite everything, I tried my best to love and care for my baby. He was a beautiful baby, very advanced. He sat up by himself from three months, crawled at five months and walked at seven months. He knew his own mind so well by the time he was one I called him Lord Fauntleroy. We gave him the best opportunities we could afford. He went to a private nursery and prep schools. And despite everything he grew to be a wonderful boy, who is loved. It took everything I had to keep all the balls in the air, to ensure Antoinette had what she needed. She too has lived a loved life and she is a loving young woman.

"Mathew hated to see the effect having Monet had had on me. He had been powerless to combat that effect, so he watched helplessly as I went downhill. In the end it was too much for us and we broke up for about six months, before the penny dropped and I realised the problems in our marriage were not solely down to me but were down to you. So I went into therapy. And the more I talked the clearer the solution became. I needed to give you what I have been carrying so I can go on to live an unburdened life and you can feel the weight of my pain and torture."

As I peered deep into her eye, I asked my ultimate question.

"Why do you hate me so much? Why?"

"I don't hate you."

"Only hate could make you do the horrible things you have done to me. You kept my father from me. Why? Why didn't you tell me his name when I asked you? You knew I was getting married. Why didn't you just write it down and send it to me? Why did you have to be so cruel?"

She averted her eyes and stared at the TV.

"I didn't want to talk about my business. You always wanted to know my business."

She irritated me. I couldn't believe she was still spouting the same old rubbish.

"Why don't you understand? It's not just your business, who my father is, it's my business too and I had the right to know."

I stared at her incredulously.

"Thankfully, my sister found me and told me who my father is and the whole story."

My so-called mother snapped her neck as she swung her head around to stare at me.

"It's not you I hate, it's your father. He lied to me and left me when I needed him the most."

"But why did you have to take it out on me?"

We locked eyes. I could see she was still hurting.

"I don't know. I shouldn't have but I just couldn't stop myself. He told me he loved me and then he went off and married your sister's mother. How could he do that to me? He knew I was pregnant, and he still left me one morning and went to marry her. I hated him for leaving me. I loved him."

"But he loved you. Uncle Auburn told me. He said he loved you, but you refused to be with him. He was left with no alternative but to try to make his marriage work but he really wanted to be with you. He was so desperate to be with you he went to Barbados to find you and me. When he couldn't find us, he started drinking heavily and eventually died."

My so-called mother looked at me intensely as if she was hearing the words for the first time.

"He loved me? He did love me?"

"Yes, he loved you and wanted to be with you, but you turned him down."

"After he married her, I just couldn't trust him. I didn't realise he did really love me. He used to come to the hospital and try to talk to me, but I refused to hear him. After a while he stopped turning up. I should have listened to him. If only I knew that he really did love me, things could have been different."

She genuinely appeared shocked. She kept muttering it over and over again.

"How do you think he would feel to know how you treated me?"

"I shouldn't have taken it out on you. I'm sorry."

She actually said sorry. I could hear her words echoing in my ears, it sounded amazing.

"Since I finished work, I have had so much time to remember things. I don't want to. I try to think of other things, but the flashbacks just keep coming. I hate it, but I can't do anything to stop them. I also watch films on the True Movies channel. I have seen the pain that children who have been given away feel. They have had such hard lives. The films made me think about you."

"But my life wouldn't have been so bad if you hadn't taken me away from my family. Why did you do that? How could you just kidnap me from my family where my dad could see me? Why would you do such a wicked thing?"

"She couldn't cope with all those children, and when I heard you nearly got burnt, I decided to give you to somebody who could care for you properly. I moved you nearer to my work, so I could see you."

"But you hardly ever came to see me. Once every six months doesn't count. Not a school show or a parents' evening. You didn't care about me. You just took me away from my father and his family because you wanted to punish him and by extension me. Nothing more and nothing less."

My so-called mother shuddered like she was cold. The pressure was getting to her, but I refused to ease up.

"How could you leave me with Auntie Viola and Toni? That was nothing short of hell and you knew it. Why did you leave me there?"

She shook her head very slowly but said nothing.

"But to really put salt in the wound, you used to look after the chosen ones with such love and care. They had the best of everything while I looked like Cinderella, in second-hand rags. How could you be so cruel? How could you treat them like gold and me like shit?"

"I had to give them what I couldn't give you."

I was so shocked by her response I was stunned into silence. I just kept replaying her words over and over again, trying to make sense of them, but when I couldn't I just stared at her, searching for greater meaning.

Her facial expressions didn't change. She didn't offer further reasoning, she just stared at the TV. It was clear she didn't have any comprehension of the pain her actions had caused me. It was irritating.

"You need to carry this. You need to know the consequence of the pain and hurt you have caused me for forty-two years, just because you wanted to get back at my father. I paid the ultimate price. Don't get me wrong, I tried, really hard, to rise, to make a life for myself. I educated myself. I had a career, a family, a husband, but it didn't matter. No matter how hard I tried to shake off my childhood, something would happen, and it would be on my back again, heavier and more difficult to carry. I refused to let your bad decisions define me but somehow, they still did because your past shapes your future. Every life decision I have ever made has been influenced by my determination to not be anything like you and so, by default, you have influenced my life. And I hate you for it."

She looked at me pathetically.

"You never gave any trouble. I know you went to university and got married to Mathew. You did well for yourself."

She smiled a weak smile as she spoke. Her fakeness made my blood boil. I didn't want fake, I deserved real emotion. I wanted her to carry my pain, to feel tormented by guilt. Looking at her was adding gas to the fire.

Luckily for her the door knocked. While she went to answer it, I phoned Mathew, from the kitchen. He was clearly shocked upon hearing my location.

"What are you doing there? Don't go upsetting yourself. She'll never understand what you have been through."

"You don't understand. This isn't about her. It's about me. I am giving her my burden. I can't carry it anymore. It's not my stuff, it's hers. Don't worry, I'll be fine. Can you pick me up?"

"Of course. What time?"

"About eight. Thanks babe."

Damn man. I wanted him to calm me down but hearing him say she would never understand what I had been through made my temperature boil. He just didn't understand. Nobody did. Most people can't comprehend or expect a mother to be vicious and vindictive to their own child.

When I walked back into the living room there was a little boy sitting watching the TV.

"This is Ocean."

I tried to stop myself from laughing.

"Ocean. Now I've heard everything. I heard a woman call her daughter Pear the other day and I thought that was bad, but Ocean is the winner of the worst name competition."

"I look after him for the neighbours, just for an hour."

The thought she was such a helpful neighbour irritated me.

"Lucky them. Imagine you helping them with childcare while we had to fend for ourselves. We didn't have anyone to collect Monet from school; Mathew had to work part-time for about eighteen months so he could do it. And you're here looking after other people's children. Boy I am so salt, it's a joke."

Just to compound my irritation she added, "We'll have to collect Keres's daughter Mia in about half an hour."

I kissed my teeth until I had no air left, while giving her a dirty look to match.

She laughed.

"Keres and Simon need my help. They are both out working. She had such a hard time during her pregnancy. She was so terrified during the labour I thought she was going to die giving birth. She couldn't do much for herself. I had to help her feed and bathe the baby. You know what she's like. She needs help."

"Some people need and get all the help while those who have nothing, or no one, must fend for themselves."

I could feel flames erupting inside of me.

"Please don't talk about her anymore, it makes me sick to think about the injustice."

"It's not her fault. She's not capable like you."

"You didn't give a shit if I was capable or not. You just threw me down without a care in the world."

"Don't say that. I did care about you. I did."

"No, you did not. You hated me, and you showed me how much every chance you got, in the most hurtful and abusive ways. I just came here today to tell you to your face the damage and impact your hate had on my life. You've won. You have virtually destroyed my life. I hope it was worth it."

I watched her face as my words landed. She offered no apology. She just got up and walked across the room to the hall where she slowly put on her coat. I was done. I had nothing left to say to her.

I went with her and Ocean to collect Mia from the nursery. The walk was refreshing. When we returned to the miserable house, I got to know my four-year-old niece a little bit in between answering my so-called mother's questions about Antoinette, Monet and Mathew.

My so-called mother appeared to be interested in my life. She even had Jamie's invitation to Monet's christening, which had his picture on it, so she knew what Monet looked like when he was a baby. It felt very strange.

Jamie came home from work so happy to see me.

"Wow. Sis. How are you guys?"

"I'm still here. Nobody's dead, so things are okay."

He laughed awkwardly. Jamie and I chatted. I hadn't spoken to him since I had the stroke. It was nice catching up with him until Mathew arrived to pick me up.

The whole day had been surreal. My body tingled with all the emotions running through it. I felt emotionally exhausted but yet free.

My emotional purge meant I had finally been able to give my so-called mother my burden. I was so happy to be free of all the unanswered questions, feelings and emotions which I had kept bottled up for so many years.

I felt so proud for being true to myself and having the courage to fulfill my lifelong ambition of confronting my so-called mother with the consequences of her actions.

⁓

Living unburdened became my new learnt behaviour. Every day I reminded myself I was free from the burden of the past. I was free to walk without all the pain and sorrow which had weighed me down for so long. I was now free to love my husband and my life without the presence of old black clouds, now I had new fluffy white ones.

Life was great, except since I had had the stroke, I was unable to work. We were behind on our mortgage and all our bills. We had tried to consolidate our debts, but we just didn't have enough income coming in.

In my new life I had a caring so-called mother who called me nearly every day. I was sceptical about her personality transplant, but the new unburdened me tried to give her a chance.

One day my so-called mother phoned me when I was distraught, after receiving a letter from the mortgage company demanding we cleared our arrears, which were about £3,000.

My so-called mother asked me what was wrong a few times. I tried to brush her off, but she was persistent. I gave in and told her about the demand letter from the mortgage company.

"I've got an insurance policy which has just finished. If you can wait until Friday, I'll pay the arrears."

I couldn't believe what she was saying. Was she really going to help me, for real? She was a woman of her word. On the Friday she went into the mortgage company and paid £3,000 into our mortgage account.

I felt amazed and excited. This act was the first time she had ever done anything to help me. I didn't have to beg or plead or even ask her. She just offered. It was a miracle.

That grand gesture went a long way in encouraging me to let my guard down with her, a little bit. So I started to visit her. After a few months I even took Monet to see her and to play with his cousin Mia.

On my visits, we spent time catching up. She talked about her life and her career. 'The Grenadian' had been true to his word and left her when Keres was twenty-one, about nineteen years ago. He had left her for some white woman who lived near his local pub.

My so-called mother's passion was talking about her career. Her work was everything to her. It never gave her any problems and in fact it had been a great distraction in her life. She had worked her way up to elderly care home management and retired when she was sixty, although she still worked as bank staff when it suited her.

She had very few friends so all she had was family. She was sad she couldn't go back to Barbados to live. But she had nothing there because her sister had robbed her out of her mother's house and land.

When she talked about her woes, she looked totally dejected and old. I struggled to accept the new so-called mother. She didn't connect to the old one. It was weird.

Getting to know her was interesting. We started to go over to hers for Sunday dinner with her and Jamie and his sons, like a real family. It was strange but fun.

Monet even went to spend the weekend with her, which was weird because he had been so scared of her on the few occasions he had seen her at Jamie's house or his kids' parties.

My relationship with my so-called mother had moved on. And even Monet enjoyed spending time with her. He didn't like the way Jamie's kids used her as a piggy bank and cleaner. But otherwise he had fun staying with her.

During the early stages of bonding there were two flies in the ointment. Antoinette wouldn't have a bar of it. She hated my so-called mother with a passion. She swore she would never forgive her for the pain she had caused me. She thought I was mad to give her the time of day.

Monet and I tried to convince her to give her a chance or to go and talk to her and tell her what she thought of her, so she could move on. But Antoinette was adamant and as stubborn as an old mountain mule. I gave up and left her to it.

The other fly in the ointment was Keres. She kept making sly remarks and comments to my so-called mother about me.

Apparently, my so-called mother was saying that she needed a new car but didn't have any money and Keres said she shouldn't have given me any money.

Hearing the words nearly made my head explode. How dare she. She, who had been given everything, had the audacity to tell my so-called mother what she should or shouldn't give me. What did my relationship with my so-called mother have to do with her?

I was pissed off to the highest level of pissitivity. I told my so-called mother to never ever tell me anything Keres had to say and vice versa. All channels of communication had to be blocked unless she wanted bloodshed.

Months passed. My so-called mother and I were getting along quite well. She wasn't in my inner circle, but things were going along smoothly.

We had even invited her to the screening of Monet's first movie. He was in *Horrid Henry The Movie* and the film company arranged a special screening for Monet, twenty friends and his family.

She was so proud of Monet. After the screening she came back to our house. It was the first time she had ever been to my house.

We showed her our welcoming hospitality and she looked quite relaxed. I noticed she didn't have any earrings in her ears. I got a pair of my gold earrings from my jewellery box and put them in her ears. She looked so proud.

Mathew remained sceptical about my so-called mother, but he enjoyed the emancipated new me. Yet my spirit felt unsettled by his smoked worried outlook. As usual he dodged my direct questions and focused on his street life.

I strove to improve my health, but it proved to be a chore, which prevented me from working. But after the emotional and physical hurdles I had jumped, being self-compassionate ensured I synchronised my mind, body and spirit for the first time in my life.

About eighteen months after I connected with my so-called mother, the relationship hit a wall. I hadn't heard from her for a few weeks, which was strange. She usually called at least once a week.

After the third week I called her to find out if everything was okay. She told me things were fine, but I could hear in her voice that she was holding something back. I prodded until eventually she opened up.

"Monet shouldn't be talking about me. He should keep what he knows to himself."

I was baffled.

"What did he say?"

"He told Caine I slept with Melissa's mum's man. Why does he have to tell them things?"

I was taken aback. It sounded very out of character for Monet but at the same time I did not raise my children with secrets. I hated secrets and the damage they could cause, so my children knew the whole sordid story.

But why was she was making it into a big thing?

"Why didn't you speak to Monet and tell him what you expected from him? Why are you holding onto it?"

"I don't need to be reminded of my past. He doesn't need to be talking about it to them. I don't want them to know anything about me. I'm too old for this. My blood pressure was so high. I don't need the stress. Just tell him not to talk about me to them."

The fuse was lit.

"Your stress. Your blood pressure. Yours isn't as high as mine and you're worrying about you."

"Why do you always have to cause trouble? You probably told him to tell them."

My emotions erupted, as I began shouting, "Me? I cause trouble?"

"He used to tell you not to upset your mother."

"Me, you are at the root of it all. You should have told your husband that. Wow. I thought we had put the past to rest. I can't believe you blame me for the past when it was all caused by you. But you don't have to worry about Monet telling them anything or me causing trouble, you won't be seeing us again."

In my fury I blammed down the phone. I thought we had come far but we hadn't moved at all. She still held me responsible for her sordid past.

Because she wasn't woman enough to stand by her own truth, she had no substance and was incapable of recounting her mistakes and learning from them. Instead, she had cast Monet out and heaped the responsibility on me.

I should have known the relationship was doomed early on. About six months after we started seeing each other, we caught a bus with my sister Hyacinth, who was visiting from Barbados. My so-called mother saw some of her work friends on the bus. She told Hyacinth and me to go and sit at the back of the bus. She never introduced us to her friends.

I should have acknowledged right then and there she hadn't changed. She was still ashamed of her past and her outside children.

Regardless of how the relationship ended, I refused to put the cross back on my back. I had come too far for that. I was determined to walk strong and walk forward and upwards and leave the burden where it belonged, with my so-called mother.

22

Six Minutes of Fumbling in the Dark!

Society's notion of a family consists of parents and children; as a consequence everyone is believed to have one. My life is a contradiction to the social norm.

I can't believe that six minutes of fumbling in the dark could saddle me with six half-siblings which collectively can't make one whole.

What is made crooked can never be straight. My parents were not free to love. My father was in a relationship with Melissa's mother.

They had no business being together, let alone making a baby. But in the passion of the moment people only think about themselves and fulfilling their own desire.

My life was created on shaky ground. No foundation. Just tears and betrayal. Every tear shed by my so-called mother determined the extent of my suffering yet to come.

My parents were a non-starter but for some crazy reason I thought my siblings would be the family I never had. Pure madness.

I had so much faith in family, I didn't give any credibility to the origin of our bloodline. If I had I would have seen the poor foundation, but instead I loved my siblings hard; I applied 100% to being a great sister, who was reliable, supportive and empowered them to be all they could be.

But it's a simple fact half-siblings rarely consider the relationship a whole relationship because you are not considered equal to those who share the same parents.

Unfortunately, my existence was a reminder of the dirt their parents had done. I was a walking and living dirty secret and that's how I was treated.

But I didn't help myself either because I wanted to talk about how horrible I had been treated by their parents. They didn't want to hear that; they wanted to have perfect parents.

Over the years it became clear, regardless of the depth of our relationship, we never really got past the starting line. In my life my siblings have been a constant source of pain and regardless of how forgiving I am or how loving, each sibling relationship had a best by date.

Even as a small child, Keres's disdain was evident from the beginning. She always had her nose in the air, with the look of self-importance. She was only about six yet the look was there.

As we grew up, we got closer, but the thing that really bonded us was the child abuse, then we got really close. Even when she started dating Simon, we would spend a lot of time together.

Simon was perfect for Keres. He worshipped her like she was a god! She had this childlike behaviour; she would whinge and whine, and he would do whatever she wanted without a care or thought for himself. They were quite sickening to watch but I knew he loved her.

But suddenly things changed. I don't know what it was but I first noticed it on one of my birthdays. I had booked a restaurant for about eight of us. She was supposed to be at my house by 7; when 7.30 came I called her. She hadn't even left home yet and she lived twenty miles away.

I urged her to hurry up because people were waiting at the restaurant. At eight we just went to the restaurant; obviously the night had a different tone because we lost our table and some of my friends had been left waiting for an hour.

But what compounded the issue was that Keres didn't even bother to turn up. I was furious and when I got home, I called her. As usual she turned it on me, it was my fault she was running late because she had left work late and she didn't have enough time to get ready etc., etc.

Everything was always about Keres. She was the centre of the universe and Mother Nature. We didn't speak for about two years after that, but she always kept in contact with Antoinette and she even had her for weekends. Keres had stated she didn't want our relationship to affect her relationship with Antoinette, because she was an innocent child.

I was happy with the arrangement because Antoinette was really close to Keres and Simon. Keres was quite childlike, so they played together like two little kids.

After the two years of silence, I suddenly got a birthday card from Keres, apologising for everything and promising we would be closer than two peas in a pod.

I loved my sister, so I was eager to put things behind us and get back to being sisters. Mathew was really sceptical, so on her first visit he took her to one side and told her if she wasn't going to be a loving sister not to bother being in our lives. Keres assured him that she was genuine and there would be no more upset.

And for two years we got along like a house on fire. I introduced her to upmarket shopping in Harrods, John Lewis and Wallis; we shared a love for the finer things in life!

Keres and Simon had got engaged and she wanted me to help her with the wedding planning. Antoinette was going to be her bridesmaid.

Planning the wedding was reminiscent of the wedding planning we did together as kids. But on the first day we were due to go bridal gown shopping, Keres called me early that morning to say she was going with her mum.

Hearing the words winded me. I tried to change her mind but she told me we were never going to be sisters, we had different parents and she wanted her mother at her wedding, so it just wasn't going to work out, and that was the final knockout punch.

Devastation doesn't fully express how I felt; we had been getting on so well, we hadn't had a cross word, but she had made up her mind.

We haven't spoken since; I heard she got married in Barbados with one of our cousin's kids for bridesmaids. That was the bit that hurt the most, Antoinette was so hurt.

Keres never even explained it to Antoinette, in fact she never spoke to her again either. Keres's actions confirmed her heartless status, she is definitely cut from the same cloth as her mother; it was clear she could cut you dead without shedding a tear.

Even as an adult Antoinette has struggled to come to terms with Keres's blatant disregard for her feelings. I pray their paths never cross, as to this day I'm sure if Antoinette sees her, she'll kick her head in.

My relationship with Jamie had always been tight. From a young age we agreed to disagree regarding his ma and pa, we parked the topic like apartheid. We rode together over life's hurdles, without a single falling out for thirty-five plus years.

But sadly, Jamie stopped talking to me after I stopped talking to my so-called mother. I may be completely wrong; he has never communicated the problem to me.

But I think it's because he was shown the vicious letter I had sent my so-called mother. I used the letter to lambast her, but I also highlighted the role the chosen ones (Keres and Jamie) had played in the way she treated me.

I admit it was harsh on Jamie, but it was true. Keres and Jamie had always been self-serving selfish brats and time had not changed that fact.

And it looked like the apple didn't fall far from the tree because Jamie's kids were behind the whole falling out between Monet and my so-called mother; they resented Monet for getting close to his grandmother.

I still miss Jamie but I'm clear our relationship was built on a weak foundation and experience has taught me that it was only a matter of time before he was going to have to choose; not at my request but life has a way of testing a relationship to see where loyalty resides.

My relationship with Melissa was really disappointing and hurtful. It really did get to me because she was my last hope. Initially, I had tried to keep her at a distance, but my heart is weak for family. So somehow I had loved her without end and unconditionally, but, just like the others, she took what she could and threw me down, like a can of coke.

Even after she abused my trust, I forgave her, which was hard because I had trusted her with my private business, my marriage, and she had shared it with all and sundry.

When I addressed it with her, she treated me like I had done something wrong. She even went as far as to stop talking to our cousin, Imani, because she blamed her for telling me. This should have been my clue about her character, but I still welcomed her into my life.

I chose to focus on the good of family and forgiveness, like a fool, family at any cost mentality, pure madness.

"You are a Christian; the Lord teaches us about loving our family and forgiveness."

I stared at her, hoping her attitude would change.

"I only go once a month!" was her feeble response. I was dumbfounded. It was clear we had gone as far as we could go.

Since the talk I watched her from a healthy distance and she continued to be devious and vicious. She even tried to use my best friend Jewel against me.

When our grandmother passed away, Melissa contacted Jewel and requested her to get our grandmother's death certificate and swore Jewel to secrecy! Who does that? When there are hundreds of lawyers in Barbados, why did she contact my friend? Because she wanted to see if she could get my friend to keep a secret with her, thus testing my friendship!

She is a wolf in a market sheepskin coat; her sweet grin masks her true intentions, wolf by nature and virtue!

But what Melissa didn't bargain on is the fact that not everyone is like her and some people do respect loyalty and friendship!

Melissa is truly disappointing, and she is a prime example of people who wish for things and then, when they get them, the excitement is done and they lack the emotional intelligence and the ability to appreciate what they had prayed for.

My brother Mark is another case in point! Mark and I had been close for many years from the age of eighteen and when he had his son, Tremaine, I used to go to Florida regularly to see him. And when he moved in with his girlfriend and Naomi and Tremaine, I used to take my family to stay with him. He loved me to come and cook for him!

Mark had always been a commitment 'phobe' so I knew he was in love. Anyway, out of the blue the girl said she was pregnant and that was the end of that! He had told her he didn't want any more kids and she had refused to have a termination, so he ended it with her and the baby! His only attachment was he paid child support and that was it, he refused to see his daughter! I had tried over and over again to convince him of the wickedness he was doing to his own flesh and blood, but he just wasn't having it!

My relationship with Mark only changed in the last few years, probably since he got married. Anyway, I thought Mark and I were good but contact had slowed to about once a year and occasionally they would come to visit us if they were in England.

A few years ago, I had planned a trip to Miami, so I called Mark. I thought it might be nice to catch up with him for a few days and then meet up with Jewel and Chrystal in Miami.

He said it would be great to catch up and I should call him with the flight details nearer the time. Two weeks before I was due to travel, I called him on every number I had for him and even emailed him, no answer.

After exhausting every number I had, I began to worry, thinking something had happened to him, so I called his son's auntie. She confirmed he was just fine; he had been to football with her brother that weekend.

And that was the end of the relationship! I just couldn't believe he would treat me like that, particularly as I had been constant in his life for the past thirty years. Even when his own blood siblings had treated him like shit, I had been there for him. None of them had visited him in Florida until two years ago when Jamie finally went to visit him. But that is how that family loves, they deserve each other.

Hyacinth and I always had a simple relationship. I always visited her when I went to Barbados, but our relationship was never really the same after the remarks she made when the sexual abuse came out. She basically backed her paedophile brother.

I guess she's part of the family boycott coz I haven't heard her since the others went silent; she leaves no footprint in my life.

〜

While considering the extent of my sibling relationships I'm struck by my passion for family. I remain unclear about the source.

Not even my start to life had put me off. I still strove to make a family out of nothing. I spent many years striving to have a family of my own. I used to look for substitute mothers everywhere but funnily I never looked for a substitute father.

As a child I was actually frightened of black men. I don't know why, my fear was probably linked to the horrible way 'the Grenadian' my stepfather rejected me when I was about four years old, when he stated, "I am not your father."

But I still looked for mothers, one to call my own, but every substitute mother I gave my affection to was quick to clarify our relationship by doing something which put me back in my place.

In the absence of parents, I fought tooth and nail to bring my siblings together in love. But one by one they have shown that this, too, is something I will not have.

We are too different; our journeys are just worlds apart. We don't have mutual ground on which to build a true sibling relationship, and definitely not where jealousy and deceit are the main ingredients.

Disingenuous people struggle to comprehend or value the genuine because they think everyone is like them.

It's funny, I thought I could make something out of nothing where my parents had failed but I should have respected their effort and realised it was an impossible feat to build a family out of six minutes of fumbling in the dark!

I am and always will be an orphan. I have no parents and I have no siblings, it is just me, myself and God!

Despite the hurt and pain, I live love; I have created a loving family of my own with God at the centre, which helps our love grow and ensures our love for each other continues to grow.

Interestingly, on reflection, despite knowing how hard my life has been, I have never wished to change places with either of my siblings because the people they are I would never want to be.

23

MY ROCK!

Throughout my trials and tribulations my career was my rock. It was the one area in my life where my painful childhood experiences rewarded me for my insightful wisdom, and the rewards were many.

After I had Monet, I returned to work part-time as a locum team manager for a children and families long-term team. The work was very different from my usual roles, but I had taken the position because it was based in Stanmore. It kept me close to home.

I stayed in the post for about nine months before I found an excellent locum post as a service manager for the fostering and adoption service in Southwark.

I ambitiously sent my CV to the social work agency advertising the position. I was not that hopeful as I had never been a service manager before and it was unlikely I could get a promotion as a locum.

I had often toyed with the idea of climbing the career ladder; however, the first time I felt the dream could really be a reality was soon after I qualified as a social worker.

Don't get me wrong, I had always been ambitious, but when I met Teresa, I knew the dream could be a reality.

I met Teresa while working for Waltham Forest council. She was a service manager. She wasn't just good, she was exceptional and an excellent role model.

Her management practice was exemplary and her social work knowledge and practice fantastic. I enjoyed watching her in meetings as she had the respect of her peers and staff.

But what impressed me the most about Teresa was that she was only thirty-four. She was so young and yet she had managed to be a senior manager.

Teresa wasn't just a consummate professional, she was also a lovely person. She differed from a lot of black people I knew, who, once they got to a certain level, drew up the ladder. No, Teresa was a fantastic mentor.

She advised me to know my stuff, keep up to date with legislation and use every opportunity to learn. I took Teresa's advice to heart. I aimed to be as good as her or even better, which would be a real challenge for me given my work ethic. So I had everything crossed while I waited to hear from the social work agency. I knew it was a big step if I got the job, but I felt ready.

But by the grace of God, I was offered an interview. Fostering and adoption was my passion, so the interview was a breeze. I was interviewed by this vivacious man called Ray, who was the head of service. Ray and I clicked immediately and at the end of the interview Ray offered me the position.

I did it. I achieved my career goal. I became a senior manager at the age of thirty-two.

My new job came with many challenges. The service had been criticised for its poor performance and had been put on 'special measures' by the Social Services Inspectorate.

So not only was this my first senior management position but I was also under the government spotlight. I embraced with both hands the opportunity to shine.

Ray was a fantastic manager. He gave me carte blanche to do whatever was necessary to get the service off special measures. I used all my natural instincts to develop management systems which I used to support the change process.

I developed a business plan for all the areas in my service and provided additional support for my staff, who had been through a really difficult time before the previous manager had been fired.

I worked really hard and within six months the service had been taken off special measures. Although this was no mean feat, my main achievement was as a result of my management approach. I increased the number of children adopted, from two to forty, in one year.

As a result of my achievements I was encouraged to apply for the permanent position, which I did.

I developed a long-term fostering policy, which meant a large number of children who had been placed with foster carers for more than two years could stay in the placement.

This policy changed those children's lives. They were able to feel secure because they knew they could stay with the family they had grown to love.

My service was also the first fostering agency in the country to use a national advertising agency to develop a marketing campaign to recruit foster carers and adopters.

I received a great deal of national press coverage due to my innovative approach and the outstanding improvement of my service. I really enjoyed my job. It made me feel successful and gave me the opportunity to use my own experience of being fostered to improve services for children.

I implemented the policy called 'Achieving the right balance', which aimed to promote transracial and transcultural placements.

I became a local and national champion for the policy, as I was able to illustrate my positive experience of being a black child who was placed with white foster parents.

My strategic instincts and business planning skills underpinned my professional firefighting skills. I didn't know it at the time, but these skills would be a brilliant commodity.

After four years I left the service. I felt it was time for a new challenge as I had achieved my goals and the service was considered to be a flagship service.

I decided to look for a position which would enable me to gain more knowledge and develop different skills. I signed on with an executive management recruitment agency and that is when I discovered that my skills and experience were sought after.

Suddenly I was in demand. Every job I applied for I was offered. My reputation preceded me. I decided to accept a position working for a unitary authority outside of London, which was pure madness as I didn't drive because of my visual impairment, but I didn't care. I refused to be confined by my disability.

My new position was as a group manager, which had a really wide portfolio. I had responsibility for a children's home, respite care service, fostering, adoption and kinship care.

I had a team of five managers. The role was huge and demanding, but I loved it. It was really different working outside of London because their social work practice was lagging behind the London boroughs. I reported to the assistant director, thankful her management style complemented mine, so we got on really well.

It was strange working in an organisation where you could count the number of black or Asian people working for the organisation on one hand, but the people were nice enough.

After about eighteen months my boss left, and she was replaced by two interim consultants who job-shared the role. From the time my boss left the energy in the organisation changed.

Initially I couldn't put my finger on what the change was, but then I was in a meeting with my new boss and it became clear.

Up until that day my being the only black senior manager, or manager, period, in the organisation hadn't been a big deal, but then my boss said, "Status is a big deal to you, isn't it?"

"What do you mean?"

"You always mention your job title. It obviously means a lot to you."

"I only mention my job title if necessary and no more than my peers."

I knew right then he wanted me out of my job. Over the next few months he made it clear. I was too expensive, and he didn't like paying a black woman so much money.

I left voluntarily before they added thumbscrews. Leaving under the cloak of racism made me feel uncomfortable, so I wrote a letter to the director to raise my concerns about the way I had been treated.

I received a 'thank you for your services' response to my letter and an invitation to work for the organisation in the future. I said, thanks, but no thanks.

We decided to take the family away on holiday, giving me time to recharge my batteries and plan my next career steps. While I was on holiday in Los Angeles, I was interviewed over the phone for another locum senior management position. Thankfully I was offered the position, which I started the day after we flew back home.

From my first senior management position I had managed to carve out a nine-year career as a firefighting consultant. The pay and conditions were excellent, but the only downside was I had become pigeon-holed as a locum, which affected my ability to progress my career to the assistant director level.

On reflection, I wonder, if I had got my dream job, would the pressure of the job, together with my personal and marital problems, have been the final block to topple me? I'm a true believer that everything does happen for a reason.

At forty-one my body gave out when I had a minor stroke. Up until then my blood pressure had become uncontrollable. My doctor had tried various medication combinations to reduce it, but nothing seemed to work. I'm sure my denial of the severity of my hypertension problem probably didn't help either.

Even on the day of the medical emergency I was clueless as to what was occurring in my body. All I knew was my vision was blurred, my eyes were a shocking red colour and would not stop itching. Mathew rushed me to Moorfields Eye Hospital.

As I approached the hospital doors, my legs gave out. Mathew leaned me against a wall and rushed inside and returned with a wheelchair. An accident and emergency nurse rushed to my aid. My initial eye exam revealed that my eye pressure was extremely high. When the nurse checked my blood pressure it was 216/188! Mathew was ordered to drive me to a nearby hospital.

By the time we reached the hospital I had lost the feeling in my legs, down my left side and I couldn't speak. After being diagnosed, it took intensive medication and six hours to get my blood pressure down. After a night's stay in hospital I was discharged to convalesce.

My recovery took nearly a year and by this time my new doctor had got my hypertension controlled by medication, but only after discovering I had been prescribed medication which is ineffective when treating people of African-Caribbean descent.

With new health I had the illusion of a fresh start. I put on my Wonder Woman costume and began working again. Well, this was my only option as we were financially bereft and Mathew offered no solutions to our financial crisis. Monet was attending a prep school, we had the mortgage and on-costs for our Florida holiday home, which we had bought in 2004, as an investment. Unfortunately, the recession which hit America hit us too, when our mortgage went from $300 per month to $1200. Add to this the usual debts associated with our standard of living, mortgage, utilities, etc.

Mathew's preoccupation with printing parking/speeding fines, smoke/buying high-grade weed and gambling ensured our financial security was precarious at best.

I took a job-share post working as a social care senior manager in a local borough. My eye remained focused on my goal to be a young assistant director, while my body was running out of steam.

On reflection the synergy between my relentless determination and failing health is obvious, but back then I thought if I put in more I'd get more.

∽

After another sickness absence of six months, I returned to work, determined to get my career back on track. But one morning, as I stood on the platform waiting for my train, I sensed sadness.

I tried to shake it off but by the time I boarded the train, with my blind stick waving, sadness overwhelmed me. A young guy gave me his seat and I sat down, and I did everything I could to fight back the tears.

I hated fighting my way to work with people pitying me. As I changed for the Tube at Finsbury Park, my tears continued silently streaming.

Persevering, I walked the few yards from Wood Green Tube Station. I kept telling myself, make it to the office, as long as I didn't see my boss, I would be all right.

Getting in the building went fine, but just as I crept along the corridor to my office, there she was, my boss, Philomena (she hated her full name).

Phil is one of the kindest people you are likely to meet. Everyone loved her, her understanding, gentle compassionate approach for service users and colleagues was renowned in the social work specialism of children with disabilities.

Phil immediately responded to my distress. She took me in her office and that was it, I bawled my eyes out.

"Dominiquè, what's wrong? What's happened?"

My attempts to compose myself were futile.

"I just can't do it anymore. The commute and the lack of IT support, it's too much."

Phil comforted me as I admitted my truth.

I had masked my true feelings. Since I had started I had felt so ill by the time I got to work I just didn't have anything left to fight the IT people, never mind fighting for the disabled children and their families, it was all too much. Devastated, I knew I had no choice but to go home.

I had worked so hard to have a successful career and over the years I had worked tirelessly to make a difference in children's lives, but at the end of the day I had to give it up because I was just too broken to carry on.

My job-share partner, J, arrived as I cleared my desk. She had spina bifida. As she watched my ending, J asserted her observation.

"It must be awful having a disability which is unstable. I feel sorry for you. My disability doesn't change, I'm the same every day."

She was luckier than me, she was able to do her job like anybody else. She just walked with her sticks and, apart from mobility difficulties, she was fine. It was a strange irony, which clearly highlighted the complexity of living with disability.

It was pointless trying to fight myself. I had come to a boulder in my career path and the fight I had used to get me this far was of no use to me now. My body was making a stand and showing me who was commander and chief.

My career was beyond my reach. The end of my career signalled a new low for me. My only comfort was knowing I had surpassed my career goals.

My thirty-year career gave me the opportunity to make a real difference in the lives of children and families. I had only aimed to be a social worker, but I found my calling as a strategic manager and finished on a high as a director.

24

THE GREEN MILE

From early on I nurtured an attachment to hope and faith as I fought to navigate my way through life. From every negative experience I developed a survival skill.

Yet as the years passed I changed elements of me with the idiosyncrasies of my life, but I had to stop running to see the true impact of pain and betrayal at the core of me.

I failed to realise the importance of emotional intelligence compatibility and the impact this would have on my relationship.

Like Rose in the film *Fences*, I planted my heart in Mathew's rotten broken soil. After a while I realised I could never blossom. By the time I had been reduced to a husk, Mathew decided he wasn't the man for me.

I thought if I gave him what he needed he would give me what I needed, but I now realise the equation does not correlate.

My decision to end the marriage nine years ago was the right thing to do but I bottled it. I wasn't ready to face the truth but blaming myself for all of our problems just compounded our woes.

But I was on overdrive, determined to do whatever it took to get our love connection back. What I failed to notice was that I was alone in my crusade.

Mathew said all the right things, but his actions spoke louder, as he carried on doing what he had always done; staying out all night until early or mid-morning at least four days a week. On the days he did come in early in the am, he wouldn't come to bed, no, he'd go in the living room, watching porn until he fell asleep.

In the early years I missed him lying in beside me in bed. In the middle of the night I'd go downstairs and get him to come to bed. But in the later years I found myself creeping downstairs to get a glass of water and creeping back to bed without waking him up.

Another thing I noticed, in the beginning we shared a great social life but as the years slipped by Mathew found my 'party spirit' too much and he went out without me.

Initially I considered changing for him, but the inner me said hell no. As a teenager in love with Anthony, I had refused to change me, so I definitely wasn't about to start as a big woman.

I wonder if Mathew considered changing himself for me? Ten years ago he decided to rock 'the bald head look'. I begged him to grow his hair back, but he refused, saying if I loved him I would love his bald head.

It never occurred to him that if he wanted me to stay attracted to him, he had to do his part, too.

I'm not like Jewel. She loves a 'bald head'; the guy from the 70s group Hot Chocolate is her heart-throb! I just see an old man. Thanks, but no thanks.

In a desperate attempt to get his attention, I bought six-inch fetish heels and sexy lingerie. I made a sexy playlist with tunes from H-Town, Tony Toni Tone, Blackstreet and Escape, etc.

One evening while he watched TV, I gave Mathew a sexy pole dance, minus the pole, in my heels and lingerie. I nearly broke my ankle trying to 'drop it like it's hot'.

Mathew enjoyed my performance, which I had hoped would stimulate his desire to love and nurture me, but his interest and input was unchanged. Deflated, I sent the shoes back. It was clear they did not have any magical powers.

There was no mistaking the absence of passion between us. When our love was new, we sizzled with desire. Making love was our addiction. Our passion was unmistakable, but my happy ending eluded me. And as our relationship aged and emotional distance grew our physical connection dwindled.

The undercurrent meant our verbal exchanges skirted around our emotional impasse. The void between us became more and more obvious but it was clear Mathew wasn't bothered about the path we were on (or willing to make any effort to chart a different one).

Deep inside, I had a niggle and I just couldn't shake it. When he was in my company he always looked down, like he didn't want to be there.

And even when we socialised with friends or family he had the same miserable demeanour, preferring to play on his phone rather than interact with our family and friends.

When I mentioned my observations, he dismissed my concerns and said he found our friends boring.

As time passed, we seemed to have less and less in common. For years I thought Mathew shared my work ethic but on reflection it's clear to see he did not.

I always marvelled at the fact he kept his job and had worked for the same organisation for many years, but then I was reminded that if I didn't wake him up to go to work every day he wouldn't go. Why should it have been my responsibility to wake him up? Surely if you want to work you get yourself up, but not Mathew.

The full extent of Mathew's work ethic became clear soon after I was diagnosed with chronic fatigue.

I had been bedridden for about three months when I realised Mathew's stressed, smoked-out appearance had nothing to do with my illness.

He finally admitted he was behind on his reports at work and his boss had given him a deadline in which to submit the reports or he faced disciplinary action.

Trying to alleviate his pressure, I offered to type the reports up for him, only to discover he needed to prepare over thirty reports. I felt beyond irritated, not to mention fatigued.

It was clear he hadn't written a report in about a year. I ended up typing thirty-two reports on a laptop from my sickbed. That's when I realised; it was because of my support he even had a job.

Mathew thought I was superwoman. He expected me to run into old age carrying him on my back. It never occurred to him to carry me.

My health continued to fail me. Begrudgingly, I realised I had to honour my body and lie down. But as obedient as I had become to following my body's orders, to my horror my health plummeted by Christmas 2015. To add to my growing list of ailments, my doctor diagnosed me with a brain tumour.

Secretly I felt relieved. The thought of dying was liberating. But my inner joy was short-lived.

Unfortunately, an enlarged pituitary gland had led to a misdiagnosis. Within a few weeks the gland returned to normal and all that was left was a small cyst on my brain. So I wasn't dying.

This was devastating news, not only for me but for Mathew. He was tired of me being sick and thought my diagnosis of a brain tumour meant he was going to be free to live again, not as a bad husband but as a grieving widower. His irritation about the misdiagnosis was written all over his face, he had had enough.

Mathew did have some caring qualities. After work, he'd wash me and change my nightclothes. He was good like that, except I think he no longer viewed me as his beautiful partner but more like his old mother.

As my illness worsened his interest and concern decreased. When he took me to my doctor and hospital appointments he disappeared into a newspaper or his phone.

☙

On top of all my illnesses, my sick eye joined the attack, which resulted in me being registered severely partially sighted, which means blind. That may have been the final straw for my body, but I don't know.

After about nine months my health hit the floor and so did my career, when I was medically retired; this nail sealed the lid on my despair. I never imagined that the end of my career would be due to ill health. I had imagined I would retire after a full and illustrious career but sadly it just wasn't to be. I'm still learning to accept this fact.

I find some comfort in reflecting on my achievements during my thirty-year career in social care management. My pride is knowing I fulfilled my career goal of making a difference in the lives of children in need and their families.

As the months passed I got a little stronger, but I noticed Mathew was completely detached. If we were out he wouldn't hold my hand and guide me across the road or hold a door open for me, but if he saw somebody else in need he couldn't move fast enough to assist them.

എ

After a dodgy Christmas, Mathew's gift to me, which was the ugliest matching hat, scarf and glove set you can imagine, showed me what he really thought of me. I couldn't even regift them, not even to my ninety-nine-year-old grandmother.

Valentine's Day brought the green mile. At about 5am I awoke to the sound of the shower. I pondered the sound, as that was the first time in twenty-five years that Mathew had ever taken a shower when he got home.

I fell asleep, aware he hadn't come to bed, but by mid-morning he was in bed. For a Valentine's Day treat I fixed him breakfast in bed.

I was about to serve him breakfast but first had to use the toilet. As I sat down, I noticed his clothes lying on the sofa in the spare room.

On the way back to get the breakfast tray, I heard the clothes call me. I picked up his boxer shorts and looked inside. My heart nearly stopped when I saw spunk all on the inside of his boxers. Trembling, I dropped the boxers.

I retrieved the breakfast tray. As I entered our bedroom I called Mathew awake. I handed him the tray and the boxer shorts.

"So, this is where we are?"

Mathew bolted upright.

"D, it's not that!"

I stared at him, incredulous.

"Now you want to take me for an idiot. I have been washing your boxers for twenty-five years and I know what shit and piss look like and they don't look like spunk! You must really take me for a fool, but I am nobody's fool."

From that day to this he never offered an explanation. The atmosphere for the rest of Valentine's Day was tense. Mathew was moving strangely but he said nothing.

He must have come back about 9 or 10am the next day. He cooked me breakfast and gave it to me in bed as if nothing had happened. He even sent some flowers up with Monet.

I was fit to burst. I could barely eat the brunch. I had a shower, got dressed and went to my Aunt Kay's and Karen's flat. I told my aunt what had happened. She agreed the evidence was quite compelling but said I should wait to hear what Mathew had to say for himself before reaching any conclusions.

I went home about 9pm. I didn't even call him to get me, I just got a cab. When I stepped into the house, he said nothing to me. I shared the silence and went straight to bed. He must have come to bed at about two or three in the morning; still he said nothing.

Monday, he didn't come home after work as he usually did, he didn't get home until about three in the morning. By Tuesday I was about to have an aneurysm, I was so mad.

I couldn't take it any longer. I sent him a text stating: *Clearly we have come to the end of the road, after twenty-five years the least I deserve is respect, so treat me with respect and let's just agree how to sort out the finances and our son, peace.*

He eventually came home about 7pm. As he entered our bedroom, he handed me his house keys and then packed his clothes; he didn't say a word. I just sat and watched him.

I couldn't believe what was happening. He hadn't even given me the courtesy of a reason or an explanation.

"Wow, so that's it, not even a word?"

"You said everything in the text, what more is there to say?"

"I sent the text, you didn't even reply, you haven't said anything to me!"

"Let's not get into it, it's done, it's done!"

I was baffled. I just kept watching him. I heard the door close and I knew he was gone. My marriage was over.

The first few weeks after he left were fine, I felt good, we had limited cordial contact. But a month later depression replaced my confidence. Again the tide of support was out. Isolated and feeling like a single parent, I buckled.

Mathew and I began building bridges; I started cooking for him on Sundays. After one lovely family dinner, we ended up having sex.

We talked, too. One Sunday evening we lay together. Mathew stared at me as he spoke.

"I can't believe we broke up after twenty-five years."

"Me neither. We used to be so good together."

"I just don't think the old Dominiquè can come back."

"She will if she can feel your love."

"If you can't feel it, it's your problem. I think the reason you ended the marriage is because you got the loan money."

I felt like I had been sucker punched.

"Do you know me? I'm not a thief."

I looked into his eyes, but I saw nothing except bloodshot eyes. I heard his words, but I still didn't see the red flags, even though he waved them in my face. Pure madness.

It didn't help that my good friend, Annemarie, had refused to accept the break-up. She nearly drove me mad. Because she had been in her relationship for over thirty years and was newlywed, she campaigned hard for staying together. No matter what I said she dismissed it and said that happens after you have been together for such a long time.

Don't get me wrong, she is a lovely 'sistren' and her heart is always in the right place, but her stance was blowing my mind.

I knew what was wrong with my marriage, but I couldn't communicate it to her. I was so used to Mathew treating me like it was all in my head, it didn't help that she was treating me the same.

Annemarie wanted me to be sure things couldn't be salvaged between Mathew and me. At times her interrogation helped me clarify my own thoughts but then she would shoot my thoughts down.

I later realised that Mathew and I had created the perfect family mask, and our family and friends were reluctant to see the truth.

Thankfully, Annemarie was alone in her approach; my other girlfriends were more nurturing, like Rose. Over the years we developed a fantastic therapeutic support system, which enabled us to make sense of the world, and I used her as a sounding board.

Even with the support of my friends, the break-up was hard. I felt a rollercoaster of emotions; rage, sadness, happiness, then sadness and rage and the ride would start all over again.

Strangely enough our children were less conflicted about the break-up. In fact, Antoinette and Monet were relieved the relationship had ended. When I discussed it with Monet his response astounded me.

"I'm not surprised. You live separate lives. I think my dad only came back the first time you separated for me, well that is what he said."

"What? No. When did your dad say that?"

"I think just after he moved back in. I thought you knew."

I felt hoodwinked. Mathew had misled me. He led me to believe he came back for me. This new revelation added a new emotional dip.

Antoinette stormed like a Tasmanian devil. She was sick and tired of seeing Mathew use me.

"You've wasted enough time on him. He doesn't do anything to make you happy, all he does is take. Move on and leave him in the dust."

The truth is I didn't want to be single. I wanted to be in a loving marriage. Why couldn't I have that?

One night, my emotions spiralled out of control and I texted Mathew after a rave. He answered my text and I told him to come over and sex me, and he did. He took so long to arrive I nearly burst waiting. I yearned for him so badly, I don't know why, but I wanted him inside me and all over me.

When he arrived, we made passionate love, but there was something missing. I tried to ignore it, but I felt it. Two years later I acquired sexual freedom, which enabled me to understand what was missing and why I couldn't enjoy a sexual happy ending with Mathew.

After that night Mathew said he'd move back in and we could work on our marriage. He was adamant, however; this would be the last time he would ever move back in if I put him out again.

It was strange how Mathew had rewritten his exit, he left without explanation. I did not put him out. Anyhow, he was moving back in and I was singing the same old song again; I can fix it. I can fix it. Yes, I can, not a 'we' in sight.

Mathew was supposed to move back home in two weeks, but two weeks turned into three weeks without explanation. After the second no show, I called him to find out what was going on.

"Dominiquè, I have to be sure."

"What's stopping you?"

"I'm not sure, but if we break up again, I will never come back again."

"Well, don't come back unless you are sure."

He was obviously conflicted, but he never shared the details of his uncertainty with me. There were only so many ways I could probe and come up empty. I left him to work through his own thoughts and to come to his own conclusion.

I tried to keep busy socialising and raving with friends. One night I went out for a meal with my girlfriend, Stephani. She nearly passed out when I told her we were getting back together. She said I had done a complete 360 and she couldn't understand how I got there.

Stephani wasn't convinced by my attempt to explain. Stephani had recently separated from her husband and she couldn't understand how we were on the same path one day and on different paths the next.

Stephani surrendered her protest with a recommendation to a great therapist, Dr Neal, a clinical psychologist. She told me he only works with people who are ready to address their issues, not clients who just want to sit and purge.

I was way beyond the moaning stage. I just wanted to stop feeling suicidal and silence the constant noise in my head.

These were my two goals and things went well from the start. I achieved the first goal in the second session. I don't know what he did, it was like magic. He asked me to imagine myself as a small child and picture what was I wearing and where I was.

I imagined myself as a three or four-year-old. I was wearing a pretty white dress and I was in an attic room at the top of the house. The room had no doors or windows. I was lying on a pink warm fleece blanket. I felt so snug and safe. I felt so free.

I loved the vision. I was tired of carrying everything. I just needed to rest.

For the week until my next session I used the vision to help me levitate as my feelings of oppression dissipated. The safety and comfort of the attic room gave me peace.

At the next session, the most amazing thing happened. Dr Neal guided me to leave the attic. I visualised my spirit flying out of the attic window, into the clear blue sky and crystal white clouds, my spirit felt like a ray of light.

During the session I spoke only a few words. My spiritual connection clarified my existence on earth, and the importance of protecting my soul from pain as the pains of this world will end with this life.

My spirit had given me peace. I had learnt how to connect to it and I no longer had to worry. I could live free without anguish. I felt wonderful. Dr Neal is a genius. Of course, he refused to take credit for my healing, but he is brilliant.

Despite my spiritual enlightenment, like a cadaver dog I stuck to my trail, to repair my marriage. Mathew had eventually moved back in, but instead of developing as a person or working on his husband skills, he focused on getting a new Mercedes.

I encouraged him to buy what he wanted. My old default record played; if he's happy, he would make me happy.

He eventually found the one he wanted. Originally, we planned to get the finance together but when we went to the car showroom, he passed by himself, the significance of which became clear a few months later.

As we journeyed in our new ride, I thought he would be happy and content driving his new, less than two-year-old Mercedes, but for the whole two hours, from the car showroom to home, he focused on showing me different Mercedes he liked more.

I felt slapped by his insatiable appetite. He could never be satisfied with what he had. So nothing I did would sustain him, yet I was compelled to keep trying.

Even though Mathew had just got a new car, I desperately wanted us to go on holiday for our 20th anniversary. I thought if we had time to connect on a one-to-one basis, without domestic life interfering, we could get back on track.

I had squirrelled away some money and got a new credit card with the aim of going to Mexico. With one eye on the price, I waited for the right deal.

A week before I was due to book, and one week after he had got his new car, Mathew called me, frantic.

The car had just stopped running on his way to work. It turned out he had put petrol in his new diesel car.

Mercedes wanted nearly £900 to flush the engine. Mathew only had £400. That was the end of my Mexico dream. I had to pay the difference. I ended up booking Egypt, Sharm El-Sheikh.

Still determined to keep us on track, I bought everything we needed for the trip. I ordered Mathew some holiday clothes, which included five tops/shirts. When they arrived, Mathew stunned me.

"You should have bought me one with flowers."

That was another little red flag. I couldn't believe it. I had bought him two polo shirts, two long-sleeved shirts and one short-sleeved shirt but it still wasn't enough. He hadn't bought me anything and yet he was complaining.

The Egypt trip started with a minor bump. I asked Mathew to look and find out what gate our flight was departing from, which he did. On the way to the gate we bought some McDonald's.

When we got to the gate it was closed. Mathew had made a mistake and read the wrong departure gate number, which for me wasn't a big deal but he began to sulk.

We walked back to the departure lounge. In his sulky mood he refused to look at the departure board. With my very poor eyesight, I had to squint and peer to see what gate it was. By the time we got to the correct gate the food was tepid. Mathew grunted and refused to eat it. He threw it in the bin.

From then on, his face was set to miserable. On board the plane, he slept for the whole six-hour flight. Luckily, I had bought some Remy Martin in duty free, so I was sorted, plus I got chatting to some of the other passengers.

The hotel was supposedly five stars, but it was a disaster. We knew from the moment the coach pulled into the driveway that we were going to be disappointed.

We arrived at about 11pm. The kitchen had been kept open for us to get something to eat, but they might as well have not bothered because the food in the warmers was not fit for human consumption.

There were little signs in front of each warmer but none of the names fit the description of what was inside. We ended up eating bread rolls and drinking Orangina.

Afterwards we were taken to our room. Bearing in mind I had notified the hotel in advance that we would be celebrating our 20th wedding anniversary, the room was disgraceful.

As we entered the room we were hit by the stench of cigarettes. The room must have been the staff smoking room, and mosquitoes were rife. We were dumped in the room while another room was sought.

I got about ten bites in half an hour. The next room we were given was only a slight improvement on the first, in that it didn't smell of smoke and there were no mosquitoes. The first thing I noticed was there were two single beds, which I mentioned to Mathew; he disputed it.

"No, they are not, they are just small doubles."

I washed the journey off me. Exhausted from the journey and Mathew's sulking, I just got into my bed. Mathew got undressed and got into his bed. Two singles. He didn't make a move to get in my bed and I made no attempt to get into his bed.

I just went to sleep, hoping a new day would bring a happier mood, but it didn't. Mathew refused to get up. He said he would only get up when he knew we were changing hotels.

Now, given we were in a Muslim country and women are considered to be second class citizens, you would have thought my husband would have wanted to take the lead and get us moved, but no, not him.

I had to go and speak to the hotel rep alone. He agreed to move us to their best five star hotel. Based on the fact that the hotel we had first was five star, I wasn't convinced it would be any better, but we had no choice but to give it a go.

Before we moved hotels, I went to the restaurant, which was another horror story. All I could get Mathew was a fried egg sandwich but even that was a challenge, as the egg station had brown things on it which looked like rat droppings, but that was all there was on offer.

The egg man tried to tell me what they were, but he couldn't speak English, although a man went off to eat what he served so I am assuming it wasn't shit. Mathew consumed the offering without complaint.

But he still looked really miserable. I struggled to overlook it, but he irritated me. His depressed demeanour pissed on my efforts to get us a holiday; all he needed to do was help us to have a nice time. Was that too much to ask?

We moved to the slightly better hotel. The brightly-painted pastel buildings gave it a cleaner feel. As we checked in, Mathew met a young mixed-raced guy who told him the place was brilliant.

Mathew was sold. I was still sceptical because I knew we had Ritz Carlton standards and this bargain basement hotel wasn't going to cut it.

At least we had an ocean view, if I squinted and tilted my head. Mathew's scowl softened slightly, so we unpacked-ish and went to the pool.

Mathew got chatting to a few people and seemed to perk up. We had brought a couple of bottles of champagne to celebrate our anniversary, so we took one to drink by the pool.

When you think of Egypt you think pyramids, desert and searing heat, but the May heat was strange, it was warm rather than hot and the pool was cold. I felt miffed but soldiered on, pretending I was in Barbados.

Mathew point blank refused to get into the pool. We decided to get some lunch at the pool bar and grill, which advertised burgers and hot dogs. I ordered a hot dog and Mathew ordered a hamburger. After the last place we were hoping for nice food.

But as I watched them serve other people my hopes were dashed. They served everything in small plate-size plastic baskets with a sheet of paper on it, which they served the chips and burger or hot dog on.

The whole time I was watching I didn't see them wash or clean any of the baskets. When the food arrived, it was tepid. The sausage in the roll was some sort of frankfurter and the burger looked like dog meat. I took two bites of the hot dog and I was done. It tasted awful. Mathew wasn't impressed either. He ate even less than me.

We went back to our loungers by the pool and after obtaining orange juice popped our champagne. Mathew filled our glasses as we lay by the pool and toasted our twenty-year marriage.

The ambiance should've been 'vacay' but Mathew seemed off to me. I couldn't quite put my finger on it, but I could feel an undercurrent.

After about an hour of lounging I suggested taking a walk down to the beach. Mathew snarled, "You know I don't like the sea."

I looked at him incredulously.

"Let's just go and have a peek and come back."

"You know it's not my thing."

I tried to shrug it off, but I thought, *you know it's my thing. You know how much I love the sea, but you couldn't give a shit about what I like.*

I was pissed off, but I tried to ignore my feelings. I decided to go by myself. It was really hard going because the resort had a lot of stairs and winding paths.

After walking for about ten minutes and trying to get directions from staff, I turned back.

I didn't want to risk falling down or getting lost. By the time I got back to the pool the sun was setting so we went back to our room to shower and get ready for dinner. Silence accompanied us in the room until I couldn't take it anymore.

"Are you okay?"

"I'm fine."

"You don't seem fine. You seem rather sulky."

"I said I am fine. You don't have to go on. I'm sorry then, if that helps!"

"What are you sorry for?"

"Being distant, if it bothers you."

"Of course it bothers me. We have only just arrived and if you're being distant already it would be concerning."

"I said I'm sorry and I don't mean anything by it, ignore me."

"Okay fine, I will!"

But I was lying. My spirit was telling me what his mood meant. He had realised he had made a mistake. He didn't know what to do or say, so he was saying nothing.

We went to experience the horror of buffet dining and a Muslim fake alcohol bar. After eating no dinner, we chatted with a gay couple on their honeymoon, who had been eaten alive by mosquitoes and discriminated against by the hotel staff.

Eventually we returned to our room in silence. We even got into bed without uttering a word. The next morning, our anniversary, I was the one with a look of someone 'chewing a wasp'. I think it was sparked by the silence, it reminded me of what life had been like before we broke up.

My attempt to rally him was futile. I couldn't be bothered. I thought to myself I had done so much to get us here and if he couldn't be arsed, then neither could I. So I just kept quiet too.

We skipped breakfast and went for paninis for lunch, only to discover there weren't any paninis despite the menu advertising them. What they actually served were rolls with fillings.

I had failed to register the fact that the hotel wouldn't serve pork, being in a Muslim country, and ordered what was on the menu, showing a lovely picture of a BLT.

The waiter presented me with a baker roll with what looked like spam, tomatoes and lettuce. I ended up taking the spam-like thing out and eating the lettuce and tomatoes until I remembered the travel advice which said to avoid salad in Egypt.

I think this ordeal was the last straw. I decided to go to the local shop and buy cookies and juice. It made me feel a bit happier knowing I had snacks I recognised.

After the shop run, we spent all day by the pool. I sunbathed in between swimming while Mathew hung out with some guys by the pool.

That evening we went to the steak restaurant for our anniversary dinner. The cutlery was dirty, and the food was again tepid. The only plus was the steak; it tasted lovely, beautifully tender and the gravy was delicious.

Our conversation during the meal was strained. We made small talk and in between Mathew talked to the waiter. After the meal we walked towards the bar.

I needed the bathroom, so I went into the nearby toilets. I was in there a while but when I came out Mathew was missing. I waited for him to come back. I was scared to walk on the white marble floor alone because with my visual impairment it was really hard to see the difference between the floor and the steps.

After about ten minutes of waiting for Mathew, I tentatively walked to the bar, where I tried to see if Mathew was in there. I felt so abandoned. I was too vexed. After what felt like ages, he appeared with a smirk.

"I was waiting for you, but then I saw the guys. I was supposed to come back for you, but I got talking."

"Got talking? Are these people your priority? Why would they be more important than me?"

I was livid. I didn't want to get into anything with him in front of people.

"If you just take me back to the room, you can do you and I'll do me!"

We walked out to the steps to go back to our room. It was pitch black. Mathew took my arm and tried to guide me down the steps, but I kept feeling for each step with my foot before I took a step, and it was right then I realised that I didn't trust him.

I couldn't relax and allow my husband to lead me down the stairs. I just couldn't risk breaking my neck. Right then I realised my marriage was over. 'No trust, no relationship!'

Mathew persisted.

"I'm here. I've got you."

I didn't bother to say anything, I just concentrated on getting back to the room. Mathew went off to socialise with his 'friends'. Twenty years of marriage and that was how he chose to celebrate our anniversary; it spoke volumes.

For the remainder of our holiday he spent every night out until five in the morning, with friends, so he said. To be honest with you I was beyond caring.

I spent every evening in the room. The steak dinner had acted like an enema. I spent hours on the toilet, every two hours and most of the next day.

The fear of a repeat toilet episode imprisoned me. I didn't want to risk getting food poisoning. From then on, I lived on cookies and boxed drinks.

But my stomach got worse. By the fifth day I felt so ill. The hotel rep told us to go to the pharmacy because the anti-sickness and Dioralyte I had brought wouldn't work on this Egyptian belly.

We took her suggestion and went to the pharmacy in the resort to get antibiotics for £10. We also had to get antihistamine tablets as we had been bitten alive by mosquitoes.

The mosquito bites were not like any I had experienced anywhere else in the world. These mosquitoes were ferocious, they took no prisoners. As soon as you were bitten your leg or arm swelled up like a hot water bottle, itching like crazy.

Mathew succumbed to both afflictions, the running bum and mosquito bites, on day six. Up until then, he was very dismissive of me and my moans of discomfort, but when he came back in the early hours of the morning covered from head to foot with bites, he suddenly had compassion.

And then at 6am, just as he was about to lie down, his belly started to work him. I don't know what time he eventually got into bed but the next day he was moaning and carrying on. I directed him to the pills and played deaf.

Looking back, the dodgy belly and mozzie bites were a good distraction. They gave me time. I didn't have to address the panic I could feel within. Mathew remained silent and made no attempt to address the tension. For the remainder of the holiday we were cordial.

I don't think we even had sex during the whole trip and apart from brief exchanges about inconsequential things we were silent. Behind my silence I felt sheer panic. It was as if I had seen a ghost and I couldn't tell anyone.

I knew the answer to his unasked question. He just didn't have the courage to ask and neither did I.

I didn't know what to do. How was I going to get out of this relationship after I had just convinced him to come back home?

On the way back from the pharmacy, we had stopped in the reception to use the WiFi. I called Jewel on Whatsapp and by the grace of God the call connected. It was a miracle because WiFi calling never worked from England to Barbados but now when I needed her the most it worked, thank God.

I pretended I was having signal problems as I took myself off, away from Mathew. I whispered my discovery and I begged for a way out. Should I just flee the country, or should I just confront him?

Jewel was her usual pragmatic self. She was fantastic, and she talked me down off the ledge and advised me to keep mum until we got home.

I could hear doubt in her voice. She didn't believe I was seriously going to finish with Mathew, which was understandable because we had been back together for less than a month, but I was as serious as a heart attack.

I sang the words to Millie Jackson's song 'No Trust, No Relationship!'

She agreed but remained somewhat undecided about whether she really believed it was over, although I knew I couldn't be with this man a minute more, but we had three days left of the holiday.

Jewel told me to hold tight, the days would soon pass, and we would be back in England. Hanging up the phone to Jewel I felt better already, the relief of sharing my feelings was immense, and time left seemed manageable.

ॐ

During the remaining days in Egypt, everything became clear, and I remembered an empowering mantra, 'fortune favours the brave'. I realised I would have to be brave; there was no other way to get out of my situation. I knew to save myself I had to end my marriage.

The 'let's go to the beach' incident typified the fundamental problem in our marriage. It clearly illustrated that Mathew had no intention of trying to meet my needs, regardless of the importance to me. He was a taker and he was not intent on doing anything else.

Suddenly everything seemed so clear. All the red flags began to illuminate and wave frantically. It was strange how I had managed to dismiss them before but now I couldn't avoid them and they all said the same thing, this is the end.

The remaining days passed at a snail's pace, but eventually the time was up, and we managed to make it home.

For the first week back, we didn't talk about the huge white elephant or red flags which were clearly visible in our marriage. I had made a number of attempts, which Mathew had managed to dodge by coming home in the early hours of the morning.

Eventually I decided I had gone as far as I could go. And on the first evening he came home early I sucked up my courage and seized the moment.

I sat on the sofa at the far end of the living room while he sat in his La-Z-Boy; I tried to look in his face as I spoke.

"I'm sorry, I just can't go any further. I just don't have capacity to do it anymore."

Mathew cut in.

"If you have that, I have even less than you."

Flabbergasted, I just couldn't believe what he had said. I looked at him incredulously as I replayed his words, "he had even less than me".

He who does the barest minimum, he who takes and gives nothing, he has less than me. Then he has nothing. Well that's exactly what he had given me for the longest time, but instead of him being honest he had continued to suck me dry, like a leech. I stared in shock and then the penny dropped.

"And that's why I don't trust you, because I never know how you feel unless your back is against the wall. The amount of times I have asked you how you feel and instead of telling me the truth, you made me feel like there was something wrong with me, like I was imagining what I could feel. But now you tell me!"

Suddenly, he got mad, raising his voice.

"If I knew you didn't trust me, I wouldn't have come back!"

"If I knew you didn't love me I wouldn't have encouraged you to come back."

"I do love you, but I'm not in love with you."

His words struck me like a bullet. I felt the thud but not the impact. It was as if I was wearing a bulletproof vest, it didn't touch me, my heart was still intact.

If I am honest I had known deep down for a while, he didn't love me. I could feel it. It was evident in the way he treated me, the way he looked at me and the fact he never wanted to go anywhere with me. He rarely looked happy in my company.

We sat looking at each other, giving the words time to marinate.

"You should have been honest with me and with yourself, it would have saved us both in the long run. I could have saved my energy and stopped fighting for something which was already dead!"

Amazingly the exchange was brief and the twenty-five-year relationship was done, finished.

Over the next few weeks, we tried to co-exist. This time, unlike when he had left in February, he was reluctant to move out and give me his keys.

Now he had to get legal advice about his rights regarding the house. It really pissed me off, but I tried to be cool until he began moving the goal posts, and then I had to show my teeth and my arse.

The day after he was supposed to tell me when he was moving out, I asked to speak to him. He told me to wait until after he got showered.

I sat patiently waiting while he showered and got dressed. The next thing I knew he was out the door and in his car. I was livid. I ran out of the front door and, as he tried to drive up the street, I stood in front of his car.

Who the hell did he think he was playing with? I think he must have forgotten what I did to his last Mercedes. I stood in the road like a lion, for about ten minutes. He wouldn't open the window and he had locked the doors, so I couldn't get to talk to him. Suddenly he reversed at speed and then whizzed past me.

He was trying to play me. Luckily for him I had dinner plans in London, so I didn't have time to plot my revenge.

Ironically, I was taking my friend for a Groupon deal, which I had bought for me and him to celebrate our getting back together. I was looking forward to the lobster and steak meal at a lovely restaurant in Canary Wharf, overlooking the Thames.

I refused to let him spoil my day, so I went as planned. The meal was fantastic, and the company was just as special. My dear friend Rose and I hadn't been out together for about two years, so we made the most of the occasion.

When I got back home, I packed for him and then I sent him a text to say, *I have packed up a few of your things, let me know what day you will be coming to collect them because if you attempt to get back in this house, I will call the police!* He had obviously seen the whites of my eyes because he texted back, he'd collect them on the Monday.

It may seem heartless, but I needed him to go so I could start to move on and adapt to my new life. I began the process as soon as he had collected his things.

Unlike before, I didn't feel heartbroken. Instead I felt relieved. I didn't shed a single tear at first. It was probably about two months before I felt grief.

But first I went to Barbados to be with Jewel and Chrystal. I needed to be with people who love me for who I am and enjoy my company. I needed to feel love. And love is exactly what I got.

Despite the urge, I refused to spend every day talking about Mathew; instead I used the time to focus on me. I stayed for two weeks. It was exactly what I needed.

On my return, I accepted Mathew's offer to pick me up from Gatwick Airport. We spoke very little during the drive except for him updating me on Monet, Antoinette and Diamond.

My inner peace ensured I listened until I heard the Jermaine Jackson song 'You Like Me, Don't You?' I hadn't heard that song for many years and it was an old-time favourite.

The music made me feel sweet. It filled me up with cotton candy feelings. The words were so ironic, but I sang the song to myself, because right then and there I liked myself for the first time in ages.

My holiday had unlocked the love I felt for myself. I didn't care that he didn't like me. I liked myself and that was far more important.

I repeated the song about twenty times on the ride home. By the time I arrived there I was buzzing, despite the journey taking two hours.

Back home the house was filled with too many memories. My feelings had been thrown back to when we separated. Suddenly, I felt the grief. I didn't feel broken-hearted, I just felt really sad. The finality of the marriage felt so real.

But this time I didn't try to fight my feelings. I acknowledged them as part of the healing process. I went to see my therapist and he made my feelings clear. Dr Neal said, "It's not that you don't love your husband, because you do, but the relationship makes you ill because you are allergic to Mathew." This statement was such a eureka moment.

I enjoyed loving him but loving him makes me sick. Allergic reactions are not by choice, they are involuntary. The effect is out of my control. The only course of action is to stay away from Mathew; he will only make me sick. From this therapy session I have continued to heal myself.

If I feel down, I just remind myself, it is normal to feel grief after so many years together, and then I remind myself, I am allergic to him and with acknowledgement the feelings of grief pass. The main drag in the process was the continual flashbacks, but apart from that I felt free.

I have provided Monet and Antoinette with the emotional support they needed to come through the break-up with minimal scars. Both Antoinette and Monet can see the benefit of the end of my marriage, they see I am happier.

I appreciated having synergy with my children but, unlike my previous 'escape', I didn't look for the support of anyone.

I continued to grow in strength on my own, which enabled me to communicate my decisions effectively. If I met any resistance to my decisions, I dismissed it with confidence and continued to rise.

As I navigated my way to a new life, I looked for inspiration. I found it in an article in *InStyle* magazine. The article was just what I needed. It helped me think about what makes me happy and the importance of doing things that lift me up. I also developed a motivational map which included short-term and long-term goals.

Detailing my goals made me feel empowered, motivated and focused. I found some online courses and I enrolled for a few, but the most important course was a ten-week mindfulness course.

The mindfulness course basically saved my life. It helped me to manage my thoughts in a positive way, which stopped the constant marriage flashbacks.

It taught me to meditate; to live in the moment and to be self-compassionate. But above all it taught me to breathe.

I had lived at such a fast pace for as long as I could remember, I never consciously breathed. In the first session I learnt to slow myself down, which is exactly what I needed to do. It was so calming, every time I inhaled and slowly exhaled, I could feel myself physically changing gears.

That was the crucial beginning of my change process. But the whole ten-week course changed the way I live my life and how I view the world.

People have tried to take me off my track, but my emotional rollercoaster has stopped, so it is easy for me to ignore the madness.

The mass exodus of our family network revealed the true value of my in-law relationships, as the years loving Mathew meant nothing when all was said and done.

Despite the great losses I felt I focused on my track. Mathew made a number of attempts to divert my journey, but I refused to let him. He even went as far as to tell our children that he had stopped loving me years ago.

He suddenly found his voice. Now he wants to share his feelings, still not with me, but he is finally telling the truth.

By chance I uncovered the true extent of Mathew's betrayal. In an attempt to separate our affairs, I systematically worked my way through our creditors and utilities.

While I was changing the direct debit details with our insurance company, I noticed a separate finance agreement for a laptop. This is how I discovered he had bought someone a laptop for Christmas, the last Christmas we spent together.

As I looked at the transaction, I felt shocked, but I also found it refreshing. I was finally seeing Mathew for who he really is. He had taken the trouble to buy someone a laptop (on finance, five years) when all he had bought me was some 'ugly bugly' hat and scarf set.

For some reason I found the situation funny and then I had doubt. I wondered if maybe the transaction was fraudulent. I called him.

"Did you buy someone a laptop?"

"Yes."

I laughed as I spoke.

"Well what is done in the dark has finally come to light!"

Suddenly he was shouting.

"Why are you calling me? Why are you calling me to tell me that?"

I tried to speak, but he wasn't listening. He was just shouting so I told him to fuck off and hung up the phone.

Wrong and strong has been his mantra from as long as I have known him, except now I didn't have to deal with his bullshit.

After that incident I refused to speak to him, hoping the divorce petition would speak for me.

Today Mathew's like a dormant volcano with occasional grumbles. On the rare occasions we communicate we are cordial. I wish him well. I have learnt to forgive him because forgiveness assures me an end to all emotional ties and negative energy.

But one thing is clear; the further away he gets, the more of his character is revealed. I can now see him for who he really is.

25

THE SEEDS I HAVE SOWN

My children are a testimony to the love I felt for Anthony and Mathew, thus visually they resemble their father and not me.

Antoinette, with her father's captivating ebony eyes, milk chocolate tone and shape, is the image of her father, while Monet is Mathew's childhood and teen twin in looks, with the cuteness of a black 'Milky Bar kid' and rich red caramel skin.

They had the holistic upbringing (including love, time, security, family and the latest things) all my childhood wishes. I refused to allow the failings of their fathers to impact on their happiness.

They are both fantastic and unique. Antoinette is thirty-two, an independent woman, who is a reflection of her generation.

She combined the talents of both her parents; thus she is an exceptional R&B singer/songwriter with a lengthy career in social care.

Despite many years of negative and destructive interference by her father's wife, Antoinette has maintained a great relationship with her father and two siblings.

Early on, Anthony's wife didn't hide her destructive intent. I remember when she had her first daughter, who was seven years younger than Antoinette. I reached out to her in an attempt to create a blended family.

"Hi, how are you doing?"

"I'm fine. Ant's not here, I'll get him to call you."

"Antoinette's desperate to spend some time with her little sister, it would be nice if they can grow together."

"E doesn't need a sister."

Her response floored me as I hung up the phone. Initially I couldn't understand her motive but some twenty years later her mother confirmed she had wanted to cut Antoinette out of her father's life.

Anthony's apathy signalled his inability to change his wife's mind. Sadly, she succeeded in creating physical and emotional distance between Anthony, Antoinette and E.

I found her position particularly puzzling, as she is one of ten. She was raised like the Waltons but yet she didn't want that for her own family.

As is often the case, no matter the circumstances, siblings will gravitate to each other with age, and Antoinette's siblings are right on trend.

Monet and Antoinette should have been separated by age. They are fifteen years apart and yet they fought like wind and rain in a tsunami.

Only recently Monet admitted he loved to see his sister roar, as she searched for things he had hidden; he had no fear of her adolescence-fuelled rage.

Occasionally he'd try to fight her, and once she tried to throw him down the stairs, but still they are as close as conjoined twins.

Monet, at eighteen, is the literal definition of art. His pure existence is determined by his multi-media creativity.

Academically he has thrived, and his private education has paid off, as he achieved A* GCSEs at fifteen. He left school with 12 GCSEs, A-C.

Our decision to move him to Barbara Speake Stage School nurtured his creative ambition, thus he has worked as a professional actor since the age of seven. His IMDb credits are extensive as he has starred in movies, West End theatres and on TV.

Monet is also on his way to being the greatest fashion director since Leon Talley. He has established his own brand, which includes urban art prints and couture apparel.

Despite my fevered intention to give my children a better life than I had, my relationship with my children hasn't blossomed as I had hoped. For some unknown reason the bond appears as flawed as my marriage.

Antoinette now has a daughter called Diamond. She is the most beautiful and intelligent little girl.

I provided emotional and practical support when Antoinette became a mother, but Antoinette treats me with the contempt which should be reserved for absent or abusive parents.

The break-up of my marriage has evoked varied emotions in my children. Loyalty has been the biggest challenge.

Unfortunately, Mathew's ability to bond with his charges, nieces and nephews didn't transcend to our children. Since the separation, his lack of care, compassion and a moral compass has increased the void between them.

Monet is now living with his father while I heal myself. But he is disappointed by my inability to carry on with him living with me regardless of my emotional state.

Thankfully, my children continue to thrive, but I now ponder the quandary; maybe if I had been a sub-standard parent, their fathers would have been forced to be better fathers and my children would love me more.

Sadly, my children are yet one more example of how I invested so much but get back so little. They love me, yes, there is no doubt, but how do they love me?

It is said you reap what you sow. I'm not sure if that is true for me, as I'm still waiting for my harvest.

Christmas Eve, I baked a rum cake with Diamond. Despite using the best ingredients and following a family recipe I've used hundreds of times, after watching the oven, one of the cakes burnt.

I felt so irritated. What more could I have done to get a perfect cake? As I pondered what could have gone wrong, I realised that, regardless of my effort, the variables of life are out of my control.

Thankfully the cakes tasted delicious.

26

Full Circle

Cinderella, I wish! I do wish I was Cinderella. She suffered terribly when her mother died and her father married her wicked stepmother, who, along with her horrible, wicked stepsisters, treated her like a slave or worse.

They made her life a misery until her fortune changed and she had magic in her life. Suddenly she had a fairy godmother, a magic pumpkin which turned into a beautiful crystal carriage, and her mice turned into coachmen.

Her rags were turned into a beautiful ballgown and she had glass shoes, which were too big so one could fall off into the path of her Prince Charming as she ran from the ball as the clock chimed twelve.

Her life changed overnight, as the next day she had her Prince Charming. She was rich and she lived happily ever after.

I definitely wish I was Cinderella; that fairy tale and others like it which always ended with happily ever after gave me hope that one day I, too, would live happily ever after.

In the face of adversity and reality I decided to lower my goal and aim for an urban fairy tale, in which I would make my fortune, find love and live happily ever after.

But instead I have come full circle. I am alone again, with nothing but shattered dreams, pain and heartache for company.

Well, that's how I felt when I surveyed the remains of my life after my marriage ended, but now, after a two-year healing process, I feel as though I have gained more than I have lost.

In the seven years from marital reunion until break-up, I endured life's periodical hurricanes. My health and eyes deteriorated, my career and finances slipped away, love vanished and just as all hope was lost my spirit emerged empowered.

In the half-century since my birth the world has experienced such monumental changes, from civil rights, racial equality, women's rights, feminism to human rights.

With the magic of television my formative years were influenced by icons such as Shirley Temple, Sydney Poitier, Mohammad Ali, John F Kennedy, Diana Ross, Luther Vandross, Michael Jackson and his siblings, Bob Marley, Bette Davis. And by my teens I was influenced by *Roots*, lovers rock, Nelson Mandela, Angela Davis, Malcolm X and the Black Panthers, UB40, Musical Youth and my love of reading, with titles such as *Sweet Dreams*, *My Guy*, *Baby Father*, Alice Walker, Maya Angelou and Terry McMillan and many more greats. Plus, my all-time TV fave, Oprah.

I am a true reflection of my era. I have utilised the opportunities of my time, thus I am a beautiful woman of substance. I am university educated with a professional career. I own my own home. I have travelled extensively and am culturally intelligent.

But in amongst historical and life changes the biggest constant has always been people, people never fail to surprise.

I have come full circle.

After fifty years, I have come to the realisation that my life has been like baking a cake. Despite sourcing the best ingredients, following the world's best recipe to the letter, setting the oven to the correct temperature and lovingly watching it bake, there is something wrong with the cake. It just doesn't taste as it should. It's either too dry or too moist or burnt.

I tried to do everything right. I applied myself more than 100%. My friends and family called me 'extra' because I aimed high and had exacting standards. My 'cakes' burnt, even though I carefully watched them bake. How did this happen? Life presents variables which cannot be predicted, that's the essence of life.

So yes, I am on my own. I have circled back to my true self, but I am mindful that if I'm not careful I will get broken again should I stop loving myself.

The biggest example of this is with my relationship with Mathew. Due to my new-found self-awareness, I realised our relationship was doomed because I gave him the love I needed, instead of attracting what I needed.

A simple analogy clarifies my point.

Twelve people are stranded on a deserted island with only one water flask. How do you share the water? Answer: share the water according to individual need. The moral is we all don't need the same love.

All my life I have loved my siblings, friends, husband and kids, with the intensity and passion I wanted for myself. Now, it's all about me, because loving me is a full-time, seven day a week, twenty-four hours a day occupation.

Two years into my separation from Mathew, my health and heart had healed. I thought. I was appointed to my dream job, as a director of a social care charity. This was a part-time position based in London.

I started my new role strong but within three months my ME (chronic fatigue) returned with a vengeance. The end of my career came while I attended a national conference, as I listened to the speaker, who described abuse trauma experienced by children in care.

I became emotional. Tears ran down my cheeks as fear churned in my stomach. I attempted to centre myself but all I could hear was my inner voice saying, *I can't bear to hear about the suffering of abused and neglected children anymore.*

Resigning from what I thought was my dream job signified a monumental change in me. I heard my inner voice and acted accordingly.

It has taken a year of gains and losses, but by living one day at a time, my health and motivation is improving. I no longer run through life like someone's chasing me. I move in time with the inner me. I have moderated my response to others and reserve 100% of my energy to loving me.

Life so far has taught me that the greatest love of all is to love yourself. People will invariably let you down, you must be your own constant. Love is beautiful until life gets in the way.

Life on earth can be really challenging and difficult but it is only temporary, so don't let challenges in your life define you or persecute your spirit. Your spirit is too beautiful to be defined by this life.

In the words of Maya Angelou: *I did then what I knew how to do. Now that I know better, I do better.*

I have started a new journey. I now fill my time with positive people and enlightening experiences. I enjoy scriptwriting, writing and performing stand-up comedy and I am working on a stage production. I continue to reach for the stars.

Deep down the child in me still wishes I was Cinderella, because I really could do with some magic and happily ever after. But until then I remain hopeful. Apparently hope is the last thing to die. I hope I will live an urban fairy tale, happily ever after.

PLAYLIST

You to Me Are Everything – The Real Thing
Stop! in the Name of Love – The Supremes
Loving You – Minnie Riperton
Leader of the Pack – The Shangri-Las
I'm in the Mood for Dancing – The Nolans
Save Your Kisses for Me – Brotherhood of Man
I Love to Love – Tina Charles
If You Leave Me Now – Chicago
Gypsies, Tramps and Thieves – Cher
Feels Like I'm in Love – Kelly Marie
Love Don't Live Here Anymore – Rose Royce
I'm Wishing on a Star – Rose Royce
I Wanna Get Next to You – Rose Royce
Dancing Queen – Abba
Mamma Mia – Abba
You're the One That I Want – *Grease*
Summer Nights – *Grease*
Young Hearts Run Free – Candi Staton
Never Knew Love Like This Before – Stephanie Mills
Hey Fatty Boom Boom – Carl Malcolm
Israelites – Desmond Dekker
Everything I Own – Ken Boothe
Hurts So Good – Susan Cadogan
Tears on My Pillow – Johnny Nash
Sugar Bum Bum – Lord Kitchener
Ain't Gonna Bump No More – Joe Tex
Car Wash – Rose Royce
Gimme D Ting – Lord Kitchener
Tiney Winey – Byron Lee & The Dragonaires
Hot Hot Hot – Arrow
Long Time – Arrow
Ouch – Byron Lee & The Dragonaires
Walk & Wine – Byron
Rocket – Merchant

Police and Thieves – Junior Murvin
Ting A Ling – The Tamlins
Sideshow – Barry Biggs

Playlist Chapters 6-11

OK Fred – Errol Dunkley
Now That We've Found Love – Third World
Sexual Healing – Marvin Gaye
Southern Freeez – Freeez
Inside Out – Odyssey
Le Freak – Chic
Get Down On It – Kool & The Gang
Let's Groove Tonight – Earth, Wind & Fire
Love Come Down – Evelyn 'Champagne' King
A Night to Remember – Shalamar
There It Is – Shalamar
And The Beat Goes On – Shalamar
Stand and Deliver – Adam Ant
My Girl – Madness
House of Fun – Madness
It Must Be Love – Madness
Feel So Real – Steve Arrington
Weak at the Knees – Steve Arrington
Last Nite, Nite Before – Steve Arrington
I Thought It Took a Little Time – Diana Ross
It's My Turn – Diana Ross
Touch Me in the Morning – Diana Ross
Do You Know Where You're Going To – Diana Ross
I'm Coming Out – Diana Ross
Upside Down – Diana Ross
I'll Be There – Jackson 5
Good Times – Jackson 5

Who's Loving You – Jackson 5
Never Can Say Goodbye – Jackson 5
Shake Your Body to the Ground – Jackson 5
Blame It on the Boogie – Jackson 5
Can You Feel It? – Jackson 5
Rock with You – Michael Jackson
P.Y.T. – Michael Jackson
Don't Stop 'Til You Get Enough – Michael Jackson
Human Nature – Michael Jackson
Billie Jean – Michael Jackson
The Girl Is Mine – Michael Jackson & Paul McCartney
Ebony & Ivory – Michael Jackson & Paul McCartney
Can't Help Falling in Love with You – UB40
One in Ten – UB40
Red Red Wine – UB40
My Way of Thinking – UB40
Please Don't Make Me Cry – UB40
Kingston Town – UB40
All Night Long – Mary Jane Girls
It's Over – The Funk Masters
Turned on to You – Eighties Ladies
And the Beat Goes On – The Whispers
Somebody Else's Guy – Jocelyn Brown
Risin' to the Top – Keni Burke
I Found Lovin' – Fatback Band
You Can't Turn Me Away – Sylvia Striplin
Don't Let Love Get You Down – Archie Bell and the Drells
So Fine – Howard Johnson
Intimate Connection – Kleeer
Key to the World – LJ Reynolds
Mind Blowing Decisions – Heatwave
At the Club – Victor Romero Evans
Love Is What You Make It – Investigators
Baby I'm Yours – Investigators

I Specialise in Good Girls – Keith Douglas
Uptown Top Ranking – Althea and Donna
Silly Games – Janet Kay
You Bring the Sun Out – Janet Kay
Hopelessly in Love – Carroll Thompson
I'm So Sorry – Carroll Thompson
Break Up to Make Up – Sandra Cross
Men Cry Too – Beshara
Can't Get Over You – Alpha
It's True – Donna Rhoden
Paradise – Jean Adebambo
Six Street – Louisa Mark
Caught You in a Lie – Louisa Mark
Good Thing Going – Sugar Minott
Dim the Lights – Winston Reedy
Key to the World – Ruddy Thomas
Slow Down – Private Collection
Sitting in the Park – Cassandra
I Will Always Love You – Heather
Natural High – Claudia Fontain
No Man Is an Island – Motion
Daughter of Zion – Winston Reedy
With You Boy – Revelation
Black Pride – Brown Sugar
When I Think of You – Ruddy Thomas
In Love – Arema
I Adore You – Sandra Cross
My Tune – Cool Notes
Feel No Way – Janet Kay
It's Over (Between Me and You) – Caroll Thompson
Oh Mr. D.C. – Sugar Minott
Here I Come – Barrington Levy
The Whip – The Ethiopians
Train to Skaville – The Ethiopians

Murderer – Barrington Levy
Under Mi Sensi – Barrington Levy
Too Experienced – Barrington Levy
Bam Bam – Sister Nancy
Zungguzungguguzungguzeng – Yellowman
Wa-Do-Dem – Eek-A-Mouse
Ring the Alarm – Tenor Saw
Golden Hen – Tenor Saw
Mr Landlord – Half Pint
Pass the Tu-Sheng Peng – Frankie Paul
Woman to Woman – Shirley Brown
54-46 Was My Number – Toots and the Maytals
She's Got Papers on Me – Richard Dimples Fields
Natural Mystic – Bob Marley
Jammin – Bob Marley
Waiting in Vain – Bob Marley
Here I Come – Dennis Brown
Revolution – Dennis Brown
Wolf and Leopards – Dennis Brown
Shame and Pride – The Mighty Diamonds
Money in My Pocket – Dennis Brown
Love Has Found Its Way – Dennis Brown
Promised Land – Dennis Brown & Aswad
What One Dance Can Do – Beres Hammond
Night Nurse – Gregory Isaacs
My Only Lover – Gregory Isaacs
Better Must Come – Delroy Wilson
The Harder They Come – Jimmy Cliff
Got to Have Your Love – Mantronix
You Are My All and All – Joyce Sims
A Little Bit of Love – Brenda Russell
Hanging on a String – Loose Ends
Sugar Free – Mtume
Outstanding – The Gap Band

Only You Can Make Me Happy – Surface
Yearning for Your Love – The Gap Band
Computer Love – Zapp & Roger
Candy – Cameo
Square Biz – Teena Marie
Encore – Cheryl Lynn
Saturday Love – Cherelle ft Alexander O'Neal
Ain't Nobody – Chaka Khan
Don't Look Any Further – Dennis Edwards
Mine All Mine – Cashflow
Cause You Love Me Baby – Denise Williams
Body Fusion – Starve
Keep Love New – Betty Wright
Love Is a Dangerous Game – Millie Jackson
I Want You Back – Sinclair
See You Along the Way – Rick Clarke
Open Your Heart – Bars Kays
Stay – The Controller
Never Too Much – Luther Vandross
Buttercup – Carl Anderson
I Wanna Be That Woman – Natalie Cole
Lovely Lady – Vernon Burch
This Feeling's Killing Me – The Jones Girls
Silver Shadow – Atlantic Starr
Mr Big Stuff – Jean Knight
Games – Frederick
Please Be Gentle – Frederick
Rock Me Tonight – Freddie Jackson
My My My – Johnny Gill
Don't Let It Go to Your Head – Jean Carne
Casanova – LeVert
People Everyday – Arrested Development
There's Nothing Like This – Omar
Greatest Love of All – Whitney Houston

Band of Gold – Rohan Wilson
I Will Always Love You – Whitney Houston
Saving All My Love for You – Whitney Houston
I Wanna Dance with Somebody – Whitney Houston
Finally – CeCe Peniston

Playlist Chapters 12–16

Gun Inna Baggy – Little Lenny
Boops – Super Cat
Mud Up – Super Cat
Fast Car – Wayne Wonder
Wicked in a Bed – Shabba Ranks
Mr Loverman – Shabba Ranks
Twice My Age – Shabba Ranks
Missing You – Sanchez
Lonely Won't Leave Me Alone – Sanchez
I Can't Wait (You Say You Love Me) – Sanchez
Here I Am – Sanchez
Fall in Love – Sanchez
Baby Can I Hold You Tonight – Sanchez
Give It a Chance – Sanchez
Old Time Something – Admiral Bailey
Bandelero & Agony – Pinchers
Rumours – Gregory Isaacs
Life Is What You Make It – Frighty & Colonel Mite
Leave People's Business Alone – Admiral Tibett
Fresh Vegetables – Tony Rebel
Just Don't Want to Be Lonely – Freddy McGregor
What One Dance Will Do – Audrey Hall
Country Living – Mighty Diamonds
She's Mine – Barrington Levy
Mi Love Mi Girl Bad – Sanchez & Flourgon

Stick by Me – Johnny P & Thriller U
Good Life – Cocoa Tea
Electric Slide – Marcia Griffiths
Candy – Cameo
Back to Life – Soul II Soul
Keep on Movin' – Soul II Soul
Just Me and You – Tony Toni Tone
It Never Rains (In Southern California) – Tony Toni Tone
Hold On – En Vogue
My Lovin' You're Never Gonna Get It – En Vogue
Superwoman – Karyn White
Win Your Love – Josie James
Love's Too Hot to Hide – Clifford Coulter
You Can't Come up in Here No More – Sandra Feva
Don't Walk Away – Jade
Holding You Loving You – Don Blackman
Written All Over Your Face – Rude Boys
Knockin' De Boots – H-Town
In the Sand – I Level
Runaway Love – Linda Clifford
Variety Is the Spice of Life – Greg Perry
Camp Katcha Kai – Latoya Jackson
Behind the Groove – Teena Marie
Just Gotta Have It – Kasif
Hold Me Tighter in the Rain – Billy Griffin
Don't Tell Me Tell Her – Phyllis Hyman
Always – Atlantic Starr
Secret Lovers – Atlantic Starr
You Know How to Love Me – Phyllis Hyman
You're My Choice Tonight – Teddy Pendergrass
Curious – Midnight Star
Casanova – Coffee
Feels Like I'm Falling in Love – Bar-Kays
Close to You – Gwen Gutherie

I'm in Love – Evelyn 'Champagne' King
Keep the Fire Burning – Gwen McCrae
Get in Touch (With Me) – One Blood
Hi Howya Doin' – Kenny G
Funky Sensation – Gwen McCrae
How Could You Break My Heart – Bobby Womack
It's My Turn – Bobby Glove
I'm the One for You – Whispers
I've Been Down – Peabo Bryson
Summer Breeze – The Isley Brothers
Let the Music Play – Barry White
If You Only Knew – Patti Labelle
Practice What You Preach – Barry White
Here and Now – Luther Vandross
Endless Love – Luther Vandross
So Amazing – Luther Vandross
Stop to Love – Luther Vandross
She's So Good to Me – Luther Vandross
Guilty – Barbara Streisand & Barry Gibb
Undercover Lover – Smooth
Tell Me – Omar
Silver and Gold – Kirk Franklin
Song in the Midnight – Raymond & Co
Fire – Raymond & Co
Real Love – Mary J Blige
All Night Long – Mary J Blige
Love No Limit – Mary J Blige
Reminisce – Mary J Blige
I'm Going Down – Mary J Blige
Everything – Mary J Blige
Sweet Thing – Mary J Blige
Be Happy – Mary J Blige
I Wanna Know – Joe
All The Things (Your Man Won't Do) – Joe

Wifey – Next
Too Close – Next
Bump 'N' Grind – R Kelly
Your Body's Calling Me – R Kelly
Honey Love – R Kelly
Ignition (Remix) – R Kelly
Can't You See – Total ft Notorious B.I.G.
Juicy – Notorious B.I.G.
Mo' Money – Notorious B.I.G. ft P. Diddy
Get Money – Notorious B.I.G. ft Little Kim
Pass The Courvoisier – Busta Rhymes
You Used to Love – Faith
Love Like This – Faith
I'll Be Missing You – Puff Daddy ft Faith Evans & 112
Rock Your Body – Justin Timberlake
Best Friend – Brandy
When I Think of You – Janet Jackson
What Have You Done for Me Lately – Janet Jackson
Let's Wait a While – Janet Jackson
Count on Me – Whitney Houston & CeCe Winans
I'm Every Woman – Whitney Houston
We Belong Together – Mariah Carey
All I Want for Christmas – Mariah Carey
Hero – Mariah Carey
Fantasy – Mariah Carey
Honey – Mariah Carey
I'll Be There – Mariah Carey
Best Things in Life Are Free – Janet Jackson & Luther Vandross
Crazy Love – Beyoncé
Sweet Like Chocolate – Shanks & Bigfoot
Flowers – Sweet Female Attitude
Regular Lover – Mellody
Friend of Mine – Major Notes ft Mellody
Head, Shoulders, Kneez & Toez – K.I.G./Miles Records

Migraine Skank – Gracious K
Nuttah – UK Apache & Shy FX
Who the Hell Is Kim – Destra
Turn It Around – Square One
Fuluma/Makelele – Alison Hinds
Pump Me Up – Krosfyah
Aye Aye Aye – Square One
All Aboard – Atlantik
One More Time – Machel Montano
Sweet Mother (Dulce Madre) – Prince Nico Mbarga
Turn Me On – Kevin Lyttle
Incredible – M Beat ft General Levy
Dude – Beenie Man ft Mrs Thing & Shawnna
Dangerous – Conroy Smith
She's Living Dangerously – Barrington Levy ft Bounty Killer
I Know The Score – Frankie Paul
Sara – Frankie Paul
If I Gave My Heart to You – John McLean
Slow Down – Private Collection
Baby I've Been Missing You – Bunny Maloney
I'm in Love with a Dreadlock – Brown Sugar
Got to Find a Way – Lorna Gee
Goodbye Little Man – Sister Love
Country Living – Sandra Cross
Am I the Same Girl – Winsome
Knight in Shining Armour – Deborahe Glasgow
Take Good Care of Yourself – Junior English
Lady of Magic – Bunny Maloney
Little Way Different – Errol Dunkley
Man in Me – Matumbi
Turn Out the Light – The Investigators
Should I – Maxi Priest
Strollin' On – Maxi Priest
In the Springtime – Maxi Priest

Love the Way It Should Be (Humanity) – The Royal Rasses
I Am Blessed – Mr. Vegas
Hear My Cry Oh Lord – Marvia Providence
Morning of My Life – John Holt
Touch Me in the Morning – John Holt
For the Love of You – John Holt

Playlist Chapters 17–26

She's Still Loving Me – Morgan Heritage
Down by the River – Morgan Heritage
Tempted to Touch – Beres Hammond
What One Dance Will Do – Beres Hammond
Sweetness – Beres Hammond
I Feel Good – Beres Hammond
Walk Away – Bitty McLean
Longing For – Jah Cure
In the Ghetto – Hero
Love So Nice – Junior Kelly
Princess Gone – Jah Mason
Can't Satisfy Her – I Wayne
No, No, No – Dawn Penn
Dry Cry – Sizzla
I'm Still in Love – Sean Paul
Get Busy – Sean Paul
Give It Up to Me – Sean Paul
Like Glue – Sean Paul
Gimme the Light – Sean Paul
Murder She Wrote – Chaka Demus & Pliers
She's Royal – Taurus Riley
Stay with You – Taurus Riley
Beware – Taurus Riley
Love's Contagious – Taurus Riley

Ganja Farmer – Marlon Asher
Make It with You – Bitty McLean
Walk Away from Love – Bitty McLean
Need U Bad – Jazmine Sullivan
Just Fine – Mary J Blige
Bust Your Windows – Jazmine Sullivan
Irreplaceable – Beyoncé
He Wasn't Man Enough – Toni Braxton
It's Not Right but It's Okay – Whitney Houston
When You Believe – Whitney Houston
Wish I Didn't Miss You – Angie Stone
Breathe Again – Toni Braxton
No More Rain (In This Cloud) – Angie Stone
Everyday – Angie Stone
Brotha – Angie Stone
Next Lifetime – Erykah Badu
On and On – Erykah Badu
Even After All – Finley Quaye
You Make Me Wanna – Usher
Confessions – Usher
Confessions Part II – Usher
Caught Up – Usher
Truth Hurts – Usher
Simple Things – Usher
Burn – Usher
That's What It's Made For – Usher
Do It to Me – Usher
Follow Me – Usher
Throwback – Usher
Boogie Tonight – Tweet
Happy – R Kelly
In Da Club – 50 Cent
Spotlight – Jennifer Hudson
Blurred Lines – Robin Thicke ft Pharrell Williams & T.I.

Get Lucky – Daft Punk ft Pharrell Williams
Happy – Pharrell Williams
Wild Thoughts – DJ Khaled ft Rihanna, Bryson Tiller
Work (Explicit) – Rihanna
Bitch Better Have My Money – Rihanna
Bodak Yellow – Cardi B
Ghetto Story – Babycham
Welcome to Jamrock – Damien Marley
In Your Arms – Maxi Priest & Beres Hammond
It's a Pity – Tanya Stephens
Sad Songs – Melanie Fiona
I'm So Special – Movado
I'm a Big Deal – Christopher Marshall
Heaven in Her Eyes – Gappy Ranks
Who Knows – Protoje ft Chronixx
Here Comes Trouble – Chronixx
Angola – Jah Bouks
Modern Day – Jesse Royal
Smile Jamaica – Chronixx
If You Want Me – Love Unlimited
Good Morning – Lia Renee Dior
So Amazing – Maskerade
Philly Brown – Cel
Body Language – Anthony David
Smile – Hil St Soul
If It's Money That I Want – Torrey Carter
Take Me Away – Stacie Orrico
Just Can't Get You Off My Mind – Profyle
How Could I – Roachford
Feelin' U – Don E
Take It Slow – Boozoo Bajou
In the Morning – Ledisi
Make Love to Me – Jill Francis
Can't Wait – Jill Scott

Let It Go – Le'andria Johnson
Rockin' You Eternally – Leon Ware
Lovely Day – Independent Divas
When I See U – Fantasia
Should've Known Better – Mica Paris
Ascension (Don't Ever Wonder) – Maxwell
Turnin' Me Up – BJ The Chicago Kid
Thinking Out Loud – Ed Sheeran
Shape of You – Ed Sheeran
Hotline Bling – Drake
You Like Me Don't You – Jermaine Jackson
There Goes My Baby – Charlie Wilson
You're My Starship – Dazz Band
Take Me to the King – Tamela Mann
I Feel Good – Fred Hammond

LIFE'S PEARLS
OF WISDOM

Loving me

◊ Life is a journey of self-discovery, which can lead to spiritual enlightenment!

◊ The greatest love of all is loving yourself and if you stop loving yourself true love will elude you.

◊ Trust your gut instinct, your gut will never lie to you or mislead you!

◊ Prioritise yourself because if you don't nobody else will. For example, what do you want to eat? I always ask everyone around me first, like what I want is secondary!

◊ Never do something which means you lose the essence of you. The moment I put Mathew's need for a baby ahead of my own needs, I lost myself and then Mathew didn't want me anyway, he didn't know who I was and neither did I!

◊ Actions speak louder than words! Don't wait for someone to confirm what their actions have already told you!

Relationships

◊ Find out what type of love you need.

◊ If love is based on what you do and not who you are it will not last.

◊ Modelling the love you want doesn't always work and particularly if the person you love is a taker and not a giver.

◊ You need to know what you need and know how to get it.

◊ Learn how to love yourself and how to meet your own needs.

◊ Do not settle you deserve your equivalent.

◊ You cannot grow a man. He is already cooked!

◊ If you have to teach your lover how to love you, you are wasting your time!

◊ Men's three main drivers are fear, their own needs and to get away with as much as possible!

◊ When attracting a partner stay in your lane. If you have a university education then only attract someone who has one too, if you own property only attract someone who owns property too. If you stack shelves for a living, then attract someone who packs groceries or stacks shelves or moves shopping trolleys. If you attract someone who is not in your lane you will have to act down or up and eventually someone will be worn out with pretending to be someone they are not! Just like a boxer who is a natural middleweight but decides to be a heavyweight, eventually his body will give up and he will have to return to his natural body weight and he will again be a middleweight!

◊ People come into your life for a reason and a season; when it's done it's done!

Family

◊ Family is overrated unless your family doesn't abuse you!

◊ I am better off as an orphan! Blood relatives have been the most abusive people in my life and I do not need them. I choose to surround myself with love and to spend my time with people who love me for who I am.

◊ If you do not have a family, you need to love yourself and make your own family. Love can be acquired if you are loving and caring. The saying "Blood is thicker than water" is only relevant to scientists; it doesn't have any relevance to families! I don't know what it's like to have the love of my mother and father but I have ensured that my children and grandchild know what it is like to be loved.

◊ If you are thinking about having children, remember my story and ensure that you do not bring a child into anything similar. A child produced out of six minutes' fumbling in the dark *with somebody else's man* will create a lifetime of misery!

◊ When children have no one who loves them, no one who is prepared to fight for them or support them, these children are extremely vulnerable, and people prey on vulnerable children; bullies, child abusers, gangs, drug dealers and evil people. We must protect vulnerable children. They have nobody else.

◊ Unloved children are everybody's responsibility! All children need love and they need to be taught how to love themselves, because loving yourself is the greatest love of all!

Therapy is fantastic if you are clear about what type of therapy you need and take the time to find the right therapist for you.